Perspectives on Deafness

Series Editors
Marc Marschark
Patricia Elizabeth Spencer

Approaches to Social Research

The Case of Deaf Studies

Alys Young
Bogusia Temple

OXFORD
UNIVERSITY PRESS

OXFORD
UNIVERSITY PRESS

Oxford University Press is a department of the University of Oxford.
It furthers the University's objective of excellence in research, scholarship,
and education by publishing worldwide.

Oxford   New York
Auckland   Cape Town   Dar es Salaam   Hong Kong   Karachi
Kuala Lumpur   Madrid   Melbourne   Mexico City   Nairobi
New Delhi   Shanghai   Taipei   Toronto

With offices in
Argentina   Austria   Brazil   Chile   Czech Republic   France   Greece
Guatemala   Hungary   Italy   Japan   Poland   Portugal   Singapore
South Korea   Switzerland   Thailand   Turkey   Ukraine   Vietnam

Oxford is a registered trademark of Oxford University Press
in the UK and certain other countries.

Published in the United States of America by
Oxford University Press
198 Madison Avenue, New York, NY 10016

© Oxford University Press 2014

Library of Congress Cataloging-in-Publication Data
Young, Alys.
Approaches to social research : the case of deaf studies / Alys Young, Bogusia Temple.
     pages cm
Includes bibliographical references and index.
ISBN 978–0–19–992953–5
1. Social sciences—Research.   2. Social sciences—Methodology.
3. Deaf—Research.   I. Temple, Bogusia.   II. Title.
H62.Y6668 2014
305.9'082072—dc23   2013039975

9 8 7 6 5 4 3 2 1
Printed in the United States of America
on acid-free paper

Contents

Abbreviations

AAA	American Anthropological Association
ANT	Actor Network Theory
ASL	American Sign Language
AUSLAN	Australian Sign Language
BPS	British Psychological Society
BSL	British Sign Language
CDC	Centers for Disease Control
CODA	Children of Deaf Adults
CORE-OM	Clinical Outcomes Routine Evaluation—Outcomes Measure
dB nHL	Decibel normal hearing level
DSDJ	*Deaf Studies Digital Journal*
DSRU	Deaf Studies Research Unit
ESRC	Economic and Social Research Council
HOH	Hard of Hearing
Dhh	Deaf and hard of hearing
ICT	Information and Communication Technologies
IM	Instant Messaging
IPCB	Indigenous Peoples Council on Biocolonialism
ISL	Irish Sign Language
JCIH	Joint Commission on Infant Hearing
LSA	Linguistics Society of America
NDCS	National Deaf Children's Society (UK)
SIL	(formerly Summer Institute of Linguistics, now SIL International)
SLN	Sign Language of the Netherlands
TTD	Telecommunications Device for the Deaf
TTY	Teletypewriter
UNHS	Universal Newborn Hearing Screening
WFD	World Federation of the Deaf
WHO	World Health Organization

1

Introduction to the Book: Its Scope and Approach

This book will trouble some readers. It provides no firm answers about how to carry out social research. It provides readers with issues and choices and some guidelines to help weigh up, on balance, the most appropriate choices for them. Those who like certainty and clear-cut answers about how to do research may feel unsettled. Indeed, the discomfort may start right at the outset, since there is a lack of agreement between social researchers about the nature of social research itself, that is, about what this book "should" be about. Researchers disagree about where to draw the line when discussing the influence of "the social," for example, in relation to disability or being deaf. They also differ in their views of what constitutes valid research. How to conduct social research, how to evaluate it, the extent to which it is comparable with research in the natural sciences, and the status of social research are highly contested issues within what has become known as "the philosophy of the social sciences."

We argue in this book that the choices researchers make about how to do research are not inevitable consequences of the application of methodology and method. How can they be, when what might be defined as a problem or what counts as evidence is neither immutable nor self-evident? Some types of knowledge are closed down and others privileged through the questions researchers begin with. The influence of researchers' biographies, allegiances, and "intellectual genealogy" (Simon, Campano, Broderick, & Pantoja, 2012) are therefore of central interest. Seemingly technical activities such as sampling, translation, and transcription have power to close down some voices and enable others through how they are practiced. Some kinds of experience count as data, while others do not, but why? We are therefore not concerned in this book with putting forward the single correct way of doing research; in fact, we argue that this is not possible. Rather, we put forward possible consequences in the choices researchers make about how to do their research and invite the critical dialogue associated with these to be front and center in thinking about methodology and method.

We make these points in the book in relation to all social research, not just with deaf people. However, research that concerns deaf people creates a strong light through which to explore these kinds of issues, challenging established ways of looking at social realities generally and research endeavors specifically. This is because there is nothing axiomatic about being deaf. At this point in the book we are deliberately using the word "deaf" in a general sense to include all identities and differentiations that might have a relationship with that term. As the book progresses, we explore and challenge the use of the word, in particular in Chapter 2, where we discuss the issue of definition. Debates over the definitions researchers use surface regularly throughout this book. We use the terms researchers themselves use when we introduce their work by putting their definitions in quotation marks. Thereafter in our discussion of the issues we use our own terminology. We note here that this sometimes makes direct comparisons of research problematic. Occasionally no definitions are given and the reader is left to speculate about whom the researchers included and how they view their findings.

As we argue throughout this text, to be deaf is to stand at multiple intersections of language, culture, disability, society, politics, ethics, and the body. Consequently, research incursions into this complexity have to deal with the consequences of such issues as the contested nature of identity, bilingual and bimodal effects, definitionally unstable populations, relationships between epistemology and language, alternative and multiple ontologies or ways of being, socially constructed hierarchies of sameness and difference, not to mention the influence of who exactly is doing the looking and the telling. Such issues of methodology and method are those which, in broad terms, we refer to in this book as pertaining to a social research perspective. They are, of course, not unique to a specialist research focus concerning deaf people. They are resonant through social research more generally. Therefore, while this book is principally concerned with social research with deaf people, it is written in such a way as to be in constant dialogue with many interdisciplinary concerns of wider social research.

This dual focus is important to us, because as the book will illustrate, those who have never had any connection with research carried out by, with, and about deaf people are likely to find themselves challenged by the insights and practices of this specialist field. Those who work within research concerning deaf people are often guilty of failing to see the connections with broader developments in epistemology, methodology, and method employed by a diverse range of social researchers. Therefore, this text will constantly signpost in both directions, within and outside its specialist interests in order to foster a greater interdisciplinary dialogue.

As authors, we seek to embody that dialogue in the production of this text. One of us has worked for many years in research with deaf people; the other has a broader methodology-specific portfolio of work, particularly in relation to minority ethnic communities. Together, we take a particular position in relation to our own social research that denies that there is any way to stand outside of the research we do. This stance involves purposeful reflexivity about our own influences on our research.

Alys has carried out research alongside, with, and about deaf people for nearly 25 years. Throughout that time her interests have centered on the relationships between deaf and hearing people in a variety of research-related and nonresearch interactions and processes. In particular, she has questioned the narrowness with which hearing people see deaf people within research. This has implications for the generation of knowledge and the validity of the research findings both she and others have produced. As an educator of the next generation of research leaders in this field, she has become frustrated with the lack of good quality methodological discussions that place the contested nature of what it is to be deaf front and center in any and all research enterprises. As a hearing, late learner, British Sign Language/English bilingual, she relishes her inadequacies of expression and the daily challenges to the basis on which she "knows" and "tells." She acknowledges that the strengths and limitations she brings to her research are in many respects two sides of the same coin. Standing outside of the experience of being deaf, she has occupied a legitimate platform from which to carry out a wide range of studies from that particular location. Yet if she were to lose her hearing tomorrow, she still would never know what it is like to be a deaf child, to have experienced a lifetime of discriminations associated with not hearing, or to have the strength of a cultural heritage deriving from a shared signed language(s). She will be forever a hearing person with an occasional travel permit into deaf worlds and the tensions of that relationship lie, reflexively, at the heart of her work.

Bogusia's interests over the years have centered on issues about the status of the research she does and the methodologies and methods available to do it. She has increasingly been concerned with issues of representation in communities who do not speak English and the reasons why these concerns continue to be marginalized within research. Her reading of the literature on research with deaf people was initially sparked by conversations with Alys about interpretation and translation and led to a joint article (Temple & Young, 2004). Since then she has picked up on research with deaf people in other areas such as identity and the politics of research. This has helped her to think through how research processes define and exclude groups whose inclusion would challenge accepted hierarchies of knowledge. In particular, it has made her aware of the challenges and benefits of looking beyond established social research thinking on issues such as language and representation within research. She intends to use what she has learned within her own areas of interest. She acknowledges her strengths are in general methodology and that her limitations lie in her lack of experience of research with deaf people.

For different reasons, therefore, and as a result of different journeys, we both write from outside of the experience of being deaf. This position itself is held up to critical reflection throughout as what it is to be an insider or an outsider or both simultaneously becomes examined within the differing components of the text. We reference at length colleagues who occupy different knowledge biographies and different ontological positions from our own, some of whom are deaf, and some of whom are not. In making this point we signal that being deaf is one of several latitudes from which others will differ from ourselves. If a reader seeks discussion about social research with deaf people written from within (rather than referenced to) a deaf professional research experience and perspective, then this is not the book for them.

While writing this book, we had in mind researchers and graduate students working on projects or studies concerning deaf people from a wide range of disciplinary fields. We do not limit ourselves exclusively to the disciplines and topics traditionally defined as the preserve of social researchers, as many valuable contributions in research with deaf people emanate from disciplines such as the arts, psychology, and education and can be approached with an interest in how people experience them. However, we use a social research perspective to interpret this research. Also we are writing for the nonspecialists, that is, those not working on research involving deaf people specifically, but for whom the material would be of parallel interest, for example, researchers with a broad-based interest in methodology, cultural studies, special education, and disability studies. Therefore, we presume a broad knowledge of research methods and methodology, but if the reader does not have this in relation to a particular topic or issue, we provide references to help. The book is, therefore, very highly referenced across many literatures, and we envisage it as a resource for readers at all levels of research experience and interest.

That said, this book is not a research methods textbook nor is it a "how to do research with deaf people" manual. Indeed, throughout much of the book we argue against the objectification of deaf people's experiences and knowledge. We largely reject the idea of writing about "deafness," except in some highly particular circumstances. We do offer guidance around some specific points peculiar to this field, but these are embedded throughout the book, rather than forming the organizational structure of the book. The book *is*, however, about methods in the sense of arguing for the need to move beyond simply describing which methods are used and why, to specifying their status and effect on the research process and the validity of findings. Specifically we argue that positions taken on epistemology, methods, and methodologies have political and ethical consequences in relation to the many ways in which it is possible to *be* deaf. We are also interested in the ways in which research concerning deaf people applies, borrows, adapts, innovates, or ignores mainstream epistemological, methodological theory and practice *and* contributes to, challenges, and changes non-deaf-related debates and practice in these areas. The aim is to avoid the silo thinking that has characterized much methods writing in this field in the past and to promote a more interdisciplinary and critical approach. Themes are not divided into issues for quantitative and qualitative researchers in the spirit of moves within academic discourse toward demolishing such binaries in research.

There is a strong leaning toward sign language users in the book, partly because of the intersection of debates about disability, language, and culture in this body of literature. Moreover, the challenges to established ways of looking at the core concerns in the book lay pre-dominately in lessons learned from research with sign language users. However, because one of the book's primary concerns is the contested nature and plurality of what it might be to be deaf, sign language users are not its only focus. Every chapter also includes research with those who would not consider themselves or be considered by others as cul-turally deaf. Our view is that without this holistic focus it is not pos-sible to identify the subtleties, challenges, creativity, and errors which might underlie various approaches to research design in this field.

NAVIGATING THE BOOK

The book is organized in two sections. The first section (Chapters 2 to 4) introduces some fundamental background about research with deaf people from a social research perspective and is organized around three core concerns: the significance of definitions, the role of episte-mology, and the ethical choices involved in research with deaf peo-ple. We have chosen these because the research process unavoidably involves assumptions about the people research is concerned with; that is, researchers have to define their concepts. Issues of represen-tation and identity are especially complex in relation to deaf people. Furthermore, how we construct our research involves making choices, implicitly or explicitly, about what counts as knowledge, who can be "a knower," and the status of the claims we are making. These are fun-damental questions of epistemology. Finally, how we set up and carry out research has ethical implications, both in the choices we make and those we do not. These implications operate at individual and societal levels with powerful consequences for marginalization, empowerment, and the control of social discourse. Inevitably, our three chosen core concerns stray into other areas. For example, we relate our discussion of definitions of deaf identities to issues of representation, our discus-sion of epistemology to issues of ontology, and our discussion of ethics to politics. Research cannot be rigidly policed and compartmentalized; hence, our three concerns are starting points rather than ending points.

The second section of the book (Chapters 5 to 8) builds on our arguments to date to explore a range of thematic areas of interest: population and sampling; narrative analysis; interpretation, transcription, and translation; and technology. Each chapter builds on previous ones with occasional reminders to readers who may need to refresh their understanding of our arguments.

In summary each chapter covers the following:

Chapter 2: Definitions and Transgressions

We begin with a chapter that explores the subtle and contested nature of what it means to be deaf. It is important for readers to understand the terminology used by researchers who specialize in this area, as without this understanding the reader may misread or miss the significant messages that such research draws out. For some readers this chapter will involve new ways of looking at what it means to be deaf, ways that they may not have encountered before and that challenge what they think they know. We begin the chapter by introducing and critiquing what are usually referred to as "models of deafness," terminology that itself is held to account. The reader is provided with an historical context for the situated definitions used with, by, or about deaf people and is challenged to consider being deaf from an ontological perspective, that is, one that takes into account the different ways it is possible to experience being deaf. We show how the personhood of deaf people has been objectified by researchers and consider the consequences of this for study design and whether there are circumstances in which it is justifiable. By the end of the chapter, the reader has been encouraged to be critically reflexive of his or her own and others' approaches to "deafness" and *being* deaf.

Chapter 3: Epistemology, Methodology, and Method

This chapter forms the basis of an argument throughout the book that understanding and challenging knowledge claims cannot remain at the level of surface discussions of the methods used in research. We foreground the importance of researchers specifying their epistemological stance, that is, what they view as valid knowledge claims, who can make such claims, and the status of the research they are producing. We introduce a small sample of possible ways of understanding the many epistemological positions academics have used and argue that specifying an epistemological perspective is the bedrock of good research. Opening up the research process by discussing its underpinnings enables critical engagement that can challenge the deliberate or unknowing silencing of alternative perspectives. This is important in research with deaf people who have only recently begun to be accepted within academic life as producers rather than subjects of research. The chapters throughout the book demonstrate that epistemological assumptions influence research and, if not spelled out, readers may make inappropriate assumptions and inferences.

We lay out our own epistemological position in this chapter and introduce the possibility that research can usefully be evaluated using other "goods" than the quest for "the truth," such as politics and ethics. Ethics and politics are inseparable from epistemology in that what is seen as ethically acceptable in research is influenced by the view of what counts as knowledge. This is illustrated by debates around, for example, who should do research with deaf people. Different perspectives may be important but deciding if, when, or how hearing and deaf researchers should work together, for example, is a political and ethical choice that is part of an epistemological position. Ethical considerations in research with deaf people are therefore a central concern for research design.

Chapter 4: Ethical Research Practice

We focus on ethics as the third core concern in our book, as research is not a value-neutral enterprise, an argument we make with reference back to discussions in Chapter 2. We explore how common ethical issues in research might be expressed differently in studies that concern deaf people and focus on specific consequences for praxis. We show how ethical issues are at the same time political when working with a culturally minoritized group and challenge the reader to think about ethics as situated epistemology rather than as formalized processes and procedures.

Chapter 5: Populations and Sampling

In this chapter we begin by focusing on the consequences for research design and process of recognizing the many ways in which it can be claimed that heterogeneity characterizes deaf populations. We ask about the relative importance of starting from similarity or difference in sampling decisions in this specific context and explore why it is important sometimes to look at whole populations even if we have to suspend the idea that deaf people(s) are very different. We explore the ethical consequences, as well as consequences for the validity of studies, of particular kinds of decisions about samples involving deaf people. The process of deciding what constitutes a deaf population or sample involves addressing deaf identities and the application of inclusion and exclusion criteria. We argue that such decisions, although often treated as technical exercises, are fundamentally epistemological decisions. Research with cultural minorities is full of examples of exclusion and academic battles to include people who have been "defined out" as both producers of knowledge and subjects worthy of inclusion in their own right. We also examine the influences of cohort and context on how knowledge is constructed with and about deaf people and the consequences of failing to situate a sample in time and place.

Chapter 6: Narrative, Epistemology, and Language

In this chapter we begin by asking why it is important to focus on narratives and give examples of how deaf people have used narratives to challenge hearing people's definitions of who they are, again raising issues of identity. Within the burgeoning social research literature on narratives, the term is used to refer to a variety of different approaches based on different epistemological assumptions. We provide one possible working definition and introduce some of the critiques of narratives as nonproblematically "truthful" accounts of experience. We address the issue of whether deaf people's narratives differ because they "are deaf" and go on to show if this might matter in some instances and why. We focus on narratives using different modalities and their perceived status and argue that the way narratives are structured and constructed is as significant as their content. We return again to the point that it is not just the choice of method that is important for what is produced but that *who* applies the method matters as well as how it is put together and whose perspectives influence the final product.

Chapter 7: Interpretation, Transcription, and Translation: Representation in Research

This chapter deals with what are generally regarded as tools in research across languages and cultures. Interest in interpretation, translation, and transcription is often dismissed as an esoteric fad that standard processes used by researchers can deal with adequately. Research with deaf people inevitably raises complex issues connected with interpretation, translation, and transcription and the relationship between the three when different modalities (signed, spoken, written) may be involved. We consider how researchers process narratives in research, generally working with bilingual researchers, and question whether there is sufficient attention paid to the identities of those working to process research data. This question encompasses the nature of ties to language, the use of different modalities, and the significance for the kinds of knowledge that can be produced given limited engagement with those who may be central to understanding what it means to be deaf.

Representing what has been signed in written form highlights issues that can remain hidden in arguments in languages that have written forms. This chapter marks these "tools" as critically complex influences on the epistemological foundations of studies, research design, and the validity of findings. They are examined in light of our previous arguments around identity.

Interpretation, transcription, and translation are all concerned with representing others and therefore involve *producing* rather than straightforwardly reflecting deaf identities. Within interpretation and translation studies it is accepted that representing people involves choices about appropriate words and concepts to portray them. Both translation and interpretation are therefore political acts that raise ethical concerns. We argue for foregrounding interpretation, transcription, and translation in research as more than practical concerns, however useful the discussion of such practicalities may be, and address them in terms of identity and representation, epistemology and ethics.

Chapter 8: The Impact of Information and Communication Technologies

Social researchers have long recognized the influence of the material on the social world. Information and communication technologies are changing how we experience and relate to our world. Communicating with and contributing to the world is a fundamental challenge for deaf people and for hearing people in dialogue with deaf worlds. If we accept that our identities are increasingly influenced by how we relate to technological innovations in communication and information, what difference is this making for deaf people and what difference does this make to aspects of the research process? These are the basic questions addressed in this chapter.

New information and communication technologies are enabling new "knowers" and new forms of knowledge, that is, epistemological considerations. They are changing assumptions about deaf people's participation as research producers, consumers, and participants while redefining notions of community and changing the terms of communicative engagement—issues of identity and representation. The new technologies are also blurring boundaries between the public and the private, creating new forms of anonymity while disallowing others and setting up new hierarchies of exclusion—issues of ethics in research production. We challenge the reader in this chapter to go beyond the functional and practical in thinking about the interaction of new technologies and social research with deaf people. Instead, we argue for a consideration of technology as epistemology within research designs that seek to explore and exploit its relationship in studies which involve deaf people.

Chapter 9: (In)conclusion

In this short final section we address our own journey in writing this text and what we have learned through our desire to juxtapose broad social research debates and deaf-research-specific concerns. We reflect on the main points of our argument throughout the book, in particular the implications of living with a research context that provides no certain and final resolutions. We assess the contribution to social research of studies that engage with, are authored by, and are about deaf people.

REFERENCES

Simon, R., Campano, G., Broderick, D., & Pantoja, A. (2012). Practitioner research and literacy studies: Toward more dialogic methodologies. *English Teaching: Practice and Critique, 11*(2), 5–24.

Temple, B., & Young, A. (2004). Qualitative research and translation dilemmas. *Qualitative Research, 4*(2), 161–178. doi: 10.1177/1468794104044430

2

Definitions and Transgressions

It has been remarked that the more clearly we define the limits and boundaries of something, the more seriously we start to think about the possibility of transgressing them (Cupitt, 1998). This happens the very moment one starts to write about deafness—let alone starting to consider deaf people. Furthermore, what has research got to do with it? The problem is that we do not just use language as an efficient way to convey what we mean. The language we use also *creates* meaning in what it telegraphs of our attitudes and of society's perspectives and values.

Take "deafness." By using the term, the attribute is objectified in such a way as to allow it to be talked about as something that happens to people, rather than being part of the person. It becomes possible to write about the impact of deafness (Gascon-Ramos, Campbell, Bamford, & Young, 2010), to categorize varieties of deafness (Bess & Humes, 2008), or to seek to understand the causes of deafness (Bajaj et al., 2009). By doing so, the writer implies that deafness is a deviation from the norm because it has to be specified. "Hearingness" would not usually be identified in the same way as an attribute associated with some individuals or communities.

This implicit social encoding of hearing as normal (no need to mention it) and deafness as different (it has to be specified) is wonderfully challenged in numerous satirical discourses by members of Deaf communities throughout the world in which the audience learns about "the impact of hearingness" or the problems associated with being "profoundly hearing." Yet for those who lose their hearing in later life, deafness does indeed happen *to* them; hearing *loss* is an apt description, and the sense of a normal (hearing) self has been forever changed (Hogan, 2001; Morgan-Jones, 2001; Young, 2006).

If we accept that terms are not just definitional but actively create as well as reflect shifting meanings, then it becomes clearer why the language used to talk about research involving deaf people is important. For those new to this field of study, the bewildering differences in when, how, and why someone might write (or sign) "deaf," "Deaf," "d/Deaf," or "DEAF" (or for that matter "hearing," "Hearing," or "HEARING") (Napier, 2002; Sutton-Spence & West, 2011) can make the corpus of research work in this specialist area seem impenetrable and inward looking. It also can make comparisons between authors and their work difficult. Differences in terminology are not inconsistencies but often indicate deliberate choices and perspectives. For those within the field, research texts are read (or watched) with antennae alert to what the authors' use of language might tell us about their political, disciplinary, and methodological positioning within the research endeavor.

In this opening chapter, we will introduce three main perspectives associated with what it is to be deaf and the language usage associated with them. They are sometimes referred to as cultural, medical, and disability "models of deafness." We generally prefer to write about "being deaf," rather than "deafness," in the same way as one might write about being a woman, rather than "having female characteristics." We will, however, use "deafness" when the biophysical condition of not hearing is intended and we are focusing attention on that aspect.

These models, the cultural, medical, and disability, are not just ways of describing variations in populations; some deaf people speak, some sign, and some can hear more than others. They are used to convey that how we understand what it is to be deaf and its implications are socially constructed (Lane, 1995). Deafness might be a biophysical condition, but being deaf is a product of influences, identities, and perspectives that transcend (but intersect) the biological fact. Just as early feminists might have proclaimed "biology is not our destiny," neither is what it is to be deaf defined by an individual's audiogram or the person's linguistic fluency. It is a product of how society behaves, commonly shared assumptions, and institutionalized priorities—Who is stigmatized? What traits are valued? What is it that explains sameness and difference? Beginning from an exploration of cultural, medical, and disability models forces a consideration of the assumptions researchers might bring about what it is to be deaf, the boundaries of our understanding, our implicit or explicit allegiances, and what sustains or challenges our preferred meanings.

This is a fundamental first step for those who might seek to carry out research which in some way involves, or is about, or is driven by deaf people. Because, as we argue throughout this text, multiple (and overlapping) constructions of what it is to be deaf exert a fundamental influence on the design, conduct, and evaluation of research studies in this field, from whatever disciplinary or methodological perspective we might begin. Furthermore, the activity of research of itself contributes to the creation and sustaining of some realities (some versions of being deaf) in comparison with others.

This chapter, therefore, is the first introduction to why it might be significant to understand competing and conflicting notions of being deaf as integral to the research enterprise. The subsequent two address the other fundamentals—epistemology and ethics—from which all subsequent discussion in the book will flow. This chapter is also a vehicle for us, as authors, to continue to define our preferred terminology and reflect on why we have made certain choices about language within the text as a whole. At this point we are simply using the term "deaf" to encompass all preferred meanings, identities, and differentiations until we have explored further. We are also consistently using the phrase "*being* deaf" to signal our fundamental interest in the ontological politics (Law, 2009) that underpins research enterprises in this field.

THE CULTURAL AND THE MEDICAL—TO DIFFERENTIATE OR TO DIVIDE?

Although signed languages have existed for centuries (Davis, 1995; Lane, 1984; Rée, 1999), they were only recently discovered by researchers. In the 1960s and 1970s pioneers like Stokoe in the United States (Stokoe, 1960), Brennan in the United Kingdom (Brennan, 1975), and Tervoort in the Netherlands (Tervoort, 1961) established, quite literally, that signed languages were real languages. They were real, both in the sense of having an identifiable linguistic and grammatical structure like all (natural) languages and in the sense of having an associated community of people who used them (living languages). More recently, evidence from brain imaging has also demonstrated their corporal reality at a neurological level (Poizner, Klima, & Bellugi, 1987). Signed languages, like spoken languages, are largely processed in the left hemisphere of the brain. They demonstrate the brain's capacity to redirect a basic function, language, via a less commonly used modality, the visual, if that is the most effective for that function in that individual.

However, the early sign-linguists' work occurred at a time when it was more common to regard signing as degraded communication, rather than language, and certainly not something to be encouraged or respected. At the time, a leading proponent of a spoken language approach to language acquisition for deaf children (van Uden, 1977) commented, in response to the new evidence of sign-linguists, that sign languages are not:

> of the same value as oral languages...signs are not arbitrary codes, but iconic and dramatizing ones, keeping thinking much too concrete...sign-language cannot be acknowledged as a fully humanizing language contra Stokoe 1970, only to be used when no other form of communication is possible. (p. 23)

His words betray that his disagreement with the evidence concerning sign language was not just about questioning its validity but also questioning whether those who did not speak could be regarded as fully human.

Out of debates such as this, and in an atmosphere of needing to differentiate positively those who used sign languages from those who did not, a new convention was born: that the "d" of deaf should be capitalized to Deaf when referring to people who use sign language and who are part of the Deaf community (Woodward, 1975). Thus, being Deaf was marked as a linguistic and cultural identity, in the same way as we would mark Polish, English, or Persian with a capital first letter. We too in this book will use the capitalized version (i.e., Deaf) when it is clear that culturally Deaf people are being referred to and d/Deaf when we include culturally Deaf people but not exclusively so in the issue being discussed.

This change in language from d to D (seen also in some sign languages as well as in written language usage) was a radical shift but not just because it distinguished one language-using group from another: those Deaf people who signed from those who spoke. Fundamentally it challenged whether the biophysically defined condition of not hearing was actually of any relevance in defining the *identity* of people who used a signed language and were part of a Deaf community.

Some of the early work that sought to describe or define Deaf culture and the Deaf community was based on this radical disassociation of the biophysical issue of "not hearing" from the sociological issues of identity and belonging. For example, Baker and Cokely (1980) wrote of Deaf community membership as something that was ascribed or given by others within that community, rather than something defined by an intrinsic physiological characteristic. Therefore, demonstrating fluency in a sign language, shared values and traditions, and a common worldview were of far more significance than how much one could hear. Consequently some hearing people might be considered Deaf; for example, those hearing children who have grown up in Deaf families, conventionally referred to as CODAs (Children of Deaf Adults, although not everyone agrees; Harris, Holmes, & Mertens, 2009). Not all Deaf people are "profoundly deaf"; many might have considerable amounts of hearing. Nor are all Deaf people deaf from birth. Also "Deaf" can legitimately be used as an adjective to describe an attitude, a perspective, or a behavior, as in "will you stop being so Deaf about this" with the corollary, "you are being very Hearing today."

Padden and Humphries (1988), pioneering writers in this field, summed up Deaf people's cultural-linguistic identity as Deaf people having a different "center." Their work is particularly important because they were among the earliest writers to seek to document being Deaf not as a static identity, obvious because of certain key attributes, but as a dynamic identity, evidenced through *orientation* to and within the world around. How a contemporary issue might be viewed, how an individual priority might be defined, how an action might be undertaken, or an interaction is understood will be influenced by *being* Deaf. It is an argument not dissimilar to ones made in other fields of study (e.g., women's studies, queer studies, Black studies) where identity is not regarded from an essentialist perspective but from a performative one. For example, how does being a woman shape how I interpret the world and act within it, and how does it shape how others seek to understand what it is to be a woman from what they experience of me?

There have been many studies from anthropological, sociological, historical, sociolinguistic, and arts-based perspectives that have sought to explore and document Deaf culture and Deaf communities (see, for example, Baker & Cokely, 1980; Delaporte, 2002; Hall, 1991; Lane, Hoffmeister, & Bahan, 1996; Padden & Humphries, 1988). Work documenting Deaf culture and cultural-linguistic practices has been criticized for taking too narrow and static a view of culture (Turner, 1994) as something to be recognized, labeled, and therefore defined by a small set of agreed characteristics and features, memorably termed "the bingo model of culture" (Ladd, 1994). However, the documentation of Deaf people's cultural life, as opposed to defining what is Deaf culture, has been highly significant. Its richness compels the argument away from dismissing a cultural model as a convenient abstraction explaining how deaf people "cope" if they do not speak, toward evidencing a way of life (De Clerck, 2010). In this sense, a case has been made that being Deaf is an *ethnicity* (Erting, 1978), based on the identification of characteristic cultural rules and values, social institutions, language, arts, history, territory, kinship, socialization, and ancestry (Lane, Pillard, & Hedberg, 2010).

However, the extent of awareness of Deaf people as a cultural group (and therefore of a cultural meaning of *being* Deaf) varies considerably around the world, as demonstrated by differences in legal rights, social practices, and prevalent attitudes in differing societies of which Deaf people may also be members. For example, in the United States, the Americans with Disabilities Act (1990) confers specific rights of equality, access, and citizenship on Deaf Americans. In Zimbabwe it is usual practice in the spoken languages of the country to refer to disabled people (including deaf people) using "the prefix for 'it,' which indicates that people with a disability are perceived as having a thing-like quality that sets them apart from full humans" (Musengi, Ndofirepi, & Shumba, 2013, p. 70). Our point is that regardless of how a cultural understanding of what it is to be Deaf might be defined, such an understanding interfaces with specific social contexts, which also mediate its significance and consequences for people who are Deaf.

Understanding Deaf people culturally is often referred to as the "cultural model of deafness," in order for it to stand not just as a *contrast to* but also as a *resistance against* the "medical model of deafness" (Obasi, 2008). The medical model is defined not just by an interest in the physiology of not hearing, but rather in the way in which it focuses on deafness as an impairment and deviation from normal functioning (Lane, 1995). As such, deafness is something to be remediated; the goal is to restore hearing in such a way as to enable the individual to function in as unimpaired manner as possible. For many professionals, parents of deaf children, and deaf adults, it is self-evident that deafness is a problem, a product of something in the human body that is not working correctly and therefore requires repair, or at least improvement.

The past 20 years 'have seen significant innovations in the science of hearing with the development of cochlear implants (Zeng, Popper, & Fay, 2004), digital programmable hearing aids (Kates, 2008), and auditory brain stem implants (Hitselberger et al., 2001). All such devices can and do restore or enhance the ability to hear. They will be more or less successful whether the comparison is the baseline from which the individual's hearing was measured, or what is usually defined as "normal" hearing. It is an interesting quirk of how hearing is measured that definitions of deafness are not necessarily consistent. In the United Kingdom, the threshold for a baby being identified as deaf through universal newborn hearing screening is a permanent bilateral hearing loss of 40 dB nHL or above (Kennedy et al., 2006); in Flanders, detection of deafness through universal newborn screening begins at 21–40 dB nHL (Verhaert, Willems, Van Kerschaver, & Desloovere, 2008).

From a medical model perspective it is not regarded as strange or discriminatory to use such terms as "hearing impaired," "partially hearing," "hard of hearing," and so forth. The assumed norm is full hearing (in terms of quality and of range) and the goal is to reach as near to those standards as possible. Furthermore, from this perspective, failure to seek to restore/improve hearing and speech can be seen as unethical in the same way as failure to treat an illness or to seek to cure someone when one had the power to do so would be seen as unethical.

However, professional practices within a medical arena (fitting hearing aids, genetic testing, and so forth) are not of themselves what define a medical model of deafness. It is the implicit assumptions, associated attitudes, and their social consequences that do. From a culturally Deaf perspective, the problem is that medical model discourse defines the Deaf *person* as deviant and impaired. If one has a view of personal and collective identity in which to be Deaf is akin to an ethnicity, then the medical model view is a dangerous assault on the basis of one's rights to be (Lane et al., 1996). It is as if someone decided that because of a particular trait the world was not going to allow a particular nation to exist. Imagine a perspective that suggested all French-speaking people should not be allowed to speak French or have a cultural identity associated with being francophone. It is that kind of strength of feeling that many culturally Deaf people feel toward a medical model approach.

Yet for many working within, broadly defined, medical fields of interest/practice, this perspective is at best puzzling. Deafness as a loss of function that brings developmental difficulties and potential social problems is so obvious and commonsensical that, as a proposition, it does not require examination. There is no medical model, because there is no need to specify it in relation to an alternative position. Regarding deafness as a medical problem requiring treatment is as axiomatic as saying the Earth is round; it is not that there are various potential models of the shape of the Earth.

However, for some writers, from a culturally Deaf perspective, the niceties of whether conscious opposition or unconscious bias lies at the heart of a medical model perspective are irrelevant because the consequences are just the same. These are defined as including the systematic denial and eradication of signed languages, Deaf communities, and Deaf cultures in a form of ethnocide (Batterbury, Ladd, & Gulliver, 2007; Ladd, 2003; Lane et al., 1996, 2010). In other words, that the medical model perspective does not just privilege one kind of understanding of normality over another, but that it actively seeks to impose a preference (being hearing) and oppresses, rather than simply denies, another (being Deaf, in a cultural linguistic sense). In stating it in this way we are drawing attention to the fact that the difference between the medical model and cultural model perspectives is not just a question of classification. It is one of ontological politics (Law, 2009). How does any given practice (including research) support, deny, enable, enact, suppress, prioritize, challenge any given reality position?

A leading hearing aid company, for example, has adopted the strap line "life is on." The intention is to reinforce the positive opportunities created for many people from improved hearing and that the individual need no longer feel socially excluded. This works as a concept for many deaf people, particularly those who might have lost their hearing as a result of the ageing process. From a culturally Deaf perspective the slogan inevitably provokes the humorously ironic reflection that it implies "we are off."

The differentiation between medical and cultural models is in one sense helpful, in clearly distinguishing between culturally Deaf people and those who are not. Such a distinction is a *fundamental* struggle Deaf people associate with human rights and is not one yet consigned to history. But the medical model/cultural model binary is not the whole story. There are points of intersection. One of the most interesting examples of how these differing perspectives might be seen as in dialogue rather than in distinction arises, somewhat paradoxically, in respect of ontological claims to Deaf identity.

DEAF ONTOLOGIES

Ontology refers to the study of being rather than that of knowing (epistemology). Recent years have seen an upsurge of interest in Deaf ontology expressed through a concern not just to examine how Deaf people experience the world (what is it like to be Deaf), but how does being

Deaf extend our understanding of what it is to be fully human (what is only seen, felt, identified, or regarded as real because Deaf people exist in the world)? Ladd (2003), for example, explores the advantage and difference that Deaf people experience such as a bigger sense of community and defines Deafhood as a state of becoming through the performance of being Deaf within the collective orientation of Deaf culture(s). Bauman's (2010) concern with "Deaf gain" focuses on enhancements to majority world realities, such as enhanced visuospatial abilities associated with sign language use (Emmorey & Kosslyn, 1996; Emmorey, Kosslyn, & Bellugi, 1993) and the significant ease of international communication between Deaf people using different signed languages (Kusters, 2009).

Central to explorations of Deaf ontology is a focus on the sensory orientation of Deaf people as primarily visual and kinesthetic. However, sensory orientation is not just important as a statement of which senses are the most significant for Deaf people's experience of the world—sight, touch, and the more neglected convergence of these through movement. But rather sensory orientation also refers to the basis on which reality has form and substance; that is, it is not contingent on hearing. A nice example of this phenomenon is provided in Maitland's (1994) novel *Home Truths*, when a young Deaf child accidentally breaks a crystal bowl. She marvels at the visual beauty of how it shatters but is puzzled by why such an experience would bring (hearing) grown-ups running to her from other rooms when they have not seen it. For her, reality is created and experienced in its visual form and consequences are immediate and defined by the materiality of the brokenness before her. For the grown-ups reality is contingent on the consequences of what they heard without being materially present as they are drawn to the site (not sight) of the breakage.

However, as Bahan (1994) points out, the sensory orientation of Deaf people is also a product of *not hearing*, both in the sense of how the world is experienced and in the sense of how the world treats deaf people. Hearing people, however enculturated into the Deaf world, can never fully share that experience. We quote his argument at length to do justice to its subtlety:

> "DEAF SAME- AS- ME." This seems to be more important than mastery of the language. The fact that the "late entry deaf people" [into the Deaf community] cannot hear is important, but more important is that they share similar experiences of what it is like to be deaf. They have met the same frustrations and learned similar ways for coping with a world which looks on them as "deviant from normal." Although they have not had the opportunity to live in the Deaf World from infancy, they have developed certain behavioral patterns and pragmatic cues, such as the reliance on the use of eye-gaze (e.g.

using the eyes to "lip-read" and "reading" the world) which make entry into the Deaf World somewhat easier.

We found that two important things exist among members of Deaf World. One is the possession of Deaf World Knowledge (DWK) and the other is having the experience of being deaf. This frame of reference may explain why CODAs do not really feel as if they totally belong in the Deaf World. They may have "Deaf World Knowledge" but not the experience of what it is like to be deaf themselves. (pp. 243–244)

His argument suggests that the biophysical function of not hearing is a significant component in an ontological understanding of being Deaf, as it is an aspect of cultural identity which cannot be shared by those who hear.

Lane et al. (2010) go one step further, in reclaiming the significance of the body that does not hear as a defining feature of a Deaf ethnicity. Their argument is that in the case of many ethnicities around the world, features of the human body are an expression of that ethnicity. They cite the example of small stature among Pygmy culture. To be Pygmy is not only a socially constructed ethnicity; it is underpinned by a physical reality. Thus: "It is the correlation of physical makeup and ethnicity that allows us to recognize a newborn Pygmy as Pygmy and a newborn Deaf child as ethnically Deaf" (p. 46). Not all would agree. Corker (2002), while acknowledging the difference between those who are culturally Deaf from those who are not, nonetheless argues that the distinction between deaf and Deaf "is a nominal one. That is, it is not intended to signify deafness as some 'natural', innate or essential human characteristic (p. 3)."

Although Bahan (1994), Lane et al. (2010), and Corker (2002) do not occupy identical positions, all are in some way putting the physicality of "deafness" back into a cultural understanding of *being Deaf*. They are challenging any simple notion of medical/cultural binaries. Such arguments have complex implications for some of the most basic practices of research such as population definition and sampling, an issue we return to later in Chapter 5.

DOES DISABILITY HAVE A PLACE?

To focus only on medical models and cultural models and the dialogue between them is to miss a significant social movement of the late 20th century, which has also affected the lives of d/Deaf people. Mostly in postindustrial and economically developed countries, the disability movement has worked to change society's perceptions of disability arising from the consequences of an individual's impairment, defined in terms of the body and its functioning.

The social model of disability, as it is commonly termed, has instead focused attention on how society, through its failures of adaptation, disables the individual and limits her or his rights of participation (Finkelstein, 1993; Oliver, 1990). From this perspective, the extent of disability experienced is not defined by an individual's deafness, but rather through the individual's interaction with the ways in which needs are not accommodated and strengths are not exploited; for example, the loudspeaker announcement indicating a change in platform at the railway station that does not have a corresponding visual announcement on an electronic display board is disabling, not because of an individual's deafness but because the information is not made accessible.

The social model of disability achieves a shift in discourse away from seeing the individual's impairment as the *cause* of disability, to the ways in which others behave and the structures of society are organized as being disabling. As such, it creates a new basis on which to discuss and determine the rights of d/Deaf people, if regarded as part of the wider category of disabled people. This approach has formed the basis of major legislative changes which have outlawed discrimination on the basis of disability, imposed conditions which force an examination of the impact of structural decisions such as policies and procedures on disabled people, and which actively promotes equality (Americans with Disabilies Act, 1990; Equality Act, 2010).

While many culturally Deaf people have supported the social model of disability and its politics and indeed benefitted from such legislative consequences, there has also been a concern to point out the ways in which Deaf people are different and set apart from "disability" discourse. From a Deaf perspective the defining issues will always be the shared language and culture of Deaf people(s) and a rejection of impairment as a defining feature of identity (Lane et al., 1996). A social model of disability which includes Deaf people in their purview is therefore potentially seen as threatening to the much more pertinent struggle for society to understand Deaf people as a cultural-linguistic group and not as disabled people (Obasi, 2008).

However, the social model analysis of the processes of disability production does not actually preclude a cultural model understanding of being Deaf. For example, culturally Deaf people can still be disabled by a socioeconomic process. Restrictions on the amount of interpreter time made available and funded within a higher education learning environment is likely to impact on a Deaf student's ability to achieve. Failure by a government to fund or implement an effective visual relay service (which enables sign language users and spoken language users to converse via a remote interpreter) will create social, personal, and occupational barriers for Deaf citizens and reinforce social disadvantage.

A social model of disability *can* explain the ways in which these processes create disability without denying the cultural identity of the Deaf individuals who are impacted by these effects. But that is not the point. To accept an analysis of inequality/discrimination from a social model of disability perspective is to privilege one kind of explanation of inequality, the disability rights discourse, over another, that of language rights.

For some scholars and activists (Ladd, 2003), any rapprochement between a social model of disability and a cultural understanding of being Deaf is a luxury that cannot be afforded when the struggle for human rights on the basis of language and culture remains largely unfulfilled. Yet for many Deaf people the only way to financial support for access to education or employment is to agree to be regarded as "disabled" and have needs assessed as a consequence. For some, an alliance with the international disability rights movement is regarded as the most effective means of achieving greater political enfranchisement for Deaf peoples throughout the world. The World Federation of the Deaf, which represents sign language users throughout the world, participates as a member of the Panel of Experts on the UN Standard Rules for the Equalization of Opportunities for Persons with Disabilities.

The social model of disability, however, is also involved in its own self-critique. Its formulation has often excluded discussion of impairment (in the sense of bodily dysfunction), and the model has been criticized for resting on an unsustainable binary: disability/impairment. As Beckett (2006) argues, the social model promotes a disembodied notion of disability if it neglects the ways in which impairment is itself socially constructed. Some kinds of impairment are in some societies more acceptable than others.

In surveys of the general public in most developed world countries, for example, forced to choose between being deaf or being blind, invariably the majority will choose to be deaf. Whether this is because sight is highly valued or blindness deeply feared remains debatable. What counts as an impairment is itself a social judgment: "impairment is always already social and disability is intertwined with impairment effects" (Shakespeare, 2006, p. 35). Compare the stigma generated by hearing aids with that associated with wearing eyeglasses (Alker, 2000). To be deaf, therefore, within a social model of disability is not simply to acknowledge the disability produced through how society fails to accommodate a person's deafness. It is also to acknowledge that the impairment associated with one's disability is itself socially constructed in the meaning attributed to it and its social effects.

Cooper (2012) takes this argument one step further in pointing out that how we might decide "whether a problem faced by an individual should be changed by altering the individual or by altering society" is itself a contextualized judgment. She cites two contrasting examples.

To tackle a problem of discrimination between a White majority and Black minority, it is not acceptable to suggest that "Black people's" skin color should be "bleached." Rather, it is society's attitudes and behaviors that should be changed. On the other hand, to tackle the difficulties an "ugly" individual might have in acquiring a partner, it is acceptable to suggest the individual's appearance be changed, rather than the attitudes of those in society who would attribute the judgment of ugliness.

Thus, the differentiation is not between an individualized perspective on impairment versus a social perspective on disability, but between the relative and relational value of judgments made about the acceptability or not of the individual or society being the locus of change. In relation, particularly to deaf children, this analysis calls us to question why it has been, for centuries, that the acceptable locus of change has been predominantly within the child (that the child is assisted to become hearing) rather than within society (i.e., that they are assisted toward a cultural understanding of being Deaf). We take up this discussion further in Chapter 3, when we consider the relationship between epistemology and politics in research designs.

BOUNDARY CROSSING

Thus far, we have largely focused on the ways in which being deaf or Deaf might be understood, as if from afar. Models are invariably structures for understanding and explaining, and the differentiation between the medical, cultural, and disability models is important. However, what happens when we start to think about people, rather than models or constructions of what it is to be d/Deaf? As we discuss at length in Chapter 5 (Populations and Sampling), people in research studies invariably transgress the boundaries of how a researcher might seek to explain, classify, or analyze them.

Picture a successful professional arriving at a board meeting. The company, acknowledging their duty under the Americans with Disabilities Act (1990), has ensured an American Sign Language (ASL) interpreter is available because this is the professional's first and preferred language; she is culturally Deaf. She prefers in this hearing environment, however, only to use the interpreter for receptive communication and uses her own voice and the English language to make her points; she is bilingual. She wears hearing aids as she enjoys the environmental sound connections they provide her with at work and on a one-to-one basis they sometimes help if she is trying to lip-read a colleague. This character has transgressed and acknowledged in her preferred ways to be, in that particular context, every model we might seek to use to explain the ways in which she is d/Deaf. Her identity is *performed* through her choices. In a different context, at home with a Deaf partner, she may well make different choices.

Our point is not just that there is a danger in assuming that boundaries between different perspectives on being d/Deaf are impermeable (Corker, 1998), but that there is something vitally important too about how people choose to transgress them. As Ladd (1994) argues: "theories of cultures should be constructed in such a way that they contain dialectical relations; e.g. they should encapsulate the dynamic that one can break cultural rules, accidentally or deliberately, yet still remain inside the culture" (pp. 331–332). Myers and Fernandes (2010) warn of the dangers of seeking to delineate too firmly the boundaries of an identity or culture in such a way as to deny the diversity of the many ways in which d/Deaf people lead their lives.

However, for any people who might struggle to have their identity legitimately recognized on terms that the mainstream might hitherto have denied, boundary-crossing can be dangerous. If the cultural and linguistic identity of Deaf people remains open to debate and denial, then a certain retrenchment into clear definitions of why Deaf is not disabled, and why deafness might have little to do with being Deaf, becomes understandable. It is what Spivak and Harasym (1990), in a different context, termed "strategic essentialism." Until Deaf people's cultural-linguistic identity is universally recognized and enfranchisement and equality attained, then the discussion of nuanced positions within that identity is a luxury that some would suggest cannot be afforded (Ladd et al., 2003).

However, there is a world of difference between saying identity or culture is recognizable through the display of certain traits and the position that to be regarded as possessing that identity or culture one must also possess a fixed set of traits. Krentz (2009), for example, argues that Dunn's (2008) research is based on a definition of Deaf as people who are from Deaf families and attended Deaf Schools and therefore excludes many other Deaf sign language users. Kelly (2008) notes the long-standing oversight of the Deaf female experience, subsumed under the universal "Deaf." Bienvenu (2008) writes that the term "Deaf" has been defined using normative baselines of sexuality. Myers and Fernandes (2010) argue that Deaf culture has come to be largely defined according to a White Deaf ASL perspective. De Clerck (2010) reminds us of the significance of generational differences among those who would describe themselves as "Deaf."

From a different starting point, the public discourse of many pediatric cochlear implant programs might well also be considered essentialist. Their overriding goals are the restoration of hearing and the improvement of speech. However, the child with a cochlear implant is rarely regarded as a child who might use multiple languages in different modalities (spoken and/or signed) and who might explore Deaf and deaf identities as she grows up. She is usually portrayed as one for whom *her implant implies her identity*; she will become a deaf child whose success will be measured in terms of her hearing and spoken language use.

In questioning essentialist perspectives in these ways, the important issue is not simply that there is diversity within Deaf communities and among d/Deaf peoples that should be recognized (Myers & Fernandes, 2010; Obasi, 2008; Parasnis, 1996), or that an individual might legitimately be in possession of several identities in relationship with each other, for example, Asian and Deaf (Foster & Kinuthia, 2003) or gay and Deaf (Luczak, 1993). But rather that at an epistemological level we need to be cautious about how we use language which seeks to define, affiliate, or classify, if as a result of using a term we imply *a* version of identity or culture to become validated while another remains denied. Can we really say "the Deaf perspective" or the "deaf point of view" and know what it is we imply? We return to this issue when considering epistemology (Chapter 3) and populations and sampling (Chapter 5).

CONCLUDING THOUGHTS

In the opening pages of this book we introduce some of the many complexities and crosscurrents in understanding what it is to be d/Deaf. While we begin with the ways in which these complexities are often presented in terms of competing models, we deconstruct the apparent binaries and divisions between them by drawing attention to the significance of ontological politics, performative identities, and the power of social constructions. We do not come down on the side of any single model per se but stress the importance of researchers engaging with the complexities of being d/Deaf. We argue that researchers have choices in who they include in research and how they label and represent people and that these choices have consequences. Research itself is a social process which contributes to the denial, reinforcement, challenge, and legitimization of what it might be to be d/Deaf. Transgressing accepted wisdom that particular models are always and in themselves valueless or valuable is a difficult balancing act, but it is more compatible with a view of research as constitutive of social reality/realities. Such realities are not posed in everyday life as clearly defined binaries.

Throughout the book we will analyze and demonstrate the significance of the complexities we introduce in this chapter for every stage of the research process from the epistemological basis of research studies, through study design, data collection, and analysis, to the dissemination of results/findings and the bases on which knowledge claims are made. Our argument is that the contested nature of what it is to be d/Deaf exerts influence on every aspect of research which involves d/Deaf people(s). By "involve" we mean d/Deaf people as producers, participants/subjects, and consumers of research. We take the reader through research stages and point to the implications of particular choices and epistemological positions. For example, we suggest that the definition and status of nar-rative is contested, as is the nature of interpretation, transcription, and translation. One researcher's transcription is another researcher's transla-tion. We suggest viewing the activity of research through the lens of such complexities, rather than seeing it merely as a pick-and-mix exercise from a menu of possible methods. This makes social research more challenging because researchers have to specify how they make decisions about the most appropriate research process for them and the criteria they use to define validity. These are issues we raise in the following chapter.

REFERENCES

Alker, D. (2000). *Really not interested in deaf people?* Darwen, Lancashire, UK: Doug Alker Associates.

Americans with Disabilies Act (1990). Retrieved March 15, 2013, from http://www.ada.gov/pubs/ada.htm

Bahan, B. (1994). Comment on Turner. *Sign Language Studies, 83,* 241–249.

Bajaj, Y., Sirimanna, T., Albert, D. M., Qadir, P., Jenkins, L., Cortina-Borja, M., & Bitner-Glindzicz, M. (2009). Causes of deafness in British Bangladeshi chil-dren: A prevalence twice that of the UK population cannot be accounted for by consanguinity alone. *Clinical Otolaryngology, 34*(2), 113–119. doi: 10.1111/j.1749-4486.2009.01888.x

Baker, C., & Cokely, D. (1980). *American Sign Language: A teacher's resource text on grammar and culture.* Silver Spring, MD: TJ Publishers.

Batterbury, S. C. E., Ladd, P., & Gulliver, M. (2007). Sign language peoples as indigenous minorities: Implications for research and policy. [Feature]. *Environment and Planning A, 39*(12), 2899–2915. doi: 10.1068/a388

Beckett, A. (2006). Understanding social movements: Theorising the disabil-ity movement in conditions of late modernity. *The Sociological Review, 54,* 734–752. doi: 10.1111/j.1467-954X.2006.00669.x

Bess, F., & Humes, L. E. (2008). *Audiology: The fundamentals* (4th ed.). London: Lippincott Williams & Wilkins.

Bienvenu, M. (2008). Queer as Deaf: Intersections. In H. D. L. Bauman (Ed.), *Open your eyes: Deaf studies talking* (pp. 264–276). Minneapolis: University of Minnesota Press.

Brennan, M. (1975). Can deaf children acquire language? *American Annals of the Deaf, 120*(5), 463–479.

Cooper, R. (2012). Can it be a good thing to be deaf? In P. Paul & D. F. Moores (Eds.), *Deaf epistemologies: Multiple perspectives on the acquisition of knowledge* (pp. 236–254). Washington, DC: Gallaudet University Press.

Corker, M. (1998). *Deaf and disabled, or deafness disabled? Towards a human rights perspective.* Buckingham, UK: Open University Press.

Corker, M. (2002). Deafness/Disability—problematising notions of identity, culture and structure, (pp. 1–18). Retrieved November 29, 2013, from http://disability-studies.leeds.ac.uk/files/library/Corker-Deafness.pdf Cupitt, D. (1998). *The religion of being.* London: SCM Press.

Davis, L. (1995). *Enforcing normalcy: disability, deafness and the body.* London: Verso.

De Clerck, G. A. (2010). Deaf epistemologies as a critique and alternative to the practice of science: An anthropological perspective. *American Annals of the Deaf, 154*(5), 435–446.

Delaporte, Y. (2002). *Les sourds, c'est comme ca.* Paris: Édition de la Maison des sciences de l'homme.

Dunn, L. (2008). The burden of racism and audism. In H. D. L. Bauman (Ed.), *Open your eyes: Deaf studies talking* (pp. 235–250). Minneapolis: University of Minnesota Press.

Emmorey, K., & Kosslyn, S. (1996). Enhanced image generation in abilities in deaf signers: A right hemisphere effect. *Brain and Cognition, 32*(1), 28–44. doi: Article number 0056.

Emmorey, K., Kosslyn, S., & Bellugi, U. (1993). Visual imagery and visual-spatial language: Enhanced visual imagery abilities in deaf and hearing ASL signers. *Cognition, 46*(2), 139–181.

Equality Act (2010). Retrieved March 15, 2013, from http://www.legislation.gov.uk/ukpga/2010/15/contents

Erting, C. (1978). Language policy and Deaf ethnicity in the United States. *Sign Language Studies, 19*, 139–152.

Finkelstein, V. (1993). The commonality of disability. In J. Swain, S. French, V. Finkelstein, & M. Oliver (Eds.), *Disabling barriers enabling environments* (pp. 9–16). London: Open University Press.

Foster, S., & Kinuthia, W. (2003). Deaf persons of Asian American, Hispanic American, and African American backgrounds: A study of intraindividual diversity and identity. *Journal of Deaf Studies and Deaf Education, 8*(3), 271–290. doi: 10.1093/deafed/eng015

Gascon-Ramos, M., Campbell, M., Bamford, J., & Young, A. (2010). Influences on parental evaluation of the content of early intervention following early identification of deafness: A study about parents' preferences and satisfaction. *Child Care Health and Development, 36*(6), 868–877. doi: 10.1111/j.1365-2214.2010.01092.x

Hall, S. (1991). Door into Deaf culture: Folklore in an American Deaf social club. *Sign Language Studies, 73*(Winter), 421–429.

Hitselberger, W. E., Brackmann, D. E., Day, J. D., Shannon, R., Otto, S., & Ghosh, S. (2001). Auditory brain stem implants. *Operative Techniques in Neurosurgery, 4*(1), 47–52. doi: 10.1053/otns.2001.25264

Hogan, A. (2001). *Hearing rehabilitation for deafened adults: A psychosocial approach.* London: Whurr.

Kates, J. (2008). *Digital hearing aids.* San Diego, CA: Plural Publishing.

Kelly, A. (2008). Where's Deaf HERstory? In H. D. L. Bauman (Ed.), *Open your eyes: Deaf studies talking* (pp. 251–263). Minneapolis: University of Minnesota Press.

Kennedy, C., McCann, D., Campbell, M., Law, C., Mullee, M., Petrou, Watkin, P., Worsfold, S., Yuen, H., & Stevenson, J. (2006). Language ability after early detection of permanent childhood hearing impairment. *New England Journal of Medicine, 354*(20), 2131–2141.

Krentz, C. (2009). Open your eyes: Deaf studies talking (review). *Sign Language Studies, 10*(1), 110–132. doi: 10.1353/sls.0.0032.

Kusters, A. (2009). Deaf on the lifeline of Mumbai. *Sign Language Studies, 10*(1), 36–68. doi: 10.1353/sls.0.0035

Ladd, P. (1994). Comment on Turner. *Sign Language Studies, 85*, 327–336.

Ladd, P. (2003). *Understanding Deaf culture: In search of Deafhood.* Clevedon, UK: Multilingual Matters.

Ladd, P., Gulliver, M., & Batterbury, S. C. E. (2003). Reassessing minority language mepowerment from a Deaf perspective: The other 32 languages. *Deaf Worlds, 19*(2), 6–32.

Lane, H. (1984). *When the mind hears: A history of the Deaf.* New York: Random House.

Lane, H. (1995). Constructions of Deafness. *Disability & Society, 10*(2), 171–189. doi: 10.1080/09687599550023633

Lane, H., Hoffmeister, B., & Bahan, B. (1996). *A journey into the Deaf world.* Washington DC: Dawn Sign Press.

Lane, H., Pillard, R. C., & Hedberg, U. (2010). *People of the eye: Deaf ethnicity and ancestry.* New York: Oxford University Press.

Law, J. (2009). Seeing like a survey. *Cultural Sociology, 3*(2), 239–256. doi: 10.1177/1749975509105533

Luczak, R. (Ed.). (1993). *Eyes of desire: A deaf gay & lesbian reader.* New York City: Alyson Books.

Maitland, S. (1994). *Home truths.* London: Hodder and Stroughton.

Morgan-Jones, R. (2001). *Hearing differently: The impact of hearing impairment on family life.* London: Whurr.

Musengi, M., Ndofirepi, A., & Shumba, A. (2013). Rethinking education of deaf children in Zimbabwe: Challenges and opportunities for teacher education. *Journal of Deaf Studies and Deaf Education, 18*(1), 62–74. doi: 10.1093/deafed/ens037

Myers, S. S., & Fernandes, J. K. (2010). Deaf studies: A critique of the predominant U.S. theoretical direction. *Journal of Deaf Studies and Deaf Education, 15*(1), 30–49. doi: 10.1093/deafed/enp017

Napier, J. (2002). The D/deaf–H/hearing debate. *Sign Language Studies, 2*(2), 141–149. doi: 10.1353/sls.2002.0006

Obasi, C. (2008). Seeing the Deaf in "Deafness." *Journal of Deaf Studies and Deaf Education, 13*(4), 455–465. doi: 10.1093/deafed/enn008

Oliver, M. (1990). *The politics of disablement.* Basingstoke, UK: Macmillan.

Padden, C., & Humphries, T. (1988). *Deaf in America: Voices from a culture.* Cambridge, MA: Harvard University Press.

Parasnis, I. (Ed.). (1996). *Cultural and language diversity and the deaf experience.* New York: Cambridge University Press.

Poizner, H., Klima, E. S., & Bellugi, U. (1987). *What the hands reveal about the brain.* Cambridge, MA: MIT Press/Bradford Books.

Rée, J. (1999). *I see a voice.* London: Harper Collins.

Shakespeare, T. (2006). *Disability rights and wrongs.* Abingdon, UK: Routledge.

Spivak, G., & Harasym, S. (1990). *The post-colonial critic: Interviews, strategies, dialogues.* New York: Routledge.

Stokoe, W. (1960). Sign Language structure: An outline of the visual communication systems of the American deaf. *Studies in Linguistics, Occasional Papers* (8), 1–41.

Sutton-Spence, R., & West, D. (2011). Negotiating the legacy of hearingness. *Qualitative Inquiry, 17*(5), 422–432. doi: 10.1177/1077800411405428.

Tervoort, B. (1961). Esoteric symbolism in the communication behavior of young deaf children. *American Annals of the Deaf, 106* (5), 436–480.

Turner, G. H. (1994). How is Deaf culture? Toward a revised notion of a fundamental concept. *Sign Language Studies, 83*, 103–126.

van Uden, A. (1977). *A maternal reflective method of teaching an oral mother tongue to deaf children: psycholinguistics in the service of the deaf.* St Michielsgestel, The Netherlands: The Institute of the Deaf.

Verhaert, N., Willems, M., Van Kerschaver, E., & Desloovere, C. (2008). Impact of early hearing screening and treatment on language development and education level: Evaluation of 6 years of universal newborn hearing screening (ALGOW) in Flanders, Belgium. *International Journal of Pediatric Otorhinolaryngology, 72*, 599–608. doi: doi:10.1016/j.ijporl.2008.01.012

Woodward, J. (1975). *How you gonna get to heaven if you can't talk with Jesus: The educational establishment vs. the Deaf community.* Paper presented at the 34th Annual Meeting of the Society for Applied Anthropology, Royal Tropical Institute, Amsterdam, The Netherlands.

Young, A. (2006). The Experience of Deafness—psycho-social effects. In V. Newton & P. Vallely (Eds.), *Infection and hearing impairment* (pp. 279–286). London: Whurr.

Zeng, F. G., Popper, A. N., & Fay, R. R. (Eds.). (2004). *Cochlear implants: Auditory prostheses and electric hearing.* London: Springer.

3

Epistemology, Methodology and Method

In the previous chapter we show how attempts to distinguish between various "models of deafness" can be unhelpful. We argue that a more ontological approach to the many ways in which it is possible to *be* d/Deaf can be more revealing of the complexities of identity and the implications for research. In this chapter we take the argument one step further in considering how researchers *represent* what it means to be d/Deaf in their research. That is, we explore the links between onto-logical approaches, views of what is valid knowledge, and what comes to be known about d/Deaf people: in other words, epistemology.

We define epistemological concerns as "how reality can be known, who is or should be a knower, what the relationship is between the knower and the knowable, and on what grounds his or her knowledge should be trusted" (Young & Ackerman, 2001, p. 180). We argue that such issues are central to research. Epistemological choices influence reasoning and judgment about what are appropriate research questions and strategies. They affect what we see as important and, equally sig-nificantly, what we do not see. When the very definition of what it is to be deaf or Deaf is contested, a researcher's epistemological position is more than an interesting esoteric philosophical conundrum. It is vital to an examination of the quality of a research study and its relative influ-ence, for whom, in what contexts, and why.

Epistemological choices affect the methodologies and methods researchers use, but relationships between them are not straightforward. In this chapter we begin by examining three issues. First, whether the "model of deafness" underpinning a research study has anything to do with a researcher's epistemological approach. Does a medical model of deafness really imply a positivist epistemology as some writers argue? Second, we show how an epistemological position is not predictive of a methodology. To illustrate this point, we give examples of research-ers who view quantitative methodologies in ways traditionally seen as limited to qualitative methodologies. And finally, we suggest that it is not possible to assume that a method is tied to an epistemological posi-tion; for example, surveys need not be positivist.

The extensive and broad literature on the "philosophy of the social sciences" (Alvesson & Skoldberg, 2009; Hutchinson, Read, & Sharrock,

2008) contains complex debates and highly nuanced positions based on different views of social reality and epistemologies such as positivism, post-positivism, social constructionism, interpretivism, realism, critical realism, postmodernism, feminism, and many more. We discuss some of these next. Our intention is not to provide detailed descriptions or commentaries on them because excellent texts exist elsewhere (Alvesson & Skoldberg, 2009; Law, 2004; May, 2001; Smith, 1998; Stanley, 1990). In this chapter we address how researchers describe the foundations of their work in epistemological terms, why and how relationships are claimed between being d/Deaf and particular epistemological positions, and on what basis we may regard the findings of their work to be valid. We stress throughout the significance of the influence of the researcher and finish by asking how much we need to know about a researcher to enable a reflexive engagement with research.

IS THERE A RELATIONSHIP BETWEEN "MODELS OF DEAFNESS" AND EPISTEMOLOGY?

It is common for researchers working with people who are d/Deaf to discuss epistemological issues in research in relationship to cultural, social, or medical models of "deafness" (see previous chapter.) For example, debates around Turner's (Turner, 1994a, 1994b) critique of essentialist notions of culture elicited responses questioning who is best placed to make claims about Deaf cultures and communities (who can be a knower) as well as recognition that the concept of culture is fluid and contestable (Bahan, 1994; Ladd, 1994; Monaghan, 1994; Montgomery, 1994; Stokoe, 1994; Street, 1994).

More recently a more direct examination has begun to take place of the relationship between the assumptions which underpin medical, social, and cultural models of being d/Deaf and those which underpin approaches to generating knowledge through research. It is argued that a medical model of deafness, for example, implicitly assumes a true standard, that is, to be hearing, and that therefore deviations from that norm (being deaf) require amelioration. Consequently, from a research perspective, it is argued that medical models of deafness imply a positivist research epistemology in which knowledge is regarded unambiguously as knowable and reality is measurable. This position has been referred to by researchers working with Deaf people as "the standard epistemology" (Holcomb, 2010; Paul & Moores, 2010a, 2012). Researchers using such epistemologies look for ways to carry out research which will help to remove their influence from it. That is, they try to remain objective and to establish the truth. Who the researcher is, the researcher's identity(ies) is of little consequence. For example, recent experiments on deafened gerbils using human stem cells to restore "damaged sensory circuitry" (Chen et al., 2012, p. 490) assume unequivocally that deafness is a biophysical phenomenon and a problem; this is not assumed to be just the position of the researchers, and it is presented as scientific fact.[1]

It is rare to find a study which begins from assumptions of deafness as impairment *and* examines the implications of that worldview for the choices made in the conduct of the research. More commonly, the deafness as impairment/medical model perspective is taken as understood—no need to regard it as a "position" (see Chapter 5). Likewise methodological decisions are rarely regarded as being shaped in any way by the professional or personal identity(ies) of the researcher and their affiliations. We make this point, because in a field where deafness as problem, impairment, or lack is both the dominant and normative discourse, it is easy to see concerns about epistemology, and its links with methodology and method, as confined only to those who might challenge this view. But to regard it as such is a misreading. The relationship is one which exists and calls for examination, regardless of where a researcher might begin in social research involving d/Deaf people.

Cultural models of being Deaf emphasize the uniqueness of a Deaf person's experience of the world, Deaf ways of knowing, and therefore cultural relativism within wider society (Bahan, 2008; Bauman & Murray, 2010; Ladd, Gulliver, & Batterbury, 2003). Consequently from a research perspective, it is argued that cultural models of being Deaf imply an epistemology in which there is no single truth, reality/(ties) is regarded as constituted through multiple perspectives, and the interactions of language and society in the creation of knowledge is central (we discuss this in more detail later). Who does the research is therefore vital as their identity, experience, and understanding is seen to have a direct influence on how knowledge is generated and interpreted. There is no assumption of objective truth, only of subjectively generated understandings which are open to change, contextually specific, and to some extent temporary (of their time). For example, in Conama's (2010, 2013) comparative study of Finnish and Irish Deaf communities, his identity as a Deaf Irish man is deemed central both to the generation of data and its interpretation.

Stated in this way, it is easy to see how an approach which links models of deafness with particular research epistemologies is attractive in its simplicity. From a Deaf perspective, it emphasizes how research studies which assume deafness is a problem utilize research approaches which seek objective truths and therefore inevitably do not allow for alternative and hidden perspectives (those of Deaf people). It is argued that this epistemological position precludes the possibility of uncovering Deaf realities and, whether intentionally or not, oppresses Deaf ways of knowing because they are considered of no relevance.

However, the argument which seeks directly to tie a model of deafness with a particular research epistemology has some distinct problems.

For example, some critics of "standard" epistemology are arguably still using positivist baselines as their gold standard. Holcomb (2010) argues that the standard epistemology and what he terms "Deaf epistemology" should not be viewed as oxymoronic but that Deaf experiences can themselves provide "the truth" (p. 476). In later work he calls for researchers to "launch scientific hypotheses to test Deaf-centered teaching practices" (2012, p. 134) and suggests that Deaf epistemologies need to be supported by empirical studies that "meet the rigor of the standard epistemology" (p. 139).

However, many researchers have pointed out that science itself is not practiced in the way presented in this account. They challenge the view that science and medicine are "objective" and question the accepted wisdom that scientists do not influence the objects of their research (Harding, 1986; Kuhn, 1964; Latour & Woolgar, 1979; Law, 2004; Mulkay, 1979; Smith, 1998; Thoutenhoofd, 2010). Some scientists themselves recognize that they do not work with objective certainties. Moreover, we argue later that researchers who subscribe to epistemologies other than those based on the drive to objectivity would not want to ape criteria such as those suggested in the call for scientific hypotheses testing.

The longing to embrace "the truth" and "objectivity" is also evident in the work of Paul and Moores (2010b), who argue for an "objective methodology" (p. 424). The quest for objectivity has here moved from epistemology to methodology (we return to this later). The work of Paul and Moores (2010b) and Holcomb (2010) show that so-called Deaf methods and methodologies can be tied to concerns that are more usually linked to standard epistemologies such as positivism.

Researchers who work with epistemologies that are based on the impossibility of removing the influence of the researcher from research argue that there is no "outside" away from the influences of the social world. For example, Law (2004) uses his work on alcoholic liver disease to show how medical professionals in his research worked with two realities—two alcohol liver diseases—rather than working with the stereotypical view of scientific epistemology. One reality is produced by medicine in textbooks, wards, and consulting rooms; this is the more powerful version. The second is partly medical too but extends to the psychiatric and social relations of the production of medical narratives. This reality is still about the body but is also about culture, social life, easy access to alcohol, stressful lives, and sometimes psychiatric illness (p. 76). Professionals in Law's research worked to find a balance between *fluid realities*. He asks: Surely the body-based and predominantly medical version of reality is appropriate under some circumstances? He notes that if the patient is dying, then a strong medical regime and medical reality is what is required.

There is without doubt a long history of research studies that, founded on a single perspective on being deaf (impairment), have predominantly pursued studies which in seeking to measure, understand, improve, and cure deafness have utilized a positivist epistemology. And in seeking to challenge and invert this dominant approach and uncover instead Deaf ways of knowing, an epistemology that is not based on the drive for objectivity has been the more compelling. But a "model of deafness" does not imply a research epistemology and vice-versa. The cultural reality(ies) of being Deaf can be of great significance within studies traditionally seen as positivist in seeking to assess, measure, and test. One example is Rogers and colleagues' (2013) study testing the reliability of a British Sign Language (BSL) version of three standard psychological instruments. A Deaf perspective on Deaf world experience leads to one of several hypotheses suggested for an explanation of an unusual result within the testing of the psychometric properties of an instrument. In a similar vein, it is the social construction of an experience of impairment which has formed the basis of studies firmly focused on rehabilitation and cure-seeking; for example, Morgan-Jones' (2001) study of the impact of hearing impairment on family life. But if there is no self-evident link between how we view (and experience) what it is to be d/Deaf and epistemological choices, is there one between epistemology and methodology?

IS THERE A RELATIONSHIP BETWEEN EPISTEMOLOGY AND METHODOLOGY?

We define methodology in this chapter as the "broad approach to inquiry that brings together and ensures reasonable fit between conceptual framework, epistemological underpinnings, theory, method, substantive concerns, the analysis of data and the drawing of appropriate conclusions from this" (Stanley & Temple, 2008, p. 277). For example, researchers discuss narrative methodologies or quantitative methodologies. Methods are the techniques researchers use.

Discussing quantitative methodologies, Montgomery (1994) argues that statistical correlations are "a harder more scientific approach to definition than the verbal" (p. 263). This positioning of statistics has been undermined by many researchers, including quantitative researchers themselves, whose epistemologies are nearer those usually attached to qualitative methodologies in that they specify how they construct their definitions "verbally" before using statistical techniques. The argument that quantitative methodologies can be viewed in the same way as qualitative ones in terms of epistemological perspective is not new (Bryman, 1988; Hughes, 1990; Law, 2009; Silverman, 1993; Stanley, 1990; Temple, 1994). Pugh (1990), for example, argues that numbers are just like words in that they "reflect their construction" (p. 110). Decisions about what theories to investigate, what questions to ask, the process of grouping answers into categories, and assigning numbers to the categories (coding) to enable quantitative analysis all affect the out-come. Such decisions are necessarily based on a researcher's experi-ence. For example, a researcher asks herself/himself: Do I think these categories make sense? How can I group categories so that cell sizes are adequate for statistical analysis? This kind of analysis requires, depends on, sensitivity to the data and what can be done with and to it. Quantitative methodologies can, therefore, equally be viewed using more constructionist epistemologies (see Young, Gascon-Ramos, Campbell, & Bamford, 2009, who discuss the analysis of quantitative narratives in this vein).

Moreover, there are debates over the status of the increasingly popular mixed (quantitative and qualitative) methodologies (Cresswell, 2003). In particular, there are differences in views concerning whether such meth-odologies necessitate a separate epistemology (Harrits, 2011; Tashakkori & Teddle, 2003), a debate which suggests that there are differences in the ways researchers tie epistemology and methodology together. For example, do the claims to a Deaf epistemology imply that there is a Deaf methodology? Ladd's (2003) construction of "Deaf-led research" would suggest so. "Deaf-led" does not refer to the lead researcher being Deaf necessarily but that methodological decisions are founded on Deaf ways of knowing (epistemology), which in turn suggest the methods to be used. On the other hand, De Clerck (2010), while acknowledging deaf epistemologies in the plural and signaling the fluid and contextual nature of identity by her use of "d," does not argue for "deaf" method-ologies. She does nonetheless examine the relationships between episte-mology and methodology which derive from being "deaf."

Although these two authors may occupy different positions and be more or less reluctant to claim "deaf" or "Deaf" methodologies as a con-cept to be named, there are points of agreement. Both are emphasizing the significance of the epistemology, values, experiences, and politics of the individual doing the research. It matters that the experiences of being d/Deaf (ontological realities) and d/Deaf ways of knowing (epistemolo-gies) shape the conceptual framework of the research; that researchers beginning from this position critically use or adapt the chosen method-ological approach to be consistent with that framework; and that they develop methods which cohere with those choices. In other words, epis-temology and methodology are inextricably but not deterministically bound together because it matters from where a researcher begins her or his engagement with a study and who that researcher might be.

IS THERE A RELATIONSHIP BETWEEN EPISTEMOLOGY AND METHOD?

The logic of our discussion so far on the epistemological status of meth-odologies suggests that particular methods are not tied to particular epistemologies. For example, qualitative interviews can be treated as if they are the only correct way to do research, that is, in a positivist way (see Chapter 6 for examples from narrative interviews). Surveys can be seen as constructed narratives (see earlier examples and Chapter 6). Schroedel's (1984) analysis of 41 surveys of adults who are deaf in the United States and Canada between 1959 and 1981 pulls out the significance of definitions of terms such as deafness, deaf population, and Deaf community and the lessons for the interpretation of results. This approach can be seen as sympathetic to constructionist views, although Schroedel never discusses epistemology.

Atkinson, Gleeson, Cromwell, and O'Rourke's (2007) study of the perceptual characteristics of voice hallucinations among a heterogeneous group of "deaf people" (their terminology) is an illuminating example of the relationship between epistemology and method. They applied principal component factor analysis to obtain clusters of individuals who described their experiences in similar ways based on the sorting of pre-prepared descriptive statements. The analysis demonstrated that the perceptual characteristics of voice hallucinations mapped closely onto individual auditory experience. However, the authors situate this seemingly strongly quantitative approach within a constructionist epistemology, using what they describe as a "deaf-led" research design in order to "maximise cultural and linguistic validity" (p. 340). In practice, this implies the deconstruction of "deaf conceptualizations" of sound-based phenomena. For example, "Concepts such as 'loud' may be understood by many deaf people as being highly intrusive and difficult to ignore rather than meaning high auditory volume, and 'quiet' might connote that the voice is not present at all" (p. 340). In turn, this deconstruction determined *how* statements concerning voice hallucinations should be represented within the statement-sorting task on which the later analysis was based. In other words, the epistemological underpinnings in this case directly influenced the method (the tools used within the statement-sorting task). The point we are making here is that we cannot assume that just because researchers use quantitative methods they must be positivists.

Our analysis that there is a justifiable and important but not fixed relationship between epistemology and method stands in contrast to many writers who would assert, as McLaughlin (2009) does, that "once a methodology is adopted the choice of method(s) becomes a *technical*, not a philosophical decision" (McLaughlin, 2009, emphasis ours). To treat method as merely technical, divorced and dissociated from epistemology, is dangerous because as Law (2004) argues: "methods, their rules, and even more methods' practices, not only describe but also help to produce the reality that they understand" (p. 5). He asserts that method "does politics" and "is not innocent" (p. 149) because *methods* enable some realities and exclude others. For example, the choice researchers make whether to use focus groups or interviews may influence what kind of data they get, as participants may discuss and present their views differently in group situations compared to one-to-one interviews. Moreover, some participants prefer focus groups, and others prefer interviews, and who becomes included or excluded as a result of the methods researchers use affects the data researchers collect.

We conclude, therefore, that methods are more than technical tools. While a method may be linked to a methodology, such a link is not predetermined. The association of methods with epistemology is vital to the assessment of a piece of research—an issue we return to later in this chapter. First, we address how our discussion so far on the complex relationships between epistemology, methodology, and method relates to the increasing call for approaches to research in this field that are based on Deaf epistemology(ies).

DEAF EPISTEMOLOGIES

A variety of alternative epistemologies to those concerned with being "objective" have developed within social research and are used by researchers working with d/Deaf people. Social constructionism, feminism, and postmodernism have been used to critique overtly or implicitly positivist/essentialist positions in respect of Deaf people (Bauman, 2008; Brueggemann, 2008; De Clerck, 2010, 2012a, 2012b; Hauser, O'Hearn, McKee, Steider, & Thew, 2010; Holcomb, 2010; Ladd, 2003; Miller, 2010, 2012; Nelson, 2006; Parasnis, 2012; Paul & Moores, 2010a, 2010b; Wang, 2010; Young & Ackerman, 2001). As De Clerck (2010) states: "A deaf knowing subject emerged, and deaf ways of seeing and being were claimed" (p. 438).

Social constructionism is now used to cover a variety of approaches that signal the interpretative nature of social reality (see Alvesson & Skoldberg, 2009 for a general overview and Hole, 2007, Miller, 2010, specifically in relation to research with Deaf people). There are subtle distinctions between social constructionist views about whether there is a reality (or realities) researchers can study, as suggested by Elder-Vass (2012), but all would agree that there is no objective way to study people's lives. Postmodernism has also been defined in a variety of ways, including a broad label used to make observations about contemporary issues as well as a way of questioning the existence of any knowledge claims that are not contingent on context (May, 2001). Feminist epistemologies are similarly widely variable but arguably center on concern with subjective consciousness, the devaluation, silencing, and oppression of girls and women which other epistemologies may underpin, and the development of theories within an acknowledgment that all knowledge is subject to critique from other viewpoints (Griffiths, 1995).

Many social constructionists, postmodernists, and feminists challenge the way language is used to represent reality. Reality is seen as constructed by people in their everyday lives and not a given that can be analyzed from outside of it. Language, it is argued, is not referential of reality in any straightforward way. Words, including those used to produce codes for quantitative data, are not tied to specific meanings; understanding is situational and unavoidably influenced by the perspective of the researcher. Language matters in that it can label people; exclude and maintain dominant discourses such as sexism, racism, and disablism; and can therefore affect life chances and well-being (Corbett, 1996; Spender, 1980).

In relation to Deaf people and discussing communication and language, Hauser, O'Hearn, McKee, Steider, and Thew (2010) argue that as a result of biology, Deaf people live "a visual reality, which leads to the acquisition of a knowledge base that is different from that of hearing individuals" (p. 487). However, this defines knowing from a position that would exclude people, for example, who have been deafened in later life. It has been challenged by Thoutenhoofd (1998) as essentializing (we discuss this view of people who sign as more visual in Chapter 6). In a similar way, Corker (1998, 1999) considers whether the concept of Deaf reintroduces deaf/hearing binaries. Increasingly, therefore, views of social reality/realities use social constructionist, feminist, and postmodern epistemologies and posit Deaf *epistemologies* (plural) which are nonessentialist and nonpositivist, as researchers have shown that previous definitions have served to exclude particular groups and in effect essentialized what being Deaf means (see Chapter 2). Researchers examine how definitions of Deaf culture have come into being, whom they exclude, and whether definitions based on other concepts would be less exclusive and more useful (Bienvenu, 2008; Brueggemann, 2008; Dunn, 2008; Kelly, 2008; Krentz, 2009). They have attempted to move away from the objective/subjective dichotomy as well as other binaries such as individual/social, deaf/hearing, emotion/reason, and impairment/disability, which are evident in positivist accounts of knowledge generation.

However, some postmodernists go further in questioning whether any research, be it text, oral, written, or signed, is "anchored in either a producer of texts (subject) or an external world" (Alvesson & Skoldberg, 2009, p. 179). For example, see Clifford and Marcus (1986); Derrida (1976, 1982); Foucault (2003, 2005); and Lyotard (1984).[2] The works of Lyotard, Foucault, and Derrida have been productively used within research with Deaf people in ways that attempt to avoid the extreme forms of postmodernism and its drawbacks (Bauman, 2008; Brueggemann, 2008; Ladd, 2003; McIlroy & Storbeck, 2011; Nelson, 2006). For example, Lane (1992) uses the work of Foucault to distinguish culturally based perspectives from infirmity-based ones, which generate technologies such as cochlear implants and genetic research (see also Friedner, 2010, for a discussion of Lane's work). These he identifies as threatening Deaf ways of knowing and being in the world. Bauman similarly (2008) builds on Derrida. He argues, quoting Derrida, that voice and insistence on phonetic writing is "the most original and powerful ethnocentrism" (Bauman, 2008, p. 7).

De Clerck (2010), looking from an anthropological, postcolonial perspective at the practice of science, adds Deaf critiques of audism and phonocentrism to those of Marxist, postcolonial, and subaltern positions, feminist and Black/Afrocentric critiques of the how scientists work in practice. Audism is "the hearing way of dominating, restructuring, and exercising authority over the Deaf community" (Humphries, quoted in De Clerck, 2010, p. 438). Phonocentrism is the conflation of a full identity with speech and sound (Bauman, 2008). Research which similarly usefully builds on feminist writing includes Kelly (2008), who focuses on feminist standpoint epistemologies, and Nelson (2006), who uses the writings of French feminists as well as those of Derrida (1976).

However, epistemologies that challenge the possibility of objectivity in research pose challenges for researchers as critics have raised charges of relativism (for a review of this critique, see Alvesson & Skoldberg, 2009). How do researchers distinguish between different research accounts if none of them are about "the truth"? We return to this later.

As a result of claims that definitions of Deaf ontology have been exclusionary, researchers increasingly refer to Deaf *epistemologies* rather than Deaf epistemology. For example, Ladd's notion of Deafhood is central to many discussions by researchers in this area (De Clerck, 2010; McIlroy & Storbeck, 2011). It "represents a process—the struggle of each Deaf child, Deaf family, and Deaf adult to explain to themselves and each other their own existence in the world" (Ladd, 2003, p. 3). Ladd points out that Deafhood is strategically essentialist (Spivak & Harasym, 1990) in that it is possible to act as if an identity were uniform to achieve political goals without implying any deeper authenticity.

However, Sutton-Spence and West (2011) point to the "difficult path between political and strategic binary redress, and damaging essentialist cul-de-sacs" (p. 424). They, for example, challenge presentations of *hearing* people as often deliberately or necessarily cast as ignorant, benevolent, philanthropic, cruel, powerful, controlling, or pathetic. They quote the work of Baker-Shenk and Kyle (1990) as an example of typologies of hearing people that they question. Although it might be argued that work such as that of Baker-Shenk and Kyle (1990) was of its time, the problem with new typologies (such as the "Deaf Wannabee")[3] remains the same: "a never-ending essentialist, epistemological, and ontological cul-de-sac" (Sutton-Spence & West, 2011, p. 424).

Despite the increasing tendency to refer to epistemologies in the plural in reference to d/Deaf people(s), researchers still make by design or default further distinctions, which in turn create layers of complexity. Atkinson, Gleeson, Cromwell, and O'Rourke (2007), for example, explicitly state that they write from a "deaf epistemology" (p. 340) and from the text it is possible to understand that not all participants could be regarded or might regard themselves as culturally Deaf. Yet the authors do not address what they intend by the term, nor their own identities in relation to this epistemological position. On the other hand, De Clerck (2012a) argues against a d/Deaf distinction as it masks the diversity of ways in which people experience the social and material world. For her there is something vitally important about the degree of fluidity and ambiguity expressed through "deaf" without distinctions. In a similar way, Cooper (2012) makes an argument for using the term "deaf" to refer to people who are physically deaf but who may or may not see themselves as part of a Deaf community. She points out that using the term "deaf" only for people who do not see themselves as part of a Deaf community means researchers are left with no term for those who are physically deaf but whose cultural affiliation is unknown. We argue that dropping the use of the term "Deaf" or not making a distinction between deaf and Deaf makes it difficult to distinguish culturally based epistemologies. In this book we generally use an author's own terminology in discussing their work (and have distinguished our own in Chapter 2), although this can make direct comparison with work by researchers who use different terms difficult.

We are showcasing this variation surrounding Deaf epistemologies because, as we contend throughout this book, research is not a straightforward gathering of theory; there are no value-free facts, and all research is situated within historical and political contexts. Furthermore, researchers and participants are involved in a creative process of *producing reality/realities* rather than reflecting them. This perspective, therefore, extends to how epistemology is itself conceived of in relation to what it is to be d/Deaf. Deaf epistemologies do not merely reflect a position on being deaf or Deaf or d/Deaf; they co-create it also in their usage and relationship with methodology and method, as we discuss earlier.

IMPLICATIONS FOR ASSESSING RESEARCH

Our discussion of different ontologies/epistemologies and the complex and varied relationships that exist between these and methodologies and methods may leave the reader wondering whether anything goes. There are so many varied and nuanced positions, so perhaps it is of no consequence what we do, especially if, as McLaughlin (2009) states: "Different methodologies provide different lenses to view the same situation" (McLaughlin, 2009, p. 74). But is this the case? As we argue, methodologies themselves may be using *different* lenses to construct realities rather than reflecting the same reality. Methods are not just technical tools; nor do they flow seamlessly and consequentially from a chosen methodology. Methodologies and methods are both rooted in the underlying epistemology of a piece of work, which needs to be explicit. These considerations should cause us to think about how we judge a piece of research, particularly within a field where what it means to be deaf or Deaf is fluid, contested, contextual, and political.

In one sense, the text with which we engage points the way. Constraints are placed on the reading/watching of a text by the need to make sense of it on its own terms (see Chapter 8 on Technologies for a discussion of the visual text). Therefore, while there may be many versions of "truth" in a text, each must be made possible by something *within* the text, by its logic, syntax, or structural resources (Norris, 1989). Our reading "must be intrinsic and remain within the text" (Derrida, 1976, p. 159). We cannot, for example, argue that a research report on Deaf people's views of cochlear implants is about all d/Deaf people's views of implants if the authors specifically point out that they are asking only people who describe themselves as culturally Deaf.

Recent debates have led to suggestions for a range of criteria for assessing research, including validity, generalization, and reliability for both quantitative and qualitative research with differences between the two in how these terms are defined (Mason, 1996). Other criteria include relevance (defined as whether the research addresses the theory being tested) and rigor (whether a particular inference has sufficient weight to make a methodologically credible contribution (Pawson, Greenhalgh, Harvey, & Walshe, 2004). We direct the reader to these writers but note here that all such criteria are themselves constructed and agree with authors who suggest that assessment should be focused on the *whole* research strategy:

> what qualifies a study as being of "good quality" is not its technical competence as such, but whether its technical infrastructure *will bear the weight of the inferences to which it lays claim.* (Pawson, undated, emphasis ours)

Whatever criteria are selected, assessment involves more than a surface tick box exercise: For us, the status of the claims being made (epistemology), assumptions about the nature of reality/ities and what it means to be d/Deaf (identity/ontology), and ethical and political issues in the representation of others are key factors to be addressed. They are inextricably interrelated. We agree with Alvesson and Skoldberg (2009) that it is not the methods you use (or the amount of data you provide) which are the hallmarks of good social research, but the interplay between philosophical ideas and empirical work. This position is a long way from aping "standard epistemology" to find "the truth" (see discussion earlier). It is more in line with moves to develop Deaf epistemologies that focus on different and multiple truths and examine *research processes as crafted works.* It also recognizes that, as feminists asserted long ago, the personal is political and part of reflexivity involves considering research ethics (Young & Ackerman, 2001; Chapter 5 on Ethics). We discuss further our view of reflexivity in Chapter 7.

Law (2009) argues that if truth cannot be set as a gold standard, then other "goods" such as politics, aesthetics and spirituality come into play. The grounds for enacting one kind of reality (in our research) over another can be debated in what he calls "ontological politics" in which: "The good of making a difference will live alongside—and sometimes displace—that of enacting truth" (2004, p. 67). This argument is one that many researchers working with people with disabilities, for example, would recognize. Oliver (1992) argues for an emancipatory epistemology which confronts oppression, and Watson (2004) suggests that responses to metanarratives such as those of sexism and disablism should be situated within specific social, cultural, and historical contexts.

Political and ethical reasons for preferring particular ontological and epistemological positions have been recognized within research with Deaf people by many commentators; these include Ladd (2003), who labels his views as "strategically essentialist" (see earlier), and Mertens and Ginsberg (2008), who argue for a transformative research epistemology and identify relevant ethical issues in qualitative research based on those suggested by Guba and Lincoln (1989) and developed by other researchers. In a similar way, Davis (1995) argues that there may be political benefits to linking deafness with disability. Alternatively, some deaf people may value research based on the traditional scientific epistemology. Which is most appropriate depends on the context, including who is involved and what they seek to achieve. Researchers do not have to choose between ethnicity and disability per se as a position from which to debate Deaf politics. They may choose to ally themselves situationally.

As Rorty (1991) and Law (2004) point out, there is no neutral place from which researchers can adjudicate between epistemologies. Paul and Moores (2012) make a similar point when they state that since there is no God's-eye view of deafness, "it should be acceptable to examine individuals who are d/Dhh from a clinical/deafness or a cultural/sociological/Deafhood framework" (p. 13). This does not deny that many medical professionals still espouse traditional views on the status of their work or that they have the power to influence the lives of children and adults who are d/Deaf. Nor does this position trivialize the point that some views are more likely to register both within the academy as well as outside of it (Young & Hunt, 2011). All academics are part of a reality/realities riddled with inequalities. We simply caution against replacing hierarchies of holders of knowledge, methodologies, and methods with other hierarchies such as "more ethical." We return to the idea that that some methodologies such as emancipatory research are seen as more ethical in Chapter 4.

Writers such as McLaughlin (2009) critique research, whether based on positivism or social constructionism, as too conservative. Rather, he suggests that constructions of reality "become manifest not through the 'mind' but, through reflective action" (p. 72). This is a misreading of both positivist and social constructionist writings and a dismissal of research based on them which aims and sometimes succeeds in bringing about change. No methodology is more ethical per se and each, including emancipatory research, comes with the need to explore its limitations. Moreover, there is no direct line from a chosen methodology to change in practice.

SITUATING THE RESEARCHER WITHIN THE RESEARCH

We argue earlier, contrary to epistemologies based on objectively finding the truth in research, that researchers use methodologies/methods to create as well as describe the realities they encounter. We point to the significance of who is doing the research. But who *should* be doing research within different communities is a contested issue. We begin this section with a discussion of the influence of the researcher's identity/identities: that is, the insider/outsider debate. We then go on to explore the consequences of the choice of researcher before asking how much do we need to know about a researcher?

The question of who should do research with particular groups of people is one that has aroused much debate in social research, for example, in early feminist writing about women interviewing women (Oakely, 1981; Ribbens, 1989; Wise, 1987), in research with minority ethnic communities (Schick, 2002; Schwabenland, 2002), and in debates about whether interpreters (including in research) should be "matched" to the people they are interpreting for (Alexander, Edwards, & Temple, 2004; Thomson, Rogers, Honey, & King, 1999). Researchers who are bilingual are often treated unequivocally as insiders. They are seen as the solution to accessing communities and they can be firmly positioned as "representative" of particular cultures. But to do so, might ignore their ties to other cultures and languages (see Chapter 7), or the place they occupy or are seen to occupy within the community. See for example, Young and Ackerman (2001), who write about being challenged whether a "different sort of Deaf person" involved in the data collection and analysis might have resulted in a different set of findings, but they were never challenged whether a different sort of hearing person might have been an issue, too.

Therefore, as we note earlier in relation to essentialism, there are dangers in selecting one social signifier or identity as the only or overriding influence on research (Gair, 2012; Schick, 2002; Twine, 2000). Schick (2002) points to some of the issues when only "insiders" defined according to one selected social identifier such as ethnicity are allowed to have input into a particular aspect of research. She argues that when a researcher is seen to have expertise only in relation to specific parts of the research, such as being Maori in her work, this reifies social categories and defines in advance what can be said by whom.

Threadgold (2000) similarly argues for the value of research carried out by an "outsider" in language terms. She carried out research with Australian Vietnamese women and cites Nast's comment that reflexivity in cross-cultural fieldwork "is less about 'self-introspection' than about 'learning to recognise *others'* constructions of us" (p. 203). Difference may be valued as stimulating conversation (Harris, 1995; Threadgold, 2000; Twine & Warren, 2000) and may provide information that would not be discussed with those "in the know" as it would be taken for granted (Boulton, 2000; Gair, 2012). It has also been pointed out that it does not follow that critical awareness resides always or only in those who have particular experiences (Gair, 2012; Ladd, 2003; Twine, 2000). The significance of particular insider/outsider divides has also been shown to vary at different points within one piece of research (Boulton, 2000; Song & Parker, 1995).

Within research with d/Deaf people there is little discussion of influences other than that of Deaf identity on the research process itself. We argue in Chapter 7 that the researcher's influence in interpretation and translation with d/Deaf people is rarely discussed in terms other than whether they are hearing or Deaf. The literature on other possible social influences is sparse. In contrast, such literature within the arts, humanities, and social research generally has mushroomed. There is now a vast literature on a range of social influences on the research process and the importance of examining whose perspective is being used in research. It owes much to groundbreaking feminist debates (Griffiths, 1995; Maynard & Purvis, 1994; Smith, 1989; Stanley, 1990; Stanley & Wise, 1993) as well as to corresponding debates in race and ethnicity (Bulmer & Solomos, 1999; Twine & Warren, 2000), disability (Barnes & Mercer, 1997; Morris, 1991; Oliver, 1990), and sexuality (Seidman, 1996; Turner, 2000). This literature suggests that our experiences influence what we select to look at and what theories and views about social reality we hold. In this sense all researchers are "insiders" in their research.

There are, therefore, a variety of theories that focus on *identities* rather than identity and can serve to remind researchers that being d/Deaf may not be the only social signifier that is important in people's lives and may sometimes be *secondary* to other factors. For example, researchers have developed theories based on hybridity (Bhabha, 1994); intersectionality and positionality (Anthias, 2006; De Clerck, 2012b; Herman, 2010; Parasnis, 2012); and identity politics/politics of difference/politics of recognition (Fraser & Honneth, 2003; Heyes, 2002; Leeb, 2009; Taylor, 1994; Thompson, 2009). All these writers celebrate the multifaceted interconnection of identities, arguing that there is no "shopping list of multiple identities" (James, 2008, p. 13) and that identities are processes and not end points.

Research with d/Deaf people has tended to focus on identity through the lens of identity politics/politics of difference, including postmodernist approaches (see earlier), although there has been some interest in the politics of recognition (Ohna, 2003). For example, McIlroy and Storbeck (2011) develop a "dialogue model" building on the celebration of marginal discourses and "second-wave identity politics," discuss fluid identities and propose "DeaF" identities to mark the fluid dividing lines between Deaf and culturally hearing identities and reconciliation between oppressor and victim.

The theories listed earlier counter drives to discuss "core identities" prevalent in some literature concerning d/Deaf people (e.g., Leigh, 2009). For example, Ohna (2004) uses the politics of recognition as a framework to examine interactions between deaf and hearing people in Norway. She eschews distinctions between deaf and Deaf, preferring "deaf" in all cases as more coherent with her theoretical approach and we follow her terminology in this example. She uses an interview with a deaf woman she calls Christina to show that her identity cannot be anchored alone in being deaf as she is the mother of two hearing children. She argues that identity is something that has to be negotiated and cannot be tied to a social category or social norms. Choices "are anchored in one's own situation, not in the norms of the hearing world or the deaf world" (p. 32). In a similar way, research by Young (1997) suggests that the ways in which hearing parents learn to be bilingual, that is, learn to sign once they have a child who is deaf, are influenced not only by the quest for proficiency but by emotional and practical considerations in the family.

CONSEQUENCES OF CHOICE OF RESEARCHER

There are, however, different consequences in the choices made about who should do research with d/Deaf people, not just what the author might or might not reveal of herself. For example, as we point out in previous work (Temple & Young, 2004), there are consequences in terms of how data are constructed and in the power relations between individuals and communities in research where hearing researchers lead on research with d/Deaf people. These are epistemological and ethical consequences. Young, Ackerman, and Kyle (1998) document how Deaf people make adaptations to their BSL in order to help hearing signers understand, and this raises the issue of acceptable and unacceptable modalities and the power society subscribes to the signed word (see Chapter 6). Ladd's (2003) discussion of the subaltern researcher (p. 275) recognizes these issues of power imbalances within the academy. He states, "To be a subaltern-researcher therefore means to come to an area of study with an experiential knowledge of one's minority community" (p. 276).

Ladd's development of the subaltern concept is interesting in his refusal to accept the idea that when the subaltern can "speak" they are no longer subaltern. He suggests that while it is too simplistic to assume that there is no "interpenetration" between subaltern and elite, he does not subscribe to the "bipolar" view that as a researcher you are either an insider or not (p. 276). His discussion of the subaltern-researcher is useful in moving beyond the idea that any researcher is either an insider or an outsider and reflects the position we discuss earlier of the fluid nature of such descriptions. We introduce earlier the idea that there are other "goods" at play in deciding who to carry out research with since it is impossible to judge "the truth" from a single vantage point. Ladd's (2003) writing as a Deaf researcher is a good example of an epistemological position that emanates from a concern with the emancipatory potential of researching from inside a culture and ensuring that insider position is seen, recognized, and regarded as of significance.

As a result of the recognition that it is not possible for any one group of people to be unequivocally judged to be the only holders of the "true" perspective in research, there is increasing interest in looking at how d/Deaf and hearing researchers can work together. Work by Jones and Pullen (1992) is an example of the complicated ways in which power works as in their research, as in many research projects with Deaf people, the hearing researcher is dependent on the Deaf researcher not only for access into communities but also for help in understanding Deaf culture. This "insider" help, they argue, enhances validity by improving quality and value.

We discuss earlier Sutton-Spence and West's (2011) critique of Baker-Shenk and Kyle's (1990) essentialist portrayal of hearing people. We would go further and argue against discussions of hearing researchers' engagement with d/Deaf researchers in ways that d/Deaf people have described as unacceptable when applied to themselves. For example, we hope that researchers have moved on from the essentialist exchanges described in Jones's exchange with Pullen (1992, p. 194) which involve descriptions of '"hearing deviousness and Deaf directness" and accounts of temper loss with the hearing researcher. The power dynamics here are not ones that we would welcome in collaborations between d/Deaf and hearing researchers. This example is also a caution against assuming that a Deaf researcher on the team or as the leader of the research automatically makes research more ethical (see Chapter 4). A more constructive examination of hearing identity and d/Deaf-hearing collaborations has begun (for example, McIlroy & Storbeck, 2011; Sutton-Spence & West, 2011; Young & Ackerman, 2001). It could usefully be developed still further within the kinds of theoretical frameworks we have pointed to earlier, with respect shown for all who are involved.

WHAT DO READERS NEED TO KNOW?

If it is the case that we need to situate researchers as well as participants within research, then the question arises of what/how much readers need to know about them. We argue earlier that no researcher can stand outside of her or his research. There are differences in the amount of information that authors give about themselves when they write themselves into their research. For example, McIlroy and Storbeck (2011) situate one of the authors within their autoethnographic research (see definition later) by stipulating his bicultural and bilingual DeaF identity (see earlier). His influence on the research is acknowledged by his completion of the interview. In contrast, some researchers discuss their research through their own life stories and explore the influence of their lives on the choice of topic, preferred methodology, methods, and analysis (e.g., Sheridan, 2001, writing about deaf children and psychological distress). Such approaches share a commitment to *overtly marking their research as situated knowledge production.*

Researchers have addressed the need to be reflexive in all aspects of their research in different ways. Alvesson and Skoldberg (2009) define *reflexive interpretation* as "a demand for reflection in research in conjunction with an interpretation at several levels: contact with the empirical material, awareness of the interpretative act, clarification of political-ideological contexts, and the handling of the question of representation and authority" (2009, p. 263). Investigating the researcher's influence is part of this reflexivity. In Chapter 7 we discuss an approach which focuses on the use of intellectual autobiographies. Here we suggest another: autoethnography which has been used to openly signal researchers' roles in the production of research. Autoethnography has been defined as "highly personalised accounts that draw upon the experience of the author/researcher for the purposes of extending sociological understanding" (Sparkes, 2000, p. 21).

Ellis (1999) provides a fascinating example in her discussion of "heartful autoethnography," in which she describes her goal as extending ethnography to "include the heart, the autobiographical and the artistic text" (p. 669). Her article is written as a story of her encounter with a student in which she explains what autoethnography involves and cites academic writers along the way. For example, she notes the difference between generalization as used in survey research and generalization in autoethnography where she argues that "Our lives are particular, but they are also typical and generalizable since we all participate in a limited number of cultures and institutions" (p. 674).

Wall (2008) notes that researchers have different emphases on self and sociocultural influences when they write. How much of the author to "reveal" is always a personal choice. Ellis (1999), Roth (2008), Wall (2008), and others point out that discussing yourself and your life inevitably raises ethical issues about how researchers represent others in their own narratives, it is never self *or* social but inevitably both. Critics of autoethnography suggest that some researchers "have little to do with the ethno and everything with the auto" (Roth, 2008, p. 8). Roth (2008) describes one Internet site for autoethnography as including many contributions as deriving from "the frequently unprincipled, egoistical and egotistical, narcissistic preoccupation with the auto-affection of the Self" (p. 8).

The decision about whether the balance between "auto" and "ethno" is "right" is ultimately made by readers who bring their own life experiences to the narratives to help them decide whether the author/ researcher has adequately established the links between her/his experiences and sociocultural, historical, political, or economic influences. What is declared adequate will, therefore, vary but the criteria for assessing autoethnographical research are not those associated with objectivity but rather whether researchers "create the effect of reality" (Ellis, 1999, p. 669) and evoke recognition or provide opportunities vicariously to experience the unfamiliar.

CONCLUDING THOUGHTS

Research used to be the preserve of a few academics, typically White, middle-class men. Arguably, the academy is now opening up to include people who traditionally would have been excluded. There are many reasons why this process of "democratization" of research is valuable, including the challenging of the basis of knowledge claims that assume we are all alike. However, in this chapter we argue that power asymmetries remain and there is a need to examine the basis of all knowledge claims. We present research as made up of more than a toolkit of methods. The issues we cover as relevant to debates on epistemology are deliberately wide-ranging and are intended as an indication that there are epistemological consequences to decisions made at all points in the research process. We do not want to give the impression that findings are not important. However, when readers engage with research findings, particularly those they do not agree with, they need to look at the underpinnings of research, that is, the researcher's knowledge claims.

In Chapter 2 we discuss the significance of diversity in experiences of being d/Deaf (ontological issues) and argue that the definitions we use affect the results we get: Researchers include and exclude particular kinds of knowledge in the definitions of being d/Deaf that they set up (epistemological issues). In this chapter we introduce a small sample of epistemological stances. Our position is that epistemology, methodology, and method are necessarily linked but that these links are not predetermined as sometimes suggested. We begin by illustrating this view in relation to models of deafness but go on to demonstrate that this is the case in research generally. We discuss our epistemological position and note that taking it on board means accepting that we cannot adjudicate between epistemologies, methodologies, and methods on the basis of which gets researchers to "the truth." We argue that researchers who do not address their own epistemological positions in effect contribute to "business as usual" in that they make it possible to debate findings as if findings produce themselves in a neutral way. This does not allow for challenge and results in researchers hiding in their texts.

We also introduce the idea that we do not view methodologies as a suitable site into which we can move the drive to objectivity and the establishment of hierarchies of more and less suitable methodologies. We go on to demonstrate that methods are not neutral tools but influence what is produced. We suggest that criteria for judging research have to come from other "goods" than truth and these goods themselves are not the preserve of any particular methodology or method. There is no methodology or method which is automatically more ethical or leads to better outcomes than any other.

If researchers want to come out from behind the shield of objectivity, they have to make decisions about who should do the research and how much readers need to know about them. There can be no automatic preference for either insiders or outsiders based on superiority of epistemological position. Concepts of "insider" and "outsider" are fluid in their influence within research and cannot be attached to one overriding social characteristic. Decisions about who to choose have consequences in terms of the kind of knowledge produced. How do researchers know that the influences they have chosen to focus on, for example, gender, class, or d/Deaf identities, are as significant as they claim? This is a question to which there can be no definitive objective response. It is rather a case of marshalling the evidence and specifying the kind of knowledge claims that the researcher wants to make. We build on these arguments in Chapter 4 when we explore ethical research practice in studies concerning d/Deaf people.

NOTES

1. Although there are other understandings of objectivity, for example, Bourdieu (1992), we discuss the view that objectivity is about removing a researcher's influence from research as it is the most commonly used in social research.
2. Here the reader should note May's (2001) caution that postmodernism can mean different things and that authors have been classified differently, so that, for example, he cites Foucault as responding to claims that he is a positivist. This caution also applies to other ontologies/epistemologies. This chapter only provides a broad overview.
3. The term "Deaf Wannabee" is colloquially used to refer to hearing and deaf people who through their attitude, behavior, and affiliations indicate that they would prefer it if they were Deaf and try to act as such. It also more radically refers to "people with a deaf fetish or hearing aid fetish, or who are deaf by

choice or wish to be deaf." There are several online fora for Deaf Wannabees, including http://dir.groups.yahoo.com/group/Deaf-Wannabee

REFERENCES

Alexander, C., Edwards, R., & Temple, B. (2004). *Access to services with interpreters: User views.* York, UK: Joseph Rowntree Foundation.

Alvesson, M., & Skoldberg, K. (2009). *Reflexive methodology: New vistas for qualitative research.* London: Sage.

Anthias, F. (2006). Belongings in a globalising and unequal world: Rethinking translocations. In N. Yuval-Davis, K. Kannabiran, & U. Vieten (Eds.), *The situated politics of belonging* (pp. 17–31). London: Sage Publications Ltd.

Atkinson, J. R., Gleeson, K., Cromwell, J., & O'Rourke, S. (2007). Exploring the perceptual characteristics of voice hallucinations in deaf people. *Cognitive Neuorpsychiatry, 12*(4), 339–361. doi: http://dx.doi.org/10.1080/13546800701238229

Bahan, B. (1994). Comment on Turner. *Sign Language Studies, 83,* 241–249.

Bahan, B. (2008). Upon the formation of a visual variety of the human race. In H. D. L. Bauman (Ed.), *Open your eyes: Deaf studies talking* (pp. 83–99). Minneapolis: University of Minnesota Press.

Baker-Shenk, C., & Kyle, J. (1990). Research with deaf people: Issues and conflicts. *Disability, Handicap and Society, 5*(1), 65–75.

Barnes, C., & Mercer, G. (Eds.). (1997). *Doing disability research.* Leeds, UK: The Disability Press.

Bauman, H. D. L. (2008). Listening to phonocentrism with Deaf eyes: Derrida's mute philosophy of (sign) language. *Essays in Philosophy, 9*(1), Article 2, 1–16.

Bauman, H. D. L., & Murray, J. J. (2010). Deaf Studies in the 21st century: "Deaf-gain" and the future of human diversity. In M. Marschark & P. Spencer (Eds.), *The Oxford handbook of deaf studies, language, and education,* Vol. 2 (pp. 196–225). New York, NY: Oxford University Press.

Bhabha, H. (1994). *The location of culture.* London: Routledge.

Bienvenu, M. (2008). Queer as Deaf: Intersections. In H. D. L. Bauman (Ed.), *Open your eyes: Deaf studies talking* (pp. 264–276). Minneapolis: University of Minnesota Press.

Boulton, D. (2000). Unusual terms: What do you mean by....? In B. Humphries (Ed.), *Research in social care and social welfare* (pp. 86–91). London: Jessica Kingsley.

Bourdieu, P. (1992). *Language and symbolic power* (G. Raymond & M. Adamson, Trans.). Cambridge, UK: Polity Press.

Brueggemann, B. (2008). Think-between: A Deaf studies commonplace book. In H. D. L. Bauman (Ed.), *Open your eyes: Deaf studies talking* (pp. 177–188). Minneapolis: University of Minnesota Press.

Bryman, A. (1988). *Quantity and quality in social research.* London: Unwin & Hyman.

Bulmer, M., & Solomos, J. (1999). *Ethnic and racial studies today.* London: Routledge.

Chen, W., Jongkamonwiwat, N., Abbas, L., Jacob Eshtan, S., Johnson, S. L., Kuhn S., Milo, M., Thurlow, J. K., Andrews, P. W., Marcotti, W., Moore, H. D., & Rivolta, M. N. (2012). Restoration of auditory evoked responses by human

ES-cell-derived otic progenitors. *Nature, 490,* 278–282. doi: doi:10.1038/
nature11415

Clifford, J., & Marcus, G. E. (Eds.). (1986). *Writing culture: The poetics and politics
of ethnography.* Berkeley, CA: University of California Press.

Conama, J. (2010). *Finnish and Irish sign languages: An egalitarian analysis of language policies and their effects.* PhD thesis, University College, Dublin.

Conama, J. (2013). Who decides? Language education policies for Deaf children—Selected findings from a comparative analysis of Finnish and Irish
policies on signed languages. In L. Leeson & M. Vermeerbergen (Eds.),
Working with the Deaf community: Education, mental health and interpreting.
Dublin: Interesource Group (Ireland) Limited.

Cooper, R. (2012). Can it be a good thing to be deaf? In P. Paul & D. F. Moores
(Eds.), *Deaf epistemologies: Multiple perspectives on the acquisition of knowledge*
(pp. 236–254). Washington, DC: Gallaudet University Press.

Corbett, J. (1996). *Bad mouthing.* London: Routledge.

Corker, M. (1998). *Deaf and disabled, or deafness disabled? Towards a human rights
perspective.* Buckingham, UK: Open University Press.

Corker, M. (1999). Differences, conflations and foundations: The limits to "accurate" theoretical representation of disabled people's experience? *Disability &
Society,* 14: 627–642.

Cresswell, J. (2003). *Research design: Qualitative, quantitative and mixed methods
approaches.* London: Sage Publications Ltd.

Davis, L. (1995). *Enforcing normalcy: Disability, deafness and the body.* London:
Verso.

De Clerck, G. A. (2010). Deaf epistemologies as a critique and alternative to the
practice of science: An anthropological perspective. *American Annals of the
Deaf,* 154(5), 435–446. doi: 10.1353/aad.0.0121

De Clerck, G. A. (2012a). Contributing to an era of epistemological equity: A critique and an alternative to the practice of science. In P. Paul & D. Moores
(Eds.), *Deaf epistemologies: Multiple perspectives on the acquisition of knowledge*
(pp. 19–44). Washington, DC: Gallaudet University Press.

De Clerck, G. A. (2012b). Valuing deaf indigenous knowledge in research
through partnership: The Cameroonian deaf community and the challenge of "serious" scholarship. In P. Paul & D. Moores (Eds.), *Deaf epistemologies: Multiple perspectives on the acquisition of knowledge* (pp. 81–104).
Washington, DC: Gallaudet University Press.

Derrida, J. (1976). *Of grammatology* (G. Spivak, Trans.). Baltimore, MD: Johns
Hopkins University Press.

Derrida, J. (1982). *Margins of philosophy* (A. Bass, Trans.). Chicago, IL: University
of Chicago Press.

Dunn, L. (2008). The burden of racism and audism. In H. D. L. Bauman (Ed.),
Open your eyes: Deaf studies talking (pp. 235–250). Minneapolis: University of
Minnesota Press.

Elder-Vass, D. (2012). *The reality of social construction.* Cambridge, UK: Cambridge
University Press.

Ellis, C. (1999). Keynote address from the First Annual Advances in Qualitative
Methods Conference: Heartful autoethnography. *Qualitative Health Research,*
9(5), 669–683. doi: 10.1177/104973299129122153

Foucault, M. (2003). *The birth of the clinic.* Abingdon, UK: Routledge.

Fraser, N., & Honneth, A. (2003). *Redistribution or recognition? A political-philosophical exchange*. London: Verso.

Friedner, M. (2010). Biopower, biosociality, and community formation: How biopower is constitutive of the Deaf community. *Sign Language Studies, 10*(3): 336–347. doi: 10.1353/sls.0.0049.

Gair, S. (2012). Feeling their stories: Contemplating empathy, insider/outsider positionings, and enriching qualitative research. *Qualitative Health Research, 22*(1), 134–143. doi: 10.1177/1049732311420580

Griffiths, M. (1995). *Feminisms and the self: The web of identity*. London: Routledge.

Guba, E., & Lincoln, Y. (1989). *Fourth generation evaluation*. Newbury Park, CA: Sage.

Harding, S. (1986). *The science question in feminism*. Milton Keynes: Open University Press.

Harris, J. (1995). *The cultural meaning of deafness*. Aldershot, UK: Avebury.

Harrits, G. (2011). More than method? A discussion of paradigm differences within mixed methods research. *Journal of Mixed Methods Research, 5*(2), 150–166. doi: 10.1177/1558689811402506

Hauser, P., O'Hearn, A., McKee, M., Steider, A., & Thew, T. (2010). Deaf epistemology: Deafhood and deafness. *American Annals of the Deaf, 154*(5), 486–492. doi: 10.1353/aad.0.0120

Herman, D. (2010). Multimodal storytelling and identity construction in graphic narratives. In D. Schiffrin, A. De Fina, & A. Nylund (Eds.), *Telling stories: language, narrative and social life* (pp. 195–208). Washington, DC: Georgetown University Press.

Heyes, C. (2002). Identity politics. In E. Zalta (Ed.), *The Stanford encyclopedia of philosophy*. Retrieved December 1, 2013, from http://plato.stanford.edu/archives/fall2002/entries/identity-politics/

Holcomb, T. (2010). Deaf epistemology: The Deaf way of knowing. *American Annals of the Deaf, 154*(5), 471–478. doi: 10.1353/aad.0.0116

Holcomb, T. (2012). Paving the way for reform in deaf education. In P. Paul & D. Moores (Eds.), *Deaf epistemologies: Multiple perspectives on the acquisition of knowledge* (pp. 125–145). Washington, DC: Gallaudet University Press.

Hole, R. (2007). Narratives of identity: A poststructural analysis of three deaf women's life stories. *Narrative Inquiry, 17*(2), 259–278.

Hughes, J. (1990). *The philosophy of social research*. London: Longman.

Hutchinson, P., Read, R., & Sharrock, W. (2008). *There is no such thing as a social science: In defence of Peter Winch*. Aldershot, UK: Ashgate.

James, M. (2008). *Interculturalism: Theory and policy*. London: The Baring Foundation.

Jones, L., & Pullen, G. (1992). Cultural differences: Deaf and hearing researchers working together. *Disability and Society, 7*(2), 189–196. doi: 10.1080/02674649266780211

Kelly, A. (2008). Where's Deaf HERstory? In H. D. L. Bauman (Ed.), *Open your eyes: Deaf studies talking* (pp. 251–263). Minneapolis: University of Minnesota Press.

Krentz, C. (2009). Open your eyes: Deaf studies talking (review). *Sign Language Studies, 10*(1), 110–132. doi: 10.1353/sls.0.0032

Kuhn, T. (1964). *The structure of scientific revolutions*. Chicago, IL: University of Chicago Press.

Ladd, P. (1994). Comment on Turner. *Sign Language Studies, 85,* 327–336.

Ladd, P. (2003). *Understanding Deaf culture: In search of Deafhood.* Clevedon, UK: Multilingual Matters.

Ladd, P., Gulliver, M., & Batterbury, S. C. E. (2003). Reassessing minority language empowerment from a Deaf perspective: The other 32 languages. *Deaf Worlds, 19*(2), 6–32.

Lane, H. (1992). *The mask of benevolence: Disabling the Deaf community.* New York, NY: Knopf.

Latour, B., & Woolgar, S. (1979). *Laboratory life: The social construction of scientific facts.* Beverly Hills, CA: Sage.

Law, J. (2004). *After method: Mess in social science research.* London: Routledge.

Law, J. (2009). Seeing like a survey. *Cultural Sociology, 3*(2), 239–256. doi: 10.1177/1749975509105533

Leeb, C. (2009). The politics of "misrecognition": A feminist critique. *Good Society, 18*(1), 70–75. doi: 10.1353/gso.0.0068

Leigh, I. W. (2009). *A lens on deaf identities.* New York, NY: Oxford University Press.

Lyotard, J. (1984). *The postmodern condition: A report on knowledge* (G. Bennington & B. Massumi, Trans.). Manchester, UK: Manchester University Press.

Mason, J. (1996). *Qualitative researching.* London: Sage Publications Ltd.

May, T. (2001). *Social research: Issues, methods and process.* Buckingham, UK: Open University Press.

Maynard, M., & Purvis, J. (Eds.). (1994). *Researching women's lives from a feminist perspective.* London: Taylor & Francis.

McIlroy, G., & Storbeck, C. (2011). Development of Deaf identity: An ethnographic study. *Journal of Deaf Studies and Deaf Education, 16*(4), 494–511. doi: 10.1093/deafed/enr017

McLaughlin, H. (2009). *Service user research in health and social care.* London: Sage.

Mertens, D. M., & Ginsberg, P. E. (2008). Deep in ethical waters: Transformative perspectives for qualitative social work research. *Qualitative Social Work: Research and Practice, 7*(4), 484–503. doi: 10.1177/1473325008097142

Miller, M. (2010). Epistemology and people who are deaf: Deaf worldviews, views of the deaf world, or my parents are hearing. *American Annals of the Deaf, 154*(5), 479–485. doi: 10.1353/aad.0.0118

Miller, M. (2012). Deaf worldviews, views of the deaf world, and the role of deaf children of hearing parents in creating a deaf epistemology. In P. Paul & D. Moores (Eds.), *Deaf epistemologies: Multiple perspectives on the acquisition of knowledge* (pp. 147–175). Washington, DC: Gallaudet University Press.

Monaghan, L. (1994). Comment on Turner. *Sign Language Studies, 83,* 139–144.

Montgomery, G. (1994). Comment on Turner. *Sign Language Studies, 84*(Fall), 251–264.

Morgan-Jones, R. (2001). *Hearing differently: The impact of hearing impairment on family life.* London: Whurr.

Morris, J. (1991). *Pride against prejudice.* London: Women's Press.

Mulkay, M. (1979). *Science and the sociology of knowledge.* London: Allen and Unwin.

Nelson, J. (2006). Textual bodies, bodily texts. In H. D. L. Bauman, J. Nelson, & H. Rose (Eds.), *Signing the body poetic: Essays on American Sign Language literature* (pp. 118–129). Berkeley, LA: University of California Press.

Norris C. (1989). *Derrida.* London: Fontana Press.

Oakely, A. (1981). Interviewing women: A contradiction in terms. In H. Roberts (Ed.), *Doing feminist research* (pp. 30–61). London: Routledge and Kegan Paul.

Ohna, S. (2003). Education of deaf children and the politics of recognition. *Journal of Deaf Studies and Deaf Education, 8*(1), 5–10. doi: 10.1093/deafed/8.1.5

Oliver, M. (1990). *The politics of disablement*. Basingstoke, UK: Macmillan.

Oliver, M. (1992). Changing the social relations of research production. *Disability, Handicap and Society, 7*(2), 101–114. doi: 1080/02674649266780141

Parasnis, I. (2012). Diversity and deaf identity: Implications for personal epistemologies in deaf education. In P. Paul & D. Moores (Eds.), *Deaf epistemologies: Multiple perspectives on the acquisition of knowledge* (pp. 63–80). Washington, DC: Gallaudet University Press.

Paul, P., & Moores, D. (2010a). Perspectives on deaf epistemologies. *American Annals of the Deaf, 154*(5), 417–420. doi: 10.1353/aad.0.0115

Paul, P., & Moores, D. (2010b). Introduction: Towards an understanding of epistemology and deafness. *American Annals of the Deaf, 154*(5), 421–427. doi: 10.1353/aad.0.0117

Paul, P., & Moores, D. (2012). Toward an understanding of epistemology and deafness. In P. Paul & D. Moores (Eds.), *Deaf epistemologies: Multiple perspectives on the acquisition of knowledge* (pp. 3–15). Washington, DC: Gallaudet University Press.

Pawson, R. (undated). *Assessing the quality of evidence in evidence-based policy: Why, how and when?* ESRC Research Methods Programme Working Paper No. 1. Retrieved January 07, 2013, from http://www.ccsr.ac.uk/methods/publications/Pawson.pdf

Pawson, R., Greenhalgh, T., Harvey, G., & Walshe, K. (2004). Realist synthesis: An introduction. *ESRC Research Methods.* Retrieved January 07, 2013, from http: //www.ccsr.ac.uk/methods/publications/documents/RMPmethods2.pdf

Pugh, A. (1990). My statistics and feminism: A true story. In L. Stanley (Ed.), *Feminist praxis: Research, theory and epistemology in feminist sociology* (pp. 103–112). London: Routledge.

Ribbens, J. (1989). Interviewing—an "unnatural situation"? *Women's Studies International Forum, 12*(6), 579–592. doi: 10.1016/0277-5395(89)90002-2

Rogers, K. D., Young, A., Lovell, K., Campbell, M., Scott, P. R., & Kendal, S. (2013). The British Sign Language Versions of the Patient Health Questionnaire, the Generalized Anxiety Disorder 7-Item Scale, and the Work and Social Adjustment Scale. *Journal of Deaf Studies and Deaf Education, 18*(1), 110–122. doi: 10.1093/deafed/ens04.

Rorty, R. (1991). Objectivity, relativism and truth. Cambridge, UK: Cambridge University Press.

Roth, W. (2008). Auto/ethnography and the question of ethics. *Forum: Qualitative Social Research, 10*(1), Art. 38, http://nbn-resloving.de/urn:nbn:de:0114-fqs0901381

Schick, R. (2002). When the subject is difference: Conditions of voice in policy-oriented qualitative research. *Qualitative Inquiry, 8*(5), 632–651. doi: 10.1177/107780002237012

Schroedel, J. G. (1984). Analyzing surveys on deaf adults: Implications for survey research on persons with disabilities. *Social Science & Medicine, 19*(6), 619–627. doi: 10.1016/0277-9536(84)90228-4

Schwabenland, C. (2002). Toward a paradigm shift: Lessons from anti-oppressive movements. In J. Merrifield, R. Tandon, C. Flower, & C. Schwabenland (Eds.), *Participation—North and South: New ideas in participatory development from India and the UK* (pp. 5–17). London: The Elfida Society.

Seidman, S. (1996). *Queer theory/sociology.* Oxford, UK: Blackwell Publishers Ltd.

Sheridan, M. (2001). *The inner lives of deaf children: Interviews and analysis.* Washington, DC: Gallaudet University Press.

Silverman, D. (1993). *Interpreting qualitative data: Methods for analyzing talk, text, and interaction.* London: Sage.

Smith, M. (1998). *Social science in question.* London: Sage Publications.

Smith, D. (1989). Sociological theory: Methods of writing patriarchy. In R. Wallace (Ed.), *Feminism and sociological theory.* London: Sage Publications.

Song, M., & Parker, D. (1995). Cultural identity: Disclosing commonality and difference in in-depth interviewing. *Sociology, 29*(2), 241–256. doi: 10.1177/0038038595029002004

Sparkes, A. (2000). Autoethnography and narratives of self: Reflections on criteria in action. *Sociology of Sport Journal, 17*(1), 21–43.

Spender, D. (1980). *Man made language.* London: Routledge & Kegan Paul Ltd.

Spivak, G., & Harasym, S. (1990). *The post-colonial critic: Interviews, strategies, dialogues.* New York, NY: Routledge.

Stanley, L. (Ed.). (1990). *Feminist praxis: Research, theory, and epistemology in feminist sociology.* London: Routledge.

Stanley, L., & Temple, B. (2008). Narrative methodologies: Subjects, silences, re-readings and analyses. *Qualitative Research, 8*(3), 275–281. doi: 10.1177/1468794106093622

Stanley, L., & Wise, S. (1993). *Breaking out again: Feminist ontology and epistemology.* London: Routledge.

Stokoe, W. (1994). Comment on Turner. *Sign Language Studies, 84,* 265–270.

Street, B. (1994). Comment on Turner. *Sign Language Studies, 83,* 145–148.

Sutton-Spence, R., & West, D. (2011). Negotiating the legacy of hearingness. *Qualitative Inquiry, 17*(5), 422–432. doi: 10.1177/1077800411405428

Tashakkori, A., & Teddle, C. (2003). *Handbook of mixed methods in social and behavioral research.* London: Sage Publications Ltd.

Taylor, C. (1994). The politics of recognition. In A. Gutmann (Ed.), *Multiculturalism: Examining the politics of recognition* (pp. 25–73). Princeton, NJ: Princeton University Press.

Temple, B. (1994). Combining methods: Epistemological considerations in the study of families and households. *Journal of Family Issues, 15*(4), 562–573.

Temple, B., & Young, A. (2004). Qualitative research and translation dilemmas. *Qualitative Research, 4*(2), 161–178. doi: 10.1177/1468794104044430

Thompson, S. (2009). Participatory parity and self-realisation. *Good Society, 18*(1), 57–62. doi: 10.1353/gso.0.0066

Thomson, A., Rogers, A., Honey, S., & King, L. (1999). If the interpreter doesn't come there is no communication: A study of bilingual support services in the North West of England. Manchester, UK: University of Manchester School of Nursing, Midwifery and Health Visiting.

Thoutenhoofd, E. (1998). Method in a photographic enquiry of being deaf. *Sociological Research Online, 3*(2), 1–18.

Thoutenhoofd, E. (2010). Acting with attainment technologies in deaf education: Reinventing monitoring as an intervention collaboratory. *Sign Language Studies, 10*(2), 214–230. doi: 10.1353/sls.0.0040

Threadgold, T. (2000). When home is always a foreign place: Diaspora, dialogue, translations. *Communal/Plural, 8*(2), 193–217. doi: 10.1080/132078700426406

Turner, G. H. (1994a). How is Deaf culture?: Toward a revised notion of a fundamental concept. *Sign Language Studies, 83*, 103–126.

Turner, G. H. (1994b). Response to comments by Bahan, Ladd, Montgomery, and further thoughts. *Sign Language Studies, 83*, 337–366.

Turner, W. (2000). *A genealogy of queer theory.* Philadelphia, PA: Temple University Press.

Twine, F. (2000). Racial ideologies and racial methodologies. In F. Twine & J. Warren (Eds.), *Racing research researching race: Methodological dilemmas in critical race studies.* (pp. 1–34). New York, NY: New York University Press.

Twine, F., & Warren, J. (Eds.). (2000). *Racing research researching race: Methodological dilemmas in critical race studies.* New York, NY: New York University Press.

Wall, S. (2008). Easier said than done: Writing an autoethnography. *Journal of Qualitative Methods, 7*(1), 38–53.

Wang, Y. (2010). Without boundaries: An inquiry into deaf epistemologies through a metaparadigm. *American Annals of the Deaf, 154*(5), 428–434. doi: 10.1353/aad.0.0119

Watson, N. (2004). The dialectics of disability: A social model for the 21st century? In C. Barnes & G. Mercer (Eds.), *Implementing the social model of disability: Theory and research* (pp. 101–117). Leeds, UK: The Disability Press.

Wise, S. (1987). A framework for discussing ethical issues in feminist research: A review of the literature. In V. Griffiths, M. Humm, R. O'Rourke, J. Batsleer, F. Poland, & S. Wise (Eds.), *Writing feminist biography: Using life histories* (Vol. 19, pp. 47–88).

Young, A. (1997). Conceptualizing parents' sign language use in bilingual early intervention. *Journal of Deaf Studies and Deaf Education, 2*(4), 264–276.

Young, A. M., & Ackerman, J. (2001). Reflections on validity and epistemology in a study of working relations between deaf and hearing professionals. *Qualitative Health Research, 11*(2), 179–189. doi: 10.1177/104973230101100204

Young, A., Ackerman, J., & Kyle, J. G. (1998). *Looking on: Deaf people and the organisation of services.* Bristol, UK: The Policy Press.

Young, A., Gascon-Ramos, M., Campbell, M., & Bamford, J. (2009). The design and validation of a parent-report questionnaire for assessing the characteristics and quality of early intervention over time. *Journal of Deaf Studies and Deaf Education, 14*(4), 422–435. doi: 10.1093/deafed/enp016

Young, A., Hunt, E. (2011). Research with d/Deaf people. Methods Review 9, NIHR School for Social Care Research. Retrieved, February 02, 2013, from http://www2.lse.ac.uk/LSEHealthAndSocialCare/pdf/SSCR%20Methods%20Review_9_web.pdf

4

Ethical Research Practice

In a study evaluating the quality of information provided to parents with deaf infants (Young, Jones, Starmer, & Sutherland, 2005), one of the fathers involved said that he thought the information on communication and language was well written, unbiased, and nicely presented, but the problem was that it did not come with a health advisory warning! From his experience there was a "raging debate out there," and it was just as important to warn new parents about the strengths of feeling and differences of opinion they were likely to encounter as to provide them with balanced information about all possible communication options for their child. We begin this chapter on ethics in research with that story because in the wider context of the ordinary lives of d/Deaf people, parents with deaf children, and Deaf communities, there are many "raging debates." Ethical dilemmas and moral issues abound whether they involve language choices, cultural perspectives, economics, technology, genetics, education, social discourse, or the dynamics of power more generally (Leigh & Marschark, 2005; Marschark, Rhoten, & Fabich, 2007). The focus of this chapter is not to review those debates but instead to consider *ethical research practice* in studies that involve d/Deaf people. However, as will become apparent, the framing of many of the wider ethical debates is of relevance and examples drawn from them will also form part of the discussion.

We begin by asking whether it is correct to assume that the same ethical principles that govern and guide all research apply to research that involves d/Deaf people? Or are there additional considerations that challenge those principles, whether absolutely or through their application in this specific research context?

SAME STANDARDS, JUST A DIFFERENT CONTEXT?

Research has come a long way from the days in which it was perfectly acceptable to involve participants in experimental procedures without consent, to remove and use tissue samples without the awareness of the person from whom they were taken (Skloot, 2010), or to use information without protection of privacy if justified for reasons of research. Numerous guidelines and standards exist for the conduct of research whether generated by governmental/federal laws, for example, Title 45, part 46, of the Federal Regulations (2005); professional bodies and subject disciplines, for example, The Economic and Social Research Council (ESRC, 2010); or interest groups such as the Summer Institute of Linguistics (SIL, undated). Research projects involving human subjects are usually required to undergo ethical scrutiny before they are permitted to proceed. In some cases legal protections coincide with that process. For example, in England and Wales, The Mental Capacity Act (2005), which concerns safeguards in the treatment of general populations of individuals who might have diminished capacities to consent to treatment, has integral "research provisions" (British Psychological Society, 2008). Nonetheless, many ethical issues can arise associated with practice in the field that may be separate to those acknowledged in formal processes of ethical scrutiny to permit research.

It would be difficult to argue that research involving d/Deaf people should not meet the same ethical standards or be guided by the same kinds of ethical principles as any other research. Indeed, in an absolute sense, it would be dangerous to do so. In the not too distant past d/Deaf people in common with many other groups, including disabled people, First Nations peoples, and groups with particular racial origins, have been prey to all manner of unethical practices in the name of research (Corbett, 1996; Lane, 1992). Invasive or experimental procedures without consent are far easier to justify if specific individuals or groups are not regarded as possessing equal human rights to those around them. The 10 principles of the post–World War II Nuremberg Code (1949) was the first step toward enshrining the equivalence of human rights, consent, autonomy, and beneficence as guiding principles within research involving human subjects.

However, the important assertion that the same standards and principles apply to all research with all peoples and which is at the heart of many codified ethical standards, guidelines, and protocols can be a problem if understood too literally or too simply. There are two issues: (1) failure to understand population-specific issues means that research practices that meet ethical guidelines might well be unethical in their application in specific contexts; and (2) lack of awareness of the culturally mediated nature of fundamental ethical principles, including informed consent, anonymity, and confidentiality. We examine these considerations, in turn, within the context of research involving d/Deaf people. Once again we use the phrase "involving d/Deaf people" as an initial catchall to encompass d/Deaf people as producers/leaders of research as well as participants/subjects, only later differentiating the position of the deaf or Deaf person within research in respect to the debates we review.

UNDERSTANDING AND RESPONDING TO
POPULATION-SPECIFIC CONSIDERATIONS

As we reflect many times in the course of this book, to refer to d/Deaf people is to refer to highly heterogeneous individuals, groups, and in some cases communities whose diversity does not solely derive from differences associated with hearing and deafness or language, communication, and culture (see Chapter 5). That fundamental issue of heterogeneity has a range of implications for ethical research practice.

Imagine, for example, a researcher states she will be following the ethical review board guidelines and will provide written information about a study to potential participants, in this case to a population of young d/Deaf people aged 16 to 18 years living in Australia. She has established that all potential participants can read English but has acknowledged that as some young people's literacy will be better than others, she will make sure the information provided is in plain English. This approach seems entirely reasonable and good practice unless you know that language and communication *preferences*, as well as abilities, vary among d/Deaf people. For some of the young people, information about the research study delivered in AUSLAN (Australian Sign Language) would not just be the most effective means of ensuring informed consent but would address their language preference and acknowledge their cultural-linguistic identity. Such acknowledgement of *language rights* is enshrined in the United Nations Declaration on the Rights of Indigenous Peoples (UN, 2007).

To see the importance of this issue, consider how comfortable you would be if asked to participate in a research study by someone who has not found out the language you use every day, which is integral to your identity and which you feel most competent in for the task. However, to recognize that language *preference* is an ethical issue in studies involving d/Deaf people, the researcher has to recognise that sign language use is an issue of cultural identity, not a reasonable adjustment in the face of disability, and accede to the idea that if a sign language is recognized as an indigenous language, then its users may be regarded as indigenous peoples with language rights (Emery, 2011; Lane, Pillard, & Hedberg, 2010).

For other young deaf people in this imaginary sample, English might well be their preferred or only language. However, depressed levels of literacy among many young d/Deaf people (Mayer, 2007) is likely to mean that added safeguards would need to be in place to ensure adequate comprehension of a written text. Would it be easier, therefore, if the information were not written down and delivered face to face in spoken language instead? A modality switch from the written to the spoken is often regarded as synonymous with a switch from the formal to the informal and many ethical review boards require written information be provided regardless. Yet for some young deaf people who use spoken language, to do so could remove the added barrier of literacy and instead prioritize comprehension, however achieved. And what of those d/Deaf young people in this sample who are from Aboriginal communities for whom both English and/or AUSLAN might not be reflective of their language strengths and preferences?

An ethical review board unaware of such basic issues of diversity among populations of young d/Deaf people would fail to see that an expected good practice—to produce written information about a research study in plain English—could actually result in failure to create the best conditions in which an individual might understand what she or he was consenting to. A circumstance Pollard (2002) refers to as "unintended deception" (p. 121), which although nondeliberate, is still unethical.

From a different perspective, consider research designs that because of the methodological approach they employ deliberately seek to exclude confounding population characteristics that arise from the heterogeneity of samples and diversity of individuals. Randomized controlled trials, for example, will often ensure that the inclusion and exclusion criteria for a study are constructed in such a way as to ensure that variables which might complicate or compromise the interpretation of results are removed. This kind of approach often affects d/Deaf people in two entirely opposite ways.

Studies of issues *unconnected* with being d/Deaf, but which might nonetheless affect d/Deaf people, rarely include them in their population samples. The problem is that deafness (in the sense of hearing disabilities), communication difficulties (in the sense of speech), and cultural identity (in the sense of being Deaf) are regarded as additional variables that might confound or skew overall outcomes. For example, a recent randomized controlled trial of intensive speech and language therapy following a stroke excluded both those who did not use English fluently and those with significant hearing impairments (Bowen et al., 2012). Both conditions would influence the delivery of the intervention and the testing of its effects. Consequently, neither British Sign Language users nor deaf people more generally were eligible for inclusion, yet both might experience strokes as part of the general population (Marshall, Atkinson, Thacker, & Woll, 2004).

Conversely, studies that *are* directly associated with d/Deaf people might seek to exclude certain kinds of d/Deaf people, as is frequently the case in research involving parents of deaf children. Routinely, Deaf parents with deaf children are not included because of the different or additional considerations they might have to the majority (hearing parents). This has happened on a worldwide basis in studies of the implementation of various newborn hearing screening programs (Young & Andrews, 2001).

In both of these examples, there is nothing unethical, judged by institutional review board standards, about either the research designs or how the research studies are being executed. However, it is the *cumulative* effect of many, many research studies which make similar choices, even though they may be for good reasons, which raises ethical concerns. Over time, our knowledge about an issue or population becomes defined by results from studies that have systematically excluded certain groups. The visibility and the personal realities of those groups/individuals with certain characteristics become written out of the collective knowledge on those topics. It is these kinds of disappearances, which are a cumulative product of otherwise ethically acceptable studies, which become potentially unethical in their longer term effects. As the American Anthropological Association's Statements on Ethics (1986) says, researchers "bear a professional responsibility to contribute to an "adequate definition of reality" upon which public opinion and public policy may be based" (paragraph 2d). Such a responsibility applies as much to the choice and definition of sample(s) in positivist forms of enquiry as it might to interpretative forms of enquiry which are more explicitly concerned with subjective epistemologies (see Chapter 3).

FUNDAMENTAL ETHICAL PRINCIPLES ARE CULTURALLY MEDIATED

A cluster of fundamental principles, largely derived from a biomedical model of ethics (Denzin, 2008), reappear in ethical guidelines, standards, and protocols associated with the design and conduct of research. They include such issues as informed consent, the right to anonymity, and confidentiality. The universality of such principles does not mean that they are not of themselves culturally mediated. For example, it has been pointed out that "do no harm" is a culturally constructed concept that in some cultures might encompass issues such as "shame" or "dishonor" (Pollard, 1992, p. 95). It would be a rather crude definition that only understood it to refer to physical pain or discomfort. In research involving culturally Deaf people, whether as leaders/producers of research and/or participants or subjects of study, there is a growing interest in understanding the implications of universal ethical principles through a Deaf cultural lens. To do so, as will become apparent, is not just an interesting theoretical pursuit but has highly practical consequences too for how one might carry out a given piece of research. In this respect, we address informed consent, anonymity, and confidentiality.

INFORMED CONSENT

Informed consent, not just in studies involving d/Deaf people, raises many difficult questions (Wiles, Crow, Heath, & Charles, 2004). Often these take the form of whether potential research participants adequately understand what it is they are consenting to. But what is "adequate" understanding? Does it imply full understanding of all potential implications or only enough understanding of what will happen to be able to make a choice whether to participate (Corti, Day, & Backhouse, 2000)? There have been studies in the wider literature investigating lay understandings of research language such as "random" and "trial" and what happens when familiar words are used in the unfamiliar context of research (Featherstone & Donovan, 2002). It has been pointed out that the whole notion of informed decision making is one that many people might not be used to. It involves the idea that an individual has a right to decide and an opinion that is valid. Not everyone has had experiences of such autonomy and rights nor necessarily possesses the self-esteem to enact personal choices (Young et al., 2006).

In research involving d/Deaf people, such concerns about informed consent are valid also, but with some additional considerations. Many d/Deaf people, particularly from older generations, have what Pollard (1998) has described as a smaller fund of information and knowledge in comparison with hearing people. Hearing children and adults pick up a vast amount of information about the world in undeliberate ways, for example, through the incidental learning that arises from listening to the radio or having the television on in the background. Hearing people generally have easy access to an infinite number of conversational partners, rather than to a restricted number of those they might be able to understand or be understood by. The written form, whether factual information or literary fiction, can be a difficult window into new knowledge for many d/Deaf people with lower than average levels of literacy in the written word (Mayer, 2007). Consequently, many adults who have been deaf from birth/early childhood have had access to less knowledge (whether formal or informal), are likely to be less familiar or aware of a range of concepts, and might face considerable barriers in seeking out understanding of something they are hitherto unfamiliar with (Graybill et al., 2010).

Therefore, while the process of informed consent, its underlying concepts, and its concerns about adequate understanding hold true for *any* research participants, researchers would be wise to question their assumptions about what might be commonly understood or does not need explanation when seeking to involve d/Deaf people in studies. In this respect, the issue is being sensitive to the preexisting knowledge on which a potential participant draws within the process of informed consent, rather than the language in which information is presented or accessed.

That said, there is also a significant danger in any a priori assumptions about d/Deaf people's lack of capacity, vulnerability, or likely unfamiliarity with concepts. Deaf people have historically being victims of others' low expectations and incorrect presumptions of lack of intelligence, understanding, autonomy, and personal agency (Lane, Hoffmeister, & Bahan, 1996). Also, as we point out many times, the population of d/Deaf people is highly heterogeneous and is changing (see Chapter 5). Traditionally Deaf children growing up in Deaf families where sign language is used in the home have been regarded by Deaf communities as being particularly fortunate because of how little restriction to knowledge, explanation, and experience they faced as they grew up. All was explicable and accessible within the family and the signing community to which they belonged from birth. From a different perspective, the long-held understanding that incidental learning is difficult for many deaf children is being challenged by the technologies of early cochlear implantation and directional digital hearing aids. As a result, some deaf children are growing up with easy access to environmental sounds, including spoken language that is not directly addressed to them (Ricketts, Picou, Galster, Federman, & Sladen, 2010).

In relation *specifically to Deaf communities*, increasingly referred to as Sign Language Peoples (Ladd, Gulliver, & Batterbury, 2003), insights gleaned from cross-cultural research ethics are being applied to the issue of informed consent in studies involving or about Deaf people (Harris, Holmes, & Mertens, 2009; Pollard, 1992). Critically, it is the *individualized* nature of the model of informed consent that is being challenged. In Western and developed world contexts, informed consent is usually conceptualized as a rational decision-making process undertaken by the individual and its consequences conceived of primarily in terms of risk, harm, or benefit to the individual. This approach is so embedded it is implicit. However, to many indigenous, First Nations peoples and other cultures largely uninfluenced by post-Enlightenment and Judaeo-Christian ethics, the individual is not the most relevant or obvious denominator in a discussion on whether to participate in research (Denzin, 2008); the collective, or the community, is (IPCB, undated). Canada's Ethical Guidelines for Doing Research with Aboriginal Peoples (Uhlik, 2006), for example, asserts the "right" to "informed *collective* consent" (p. 11). Questions of risk, benefit, or harm (or indeed uncertainty) are not weighed up in terms of the consequences for an individual but rather for the community or group as a whole. As the Linguistics Society of America (LSA) Ethics Statement acknowledges:

> In many communities, responsibility for linguistic and cultural knowledge is viewed as corporate, so that individual community members are not in a position to consent to share materials with outsiders, and linguists must try to determine whether there are individuals who can legitimately represent the community. (unpaginated)

In addition, among many indigenous/First Nation peoples the definition of "community" is not necessarily confined to those who are living,
but quite commonly might encompass those who are dead but present
(ancestors). Community might also be defined by land, spirit, tradition,
and characteristic ways of being, telling, and seeing (IPCB, undated;
McKennitt & Fletcher, 2007). Therefore, even when informed consent
is understood in collective rather than individualistic terms, it is likely
to be considered on behalf of a far greater notion of community than
many, largely Western, cultures might imagine. Consequently, the definition of what might count as risk, benefit, or harm might also be considerably larger than the experience of many researchers from outside
of those communities/cultures.

If we accept that Sign Language Peoples constitute indigenous communities that are collective, rather than individualistic in their cultural
orientation (Mindess, 2006), then approaches to informed consent which
have been developed with and by other indigenous communities, become
highly relevant. Mertens and Ginsberg (2008) draw a parallel with the
position taken by Botswanen, American Indian, and Maori cultures:

> which rather than valuing individual privacy, confidentiality and
> anonymity, value instead protections safeguarding the group. These
> include community, clan, and/or family consent to pursue any spe-
> cific research agenda with accompanying assurance at the group
> rather than the individual level. (p. 496)

Pollard (1992) argues that it is the "host community" who should be
regarded as the participant, not the individual (p. 90).

The vast majority of codified ethical guidelines for research, including
those commonly used by institutional review boards, are not written in
such as way as to acknowledge this culturally mediated understanding
of informed consent as collective. Consequently, various attempts have
been made to draw up alternative ethical guidelines for research with
Deaf communities/Sign Language Peoples (Harris et al., 2009; Ladd,
2003; Pollard, 1992). The issue of collective/community/group orientation in informed consent is not the only motivator for these alternative
guidelines, but it is central to them. Although beginning from slightly
different theoretical bases, these approaches share a common emphasis
on four issues of relevance to informed consent and research with Deaf
communities/Sign Language Peoples: communication, concordance,
ownership, and benefit.

The Conditions for Communication Between
the Researcher and the Host Community

Communication refers to the fact that it might not be self-evident who a
researcher seeking access to a community, sample, or participants should
contact or how the researcher should do so. For Pollard, this amounts to

respecting and using formal channels of communication with the Deaf community to explain, negotiate, present, and seek permission for the carrying out of specific research. He refers in 1992 to "the host community's political and scientific bodies" (p. 90) and laments in 2002 that these still remain unestablished. Harris, Holmes, and Mertens (2009) emphasize the precondition of researchers having credibility within the community in which they are carrying out research. They define credibility as researchers who are Deaf and/or have trusted and verifiable cultural competence to engage in research alongside, with and for Deaf people. The work of Emery (2011) and Conama (2010), both Deaf researchers working within Deaf communities, provide good examples of how in practice positive communication can be established between researcher and host community. Interestingly, both do not assume in any blasé manner that such communication will be self-evident as they are from within those communities. Rather they describe how the identity of "researcher" must still be negotiated and that they had to work hard to achieve consent in a way that satisfied them that it was not simply given because the researcher was "one of us" (see also Chapter 3 for a discussion of insider status).

The Concordance of the Research Agenda With Host Community Needs, Interests, and Preferences

The issue of concordance of research agenda in relation to informed consent does not just refer to the subject or objectives of a piece of research but also to its methodology and its philosophical/political basis. Ladd (2003) discusses at length the ways in which research inquiry, even while acknowledging the legitimacy of sign languages, might nonetheless be at odds with Deaf people's interests. He asserts, for example, that the primacy of linguistic studies has resulted in a failure to explore with equal vigor the cultural lives of Deaf people, resulting in an impoverished understanding of the users of those languages. Harris, Holmes, and Mertens (2009) remind us of the significance of researchers being in a position adequately to interpret, understand, and reflect data derived from and with Deaf people. Therefore, to them, collaborative and participatory research approaches are important in which boundaries between the researcher and the researched are blurred. This is crucial because as Emery (2011), researching citizenship and the Deaf community reminds us, participatory approaches are not truly participatory if they only address the agenda of the researcher.

There are also some studies whose topic, basis, or orientation might simply be unacceptable to some communities and cultures. For many Deaf people, studies that might seek to "cure" deafness or studies pursued to demonstrate the ways in which Deaf people are aberrant in comparison with hearing norms are deeply offensive.

Plenty of research studies within genetic, medical, and audiological arenas now begin with the premise that the advances they are making will lead to the prevention of deafness. If one switched the term "prevention of deafness" to the "prevention of Deaf people," the lack of concordance with the agenda of a Deaf host community becomes obvious. Several scholars have drawn parallels with colonialism that has repeatedly sought to impose a preferred way to be ("civilized" rather than "savage") or a preferred identity (that of the colonizer over that of the indigenous peoples). However, as many Deaf activists and researchers point out, they are largely powerless to argue that as a community and culture they do not give their informed consent to such studies taking place. If all d/Deaf people are subsumed under "deafness" as a homogenous group, then their very status as a host community from whom consent might be sought is not recognized anyway.

Ownership of Research and Benefit

The ownership of research is identified as an important condition associated with informed consent from a collective perspective. Ownership encompasses such notions as whose interpretations of data are given primacy, to whom do the results of the research belong (the community or the university?), and the extent to which those researched are rendered visible and afforded appropriate attribution for *their* knowledge (not the researcher's who might record it). The issue of ownership is seen as particularly sensitive because of the ways in which those who are not Deaf and/or those not within the community have controlled the construction of knowledge about Deaf people and therefore the terms on which Deaf people are known.

Whether any research is of benefit to the Deaf community is proposed as a key consideration within a process of informed consent, from a collective perspective. For Pollard (1992) it is vital that benefit is defined by the Deaf community, not by the researcher, and therefore a process of negotiation both about research direction and research process is appropriate to discern what is beneficial. He suggests that research which contributes to the "self-sufficiency" (p. 90) of Deaf people is an important yardstick. However, as Denzin (2008) (after Smith, 1999), writing more generally about indigenous research ethics, points out, research that sets out to empower or enable communities can be regarded as another form of neocolonialism. The intent to empower still "inscribes" the community's "otherness" and is a subtle form of "continued subjugation" (Bishop, 1998, p. 208). From their perspective, benefit consists in approaching the community/culture as is, with research understood as a "gift" (Denzin, 2008) that is given to be received (or not) on terms defined by the community and as the first step in a shared understanding of how it might proceed. A similar approach is taken by

Ladd (2003), who is also distrustful of research which seeks to emancipate or give voice to Deaf people rather than simply to *see* Deaf people, a task which requires, in his view, a bigger field of vision than most researchers to date have demonstrated (see Chapter 3 for a related discussion on epistemology). For Harris et al. (2009) the benefit of research is best regarded as a transformative process, rooted in social justice. Both research process and aim must be of primary benefit to the community with which the researcher participates.

ANONYMITY

For a long time, anonymity for participants within the research process has been a principle, so fundamental, that to challenge it has been regarded as unethical. Participant anonymity is regarded as an important safeguard from unintended harm (Grinyer, 2002). It is considered a key component in the preservation of confidentiality, although of itself it is not synonymous with confidentiality (see later). Anonymity also supports respect for participants' privacy; taking part in a research project does not imply that any and all aspects of one's life are open for scrutiny. However, research studies which entail data capture in signed languages present significant challenges to these assumptions and contribute to the broader debate in the social sciences about anonymity within visual research methods (Wiles, Coffey, Robinson, & Heath, 2012).

On a purely practical level, because the grammar of signed languages is expressed in part through the face, it is not possible to obscure the face as a means of preserving the anonymity of the signer (Crasborn, 2010). The consequences of that simple fact are many and varied from an ethical perspective. For example, it is not common for ethical review boards to enquire *where* data will actually be analyzed. If data are in the form of an anonymous written transcript or in statistical form, there is no problem if a researcher is located in a shared office. If the data consist of viewing sign language, then a shared office might be a consideration as the identity of the data producer is easily overseen.

Many project grants now include a contractual obligation to archive data for purposes of secondary data analysis by others. Qualitative data in signed languages cannot be archived in its raw form without breaches of confidentiality. But what is the alternative? To produce a written transcript removes a whole language corpus from the stock of data held in national research archives. This is a slightly different issue than that of the storage of visual images such as photographs because it is about language, not just image. In removing the image one removes the language. Furthermore, the language has no other form in which it might exist, unlike audio recordings, for example, which might exist separately from the filmed form of their expression.

Resigning data by an actor would be a long and tedious process, calling into question whether the effort justifies the gain. More fundamentally it also removes the person from the data who was the originator of the narrative. New technologies are beginning to offer alternatives, such as signing avatars (Crasborn, 2010) or the digital manipulation of the image. While not losing the facial expression and other grammatical markers, a person can be made not to look like herself; for example, a White face becomes a Black face, a woman becomes a man, short stature becomes tall, and so forth. However, the manipulation of visual form is also the manipulation of identity and representation. Content and form of language may well be preserved, but its contextual roots and therefore the place of particular individuals and characters are lost. What is said or signed is only partial data without the "who."

Some researchers and commentators working in studies involving Deaf people (e.g., Crasborn, 2010; Kusters, 2012), in common with those involved in studies with other minority cultural-linguistic populations, have begun to question the very basis of the principle of anonymity (Bowker & Tuffin, 2004; Grinyer, 2002; Svalastog & Eriksson, 2010; Waskul & Douglass, 1996). From the perspective of communities and more particularly languages whose validity has been consistently denied for centuries, anonymity can easily seem like an agent of further oppression, rather than of protection. If data in signed languages remain hidden or unavailable in research repositories for reasons of anonymity, then the status of those signed languages remains unequal with other languages. There is no searchable history of the language itself, let alone the experiences, knowledge, and histories of its users. A similar argument exists in feminist archive research methodologies (Moore, 2012).

The multiliteracies project in Canada, for example, aims to encourage children's skills in several languages by first working with them to establish their "identity" texts in their first language (Snoddon, 2010). These are stories about themselves, rendered in their own language, which form the basis of a range of activities that teach them about discourse, how to read others culturally as well as literally, and that develops their own skills in additional languages. This national demonstration project has an updated Web presence that shows off examples of children's emerging and sustained multiliteracy activities, including their "identity texts." The achievements and "evidence" of participating Deaf children's multiliteracy skills and identity texts are, however, missing and therefore on a worldwide basis, literally, unseen. As Snodden (2010) explains: "Because of concerns about protecting students' identities, their American Sign Language (ASL) stories are not directly featured on the project's web site" yet he sees little contradiction in adding: "ASL identity texts serve to validate and normalize ASL literacy and linguistic diversity and can result in more effective practise and policies that involve the use of technology in school" (p. 209).

It may well be the case that concerns associated with being an identifiable child were regarded as a greater moral imperative than concerns to disseminate a largely hidden language. Yet why then, for example, have the children's identity texts been shown at academic conferences? Such dilemmas are not unique to sign language data. They have been reported also in the use of still images within visual methods where issues of safeguarding might take precedence over participants' legitimate desires to be recognized as collaborators or co-constructors of knowledge. Wiles et al. (2012) point out that the judgements made to reject anonymity are situated ones, dependent on context rather than absolutes. However, the question still remains who controls those situated decisions and who owns the data, a subject we return to next.

From a slightly different perspective, there is also a cultural argument which challenges traditional views of anonymity. The notion of individual privacy often associated with research anonymity is not a self-evident truth for many communities and cultures. As we have already discussed, the collective nature of those communities might imply an orientation away from the preservation of individual anonymity and toward a public openness for similar reasons to those underpinning more conventional views of anonymity. For example, safeguarding from unintended harm arising from participation in research might equally be assured by a community knowing exactly who provided data, rather than keeping it secret. This point is of particular importance if the participant is being regarded by a researcher as representative of the group/community, when she or he may not be.

Often attempts to preserve anonymity result in compromises in how someone's data is reported, even if the person's name is not used or her or his face is not seen (Grinyer, 2002; Wiles et al., 2008). It is not unusual to see identifiers marked by role and/or for characteristics that preserve a sense of perspective or context but stop short of revealing identity (Morse, 1998). For example, quotations followed by epithets such as "a senior teacher in an elementary school" or "a psychologist specializing in eating disorders." However, among cultural groups who have been subject to histories of oppression and/or who exist as small communities (for example, Lesbian/Gay/Bisexual/Transgender communities in specific locations), it is often the case that there are only a few people who might break through into any given roles and they become highly visible (Schank, Helbok, Haldeman, & Gallardo, 2010). Consequently, stating an identity through role or characteristics can often amount to broadcasting an individual's identity regardless of lack of name or presence of pseudonym. Compare, for example, the statement "a White President of the United States" and "a Black President of the United States." Both descriptors are nonspecific, but in the first it could refer to over 40 people, whereas the latter can only refer to one person. Similarly in Deaf communities at different points in time and in various locations, generalized descriptors of research participants hardly hide an identity. In the United Kingdom 20 years ago, if a quotation in a research publication said after it: "a Deaf qualified social worker," there were fewer than 15 people it could refer to. If the research also gave the location of the data collection, even in regional terms, it would be easy enough to identify the originator of the quotation. As Waskul and Douglass (1996) argue, anonymity is not a given or created status; it is more properly conceived of as a "situated social condition" (p. 134).

However, high identity visibility in research is not necessarily a problem and attempts to safeguard an individual's identity might be highly questionable from a sociocultural perspective. If the priority is the preservation of individual anonymity, the cost is often a failure to recognize and record an outstanding achievement or individual. More broadly, the preservation of anonymity can also serve to obscure from history(ies) the proud contributions of a people or culture. The Linguistic Society of America's (LSA, undated) statement on Human Subjects in Linguistics Research declares:

> Those who participate in [research] often do so with pride in their command of their language and may wish to be known for their contribution. Not to disclose their names would do them a disservice. Native Americans sometimes justly criticize earlier work with their language for not having adequately proclaimed the contributions of the Native Americans themselves. (unpaginated)

Svalastog and Eriksson (2010) in their critique of anonymity in indigenous studies argue participants' insistence on the use of their names is also a form of subversion of the power of research to own and define what is known about those who are researched. To insist on being named (rather than anonymously represented) is to assert the *ownership* of knowledge through producing a traceable origin of that knowledge:

> Ownership of one's identity and history is tied to the process of naming. In this respect, anonymity implies stealing someone's identity and history. (p. 109)

Challenging the imperative to protect identity is a particularly critical issue for those from cultural groups whose language has no written form because there are far fewer ways for them to be "read" (and therefore known), if not through being directly visible. The significance of *visibility over anonymity* is becoming a more debated issue in research involving Deaf people, signed languages, and within Deaf-led research.

CONFIDENTIALITY

Confidentiality is another example of a core principle in research ethics that nonetheless is open to cultural mediation. Conventionally, confidentiality is stressed in ethical research practice in order to protect people against the misuse of their data (Svalastog & Eriksson, 2010). It is instrumental in building trust and confidence between the participant and the researcher and its assurance of privacy, both in relation to participation and data, is generally regarded as positively beneficial (Wiles, Crow, Heath, & Charles, 2008). However, confidentiality in research involving small communities, such as the Deaf community, can be highly problematic. Small community effects raise questions about how realistic it might be to assure confidentiality in research and whether a conventional understanding of what is confidentiality requires reframing.

Literature on professional practice in remote and rural communities (Pugh, 2007), as well as in other small communities of practice (Schank et al., 2010), has identified two major effects in relation to conventional notions of confidentiality: dual/multiple relationships and heightened visibility. Although originally derived from issues in professional practice as a social worker or psychological therapist, they are of direct relevance to someone fulfilling a research role.

Dual or Multiple Relationships

In small communities it is likely that the professional/researcher is known outside of the role she or he is fulfilling as a result of everyday encounters arising from community membership. There is a much greater chance of the researcher having been known by potential participants before they meet the researcher in her or his formal role and equally a much greater chance of them meeting the researcher in other roles afterward, including social encounters. These multiple relationships raise inevitable questions from participants about whether their data would truly remain confidential. However, it also opens up channels for participants to scrutinize the researcher and make informed decisions about the extent to which they are prepared to trust her or him. Pugh (2007) comments in relation to social workers in remote and rural communities that there is a desire to "place the worker" who:

> may be expected to answer questions or provide information themselves that would rarely be sought in an urban setting. This might include information about local links, previous experience, family background...This may then be used...to decide whether, and to what degree, to engage with the worker. (p. 1406)

These kinds of checking-out and placing behaviors are well documented in research involving Deaf people, particularly in cases where the researcher is Deaf (Pollard, 2002). Asking about family, where one went to school, and mutual friends and connections is a form of cultural matching that is a vital precursor to any kind of face-to-face data collection. It will routinely involve the researcher in a higher level of self-disclosure than is generally regarded usual but is entirely culturally appropriate. In fact, to hold back or to seek to maintain a kind of professional distance would likely be seen as suspicious and certainly not culturally appropriate.

A more complicated circumstance, however, arises when the encounter is not necessarily face to face, but the participant might know, in a different relationship, someone who would legitimately have access to her or his data. For example, a research supervisor might need to review data captured by a student or associate. In reviewing the data the research supervisor literally sees the participant whose identity cannot be hidden as it might in an anonymous written transcript. These more remote research relationships are nonetheless important because the participant might well encounter those individuals in other settings and roles. Good research practice dictates that potential research participants are therefore provided with information about everyone who might *see* (literally) identifiable data so these remote individuals can be "placed" too by the participant within her or his community landscape. In this respect, using photographs of researchers and others who would view data later on participant information sheets is often more helpful and more culturally appropriate than using a written name. In Deaf communities, people are more commonly recognized by their face or their sign name (Day & Sutton-Spence, 2010), rather than by their written/family name.

The potential pressures and conflicts experienced by Deaf people who are researchers *and* ordinary members of the Deaf community are not as well documented or explored by Deaf researchers themselves as they might be (Guthmann & Sandberg, 2002). Common issues include problems that might arise over the origin of information. For instance, a Deaf researcher might have specific knowledge about a person that has arisen in data collection while being a researcher, and then quite naturally will re-encounter the research participant in an entirely different role, for example, as a colleague on a community-based committee, or within a shared interest or social group. In this instance, the problem is not one of keeping confidentiality but more subtly that the researcher's relationship with the other is now inevitably influenced by her or his data knowledge.

Schank et al. (2010), writing about being a practicing therapist in a small community, suggests a key lesson to learn is *how to keep information confidential from oneself* when involved in an encounter with someone for a different reason/in a different context (p. 503). However, she also points out that this can sometimes involve prodigious feats of remembering from where the information about the other derives in the first place, as well as prodigious feats of deliberate forgetting when one meets the individual again.

Heightened Visibility

Outside of the professional role, the researcher nonetheless remains easily visible in small communities. The researcher's heightened visibility can potentially threaten, be it undeliberately, the privacy and confidentiality of a research participant who might not wish it known that she or he is participating in a research project. For example, among researchers who are Deaf, it is not unusual to leave one's car some streets away from the Deaf home one might be visiting for research purposes because the car is likely to be "known" by other Deaf people and the researcher's visit would not go unnoticed.

This heightened visibility may also pose a problem in relation to the "consistency of personal presentation" (Pugh, 2007) across a variety of contexts for the researcher. They are open to observation by those involved in research when they are acting outside of their research role. As Schank et al. (2010) remark, "Acts of everyday living are self-disclosures" (p. 503). While this might in one sense be experienced as a pressure for the researcher, in another sense it is a benefit for research participants who are able to make judgements about the extent of their trust, liking, and willingness to disclose personal or sensitive information to someone whom they can observe outside of role, too. Pugh (2000) remarks:

> in smaller communities, people may have more opportunities to observe each other's behaviour in a range of different situations and are thus, well placed to observe discontinuities between the personal style and manner that is used within work and their behaviour and presentation elsewhere. (p. 102)

Privacy

Finally with respect to confidentiality, it is important to consider the issue of privacy. As discussed earlier, one of the effects of small communities is that privacy becomes a more complex consideration. It is often something enacted and demonstrated in how a researcher behaves toward a participant outside of the research relationship in their *continued association* and encounters with them for nonresearch reasons. By contrast, outside of small communities privacy more commonly is something assured, in part, through *a lack* of continued contact between a researcher and a participant.

In addition, in terms of signed languages, content of conversations can be easily overseen and at a distance; therefore, even the precursors to data collection, including for example processes of information giving about research, have to be considered for their visibility to others. For example, an informal remark in spoken language indicating that someone would be willing to take part in a research study is unlikely to make her or his future participation public knowledge when muttered in a crowded room. When the same remark is casually signed in a Deaf space, it amounts to a public self-disclosure of intent—someone is bound to have seen it. From a different perspective, it is also important to remember mistakes easily made with radio microphones which might have been used during an interview, for example. If inadvertently left on by a researcher when a participant has left the room but remains in range, any postinterview comments by the researcher to another become accessible to the participant who is a hearing aid wearer.

Privacy also is a concept open to cultural interpretation and influence. Its boundaries are not fixed, and different communities will have their own considerations about what counts as a violation of privacy and what does not. For example, in a study of choices in healing method for psychological health in Sri Lanka, Western researchers reported how they unwittingly created unease and discomfort by seeking to interview participants in a nonpublic space for reasons of privacy (Monshi & Zieglmayer, 2004). The participants interpreted this as being taken to somewhere which was "hidden" and were suspicious because health-related consultations are usually conducted in public and visible settings, and not on a one-to-one basis. The boundary of privacy began with the touching of the physical body, not with the physical space surrounding the communicative encounter.

Among Deaf people it is commonly reported that Deaf communities have very fluid and open notions of privacy. For example, it is not uncommon to see people's personal information and concerns discussed openly, sometimes when the person concerned might be present and could oversee the discussion. Lane et al. (2010) suggest that two reasons underlie this tendency to more direct candor; first, the high value placed on the obtaining and sharing of information and knowledge and, second, the value of allegiance to the group which regards all Deaf people as kin and like an extended family. The consequences for research practice of culturally mediated notions of privacy within Deaf communities are barely explored. Reassurances about privacy within the research process are potentially easily misunderstood if the researcher and the participant do not share a culturally equivalent notion of privacy.

CONCLUDING THOUGHTS

In this chapter we have sought to explore how both ethical principles and ethical praxis are shaped when they intersect with conditions inherent within and associated with being deaf or Deaf. We have largely concentrated on what happens when research engages with or seeks to be influential among Deaf people(s) because in many respects this circumstance creates the most demanding challenges to good ethical practice in research. Throughout, our concern has not been to show how standard principles or procedures require modification because participants (or lead researchers) might be d/Deaf. Rather we have used the ontological realities of d/Deaf lives as the starting point for examining seemingly taken for granted notions such as informed consent, privacy, and anonymity. Through this examination the meanings and implications of core issues in ethical research practice are expanded in a general sense but also made more detailed in a specific sense. We have deliberately steered clear of the debate about whether some research designs, methodologies, or methods are more ethical than others. Our argument throughout this book, and particularly in Chapter 3, is that no methodology or method is per se more truthful, preferable, or ethical than any other. This chapter reinforces this argument. Social researchers continue to argue against the tick box approach to ethics in research and for a more situated and culturally nuanced discussion of what is and is not ethical in practice.

In this chapter we focus on arguments for more collective and community approaches to research ethics. This focus does not mean that we are arguing against the need to consider the individual within research. Rather, we try to reintroduce some idea of the social within ethical decisions. Again, we give no solutions, just choices with consequences and some suggestions of safeguards. The chapter addresses the historical exclusion of d/Deaf people from both participating in research and from doing it. It should be read in tandem with debates in Chapters 2 and 3 about the dangers of reifying communities and community leaders and of introducing gatekeepers and arbiters of who should be included in research, who should do research, and how it should be done. Although we slant our discussion away from individuals toward communities, we do not mean to imply that there is no place in research for those who are defined as community "outsiders." We take up these issues of insiders and outsiders from different perspectives in subsequent chapters.

REFERENCES

American Anthropological Association (1986). Statement on ethics. Retrieved May 05, 2011, from http://www.aaanet.org/stmts/ethstmnt.htm

Bishop, R. (1998). Freeing ourselves from neo-colonial domination in research: A Maori approach to creating knowledge. *International Journal of Qualitative Studies in Education, 11*(2), 199–219. doi: 10.1080/095183998236674

Bowen, A., Hesketh, A., Patchik, E., Young, A., Davies, L., Vail, A., Long, A. F., Watkins, C., Wilkinson, M., Pearl, G., Lambon Ralph, M. A., & Tyrell, P. (2012). Effectiveness of enhanced communication therapy in the first four months after stroke for aphasia and dysarthria: A randomised controlled trial. *BMJ, 345*, e4407. doi: 10.1136/bmj.e4407

Bowker, N., & Tuffin, K. (2004). Using the online medium for discursive research about people with disabilities. *Social Science Computer Review, 22*, 228–241. doi: 10.1177/0894439303262561

British Psychological Society (2008). Conducting research with people not having the capacity to consent to their participation. Retrieved October 04, 2012, from http://www.psy.ed.ac.uk/psy_research/documents/BPS%20 Guidelines%20for%20Conducting%20Research%20with%20People%20 not%20having%20Capacity%20to%20Consent.pdf

Conama, J. (2010). *Finnish and Irish Sign Languages: An egalitarian analysis of language policies and their effects.* PhD thesis, University College, Dublin.

Corbett, J. (1996). *Bad mouthing.* London: Routledge.

Corti, L., Day, A., & Backhouse, G. (2000). Confidentiality and informed consent: Issues for consideration in the preservation of and provision of access to qualitative data archives. *Forum: Qualitative Social Research, 1*(3), Article 7, 1–16.

Crasborn, O. (2010). What does "informed consent" mean in the internet age? Publishing sign language corpora as open content. *Sign Language Studies, 10*(2), 276–290. doi: 10.1353/sls.0.0044

Day, L., & Sutton-Spence, R. (2010). British sign name customs. *Sign Language Studies, 11*(1), 22–54. doi: 10.1353/sls.2010.0005

Denzin, N. K. (2008). IRBs and the turn to indigenous research ethics. *Advances in Program Evaluation, 12,* 97–123. doi: 10.1016/S1474-7863(08)12006-3

Department of Health and Human Services (2005) Code of Federal regulations, Title 45, public welfare, part 46, protection of human subjects. Retrieved November 05, 2011, from http://ohsr.od.nih.gov/guidelines/45cfr46.html

Emery, S. (2011). *Citizenship and the Deaf community.* Nijmegen, The Netherlands: Ishara Press.

ESRC (2010). ESRC Framework for Research Ethics (FRE). Revised 2012. Retrieved February 10, 2013, from http://www.esrc.ac.uk/_images/ Framework-for-Research-Ethics_tcm8-4586.pdf

Featherstone, K., & Donovan, J. L. (2002). "Why don't they just tell me straight, why allocate it?" The struggle to make sense of participating in a randomised controlled trial. *Social Science & Medicine, 55,* 709–719. doi: 10.1016/ S0277-9536(01)00197-6.

Graybill, P., Aggas, J., Dean, R. K., Demers, S., Finigan, E. G., & Pollard, R. Q., Jr. (2010). A community-participatory approach to adapting survey items for deaf individuals and American Sign Language. *Field Methods, 22*(4), 429–448.

Grinyer, A. (2002). The anonymity of research participants: Assumptions, ethics and practicalities. *Social Research Update 36.* Retrieved February 14, from http://sru.soc.surrey.ac.uk/SRU36.html

Guthmann, D. S., & Sandberg, K. (2002). Dual relationships in the Deaf community. In A. Lazarus & O. Zur (Eds.), *Dual relationships and psychotherapy,* (pp. 287–298). New York, NY: Springer.

Harris, R., Holmes, H. M., & Mertens, D. M. (2009). Research ethics in sign language communities. *Sign Language Studies, 9*(2), 104–131. doi: 10.1353/ sls.0.0011

IPCB. Indigenous Peoples Council on Biocolonialism (undated). Indigenous Research Protection Act. Retrieved July 12, 2011, from http://www.ipcb. org/pdf_files/irpa.doc

Kusters, A. (2012). "The gong gong was beaten"—Adamorobe: A "deaf village" in Ghana and its marriage prohibition for deaf partners. *Sustainability, 4,* 2765–2784. doi: 10.3390/su4102765

Ladd, P. (2003). *Understanding Deaf culture: In search of Deafhood*. Clevedon, UK: Multilingual Matters.

Ladd, P., Gulliver, M., & Batterbury, S. C. E. (2003). Reassessing minority language mepowerment from a Deaf perspective: The other 32 languages. *Deaf Worlds, 19*(2), 6–32.

Lane, H. (1992). *The mask of benevolence: Disabling the Deaf community*. New York, NY: Knopf.

Lane, H., Hoffmeister, B., & Bahan, B. (1996). *A journey into the Deaf world*. San Diego, CA: Dawn Sign Press.

Lane, H., Pillard, R. C., & Hedberg, U. (2010). *People of the eye: Deaf ethnicity and ancestry*. New York, NY: Oxford University Press.

Leigh, G., & Marschark, M. (2005). Ethics and deafness: A matter of perspective? *Journal of Deaf Studies and Deaf Education, 10*(2), 109–110. doi: 10.1093/deafed/eni023

LSA. Linguistic Society of America. (Undated). Human subjects in linguistics research. Retrieved September, 11, 2011, from http://www.lsadc.org/info/lsa-res-human.cfm

Marschark, M., Rhoten, C., & Fabich, M. (2007). On ethics and deafness: Research, pedagogy and politics. *Deafness & Education International, 9*(1), 45–61. doi: 10.1179/146431507790560057

Marshall, J., Atkinson, J. R., Thacker, A., & Woll, B. (2004). Stroke in users of BSL: Investigating sign language impairments. In S. Austen (Ed.), *Deafness in mind: Working psychologically with deaf people across the lifespan* (pp. 284–301). London: Whurr.

Mayer, C. (2007). What really matters in the early literacy development of deaf children. *Journal of Deaf Studies and Deaf Education, 12*(4), 411–431. doi: 10.1093/deafed/enm020

McKennitt, D. W., & Fletcher, F. L. (2007). Engaging with Aboriginal communities in collaborative research. *University of Alberta Health Sciences Journal, 4*(1), 30–32.

Mental Capacity Act (2005). Retrieved November 5, 2012, from http://www.dh.gov.uk/en/SocialCare/Deliveringsocialcare/MentalCapacity/MentalCapacityAct2005/index.htm

Mertens, D. M., & Ginsberg, P. E. (2008). Deep in ethical waters: Transformative perspectives for qualitative social work research. *Qualitative Social Work: Research and Practice, 7*(4), 484–503. doi: 10.1177/1473325008097142

Mindess, A. (2006). *Reading between the signs: Intercultural communication for sign language interpreters* (2nd ed.). Boston, MA: Intercultrual Press.

Monshi, B., & Zieglmayer, V. (2004). The problem of privacy in transcultural research: Reflections on an ethnographic study in Sri Lanka. *Ethics & Behavior, 14*(4), 305–312. doi: 10.1207/s15327019eb1404_2

Moore, N. (2012). The politics and ethics of naming: questioning anonymisation in (archival) research. *International Journal of Social Research Methodology, 15*(4), 331–340. doi: 10.1080/13645579.2012.688330

Morse, J. M. (1998). The contracted relationship: Ensuring protection of anonymity and confidentiality. *Qualitative Health Research, 8*(3), 301–303. doi: 10.1177/104973239800800301

Pollard, R. Q. (1992). Cross cultural ethics in the conduct of deafness research. *Rehabilitation Psychology, 37*(2), 87–101.

Pollard, R. Q. (1998). Psychopathology. In M. Marschark & D. Clark (Eds.), *Psychological perspectives on deafness, Vol. 2* (pp. 171–197). Mahwah, NJ.: Lawrence Erlbaum.

Pollard, R. Q. (2002). Ethical conduct in research involving deaf people. In V. A. Gutman (Ed.), *Ethics in mental health and deafness* (pp. 162–178). Washington, DC: Gallaudet University Press.

Pugh, R. (2000). *Rural social work.* Lyme Regis, UK: Russell House Publishing.

Pugh, R. (2007). Dual relationships: Personal and professional boundaries in rural social work. *British Journal of Social Work, 37*(8), 1405–1423. doi: 10.1093/bjsw/bcl088

Ricketts, T. A., Picou, E. M., Galster, J. A., Federman, J., & Sladen, D. P. (2010). Potential for directional hearing aid benefit in classrooms: Field data. In R. C. Seewald & J. Bamford (Eds.), *A sound foundation through early amplification 2010* (pp. 143–165). Stäfa Switzerland: Phonak A.G.

Schank, J. A., Helbok, C. M., Haldeman, D. C., & Gallardo, M. E. (2010). Challenges and benefits of ethical small-community practice. *Professional Psychology: Research and Practice, 41*(6), 502–510. doi: 10.1037/a0021689

SIL. Summer Institue of Linguistics (Undated). Basic principles of research ethics in SIL fieldwork. Retrieved June 18, 2011, from http://www.sil.org/sil/research_ethics.htm

Skloot, R. (2010). *The immortal life of Henrietta Lacks.* London: Macmillan.

Smith, L. T. (1999). *Decolonizing methodologies: Research and indigenous peoples.* Dunedin, New Zealand: University of Otago Press.

Snoddon, K. (2010). Technology as a learning tool for ASL literacy. *Sign Language Studies, 10*(2), 197–213. doi: 10.1353/sls.0.0039

Svalastog, A. L., & Eriksson, S. (2010). You can use my name: You don't have to steal my story—a critique of anonymity in indigenous studies. *Developing World Bioethics, 10*(2), 104–110. doi: 10.1111/j.1471-8847.2010.00276.x

Uhlik, C. (2006). Ethical guidelines and principles for doing research with Aboriginal peoples. Retrieved June 2, 2011, from http://www.usask.ca/research/aboriginal_working_group/ Downloads/AEWG-Principles-25-April-2006-FINAL.doc

United Nations (2007). United Nations Declaration on the Rights of Indigenous Peoples. Retrieved September 11, 2011, from http://www.un.org/esa/socdev/unpfii/en/drip.html

US Government (1949). *Trials of war criminals before the Nuremberg military tribunals under control council law.* Washington, DC: US Government. Retrieved from http://history.nih.gov/research/downloads/nuremberg.pdf.

Waskul, D., & Douglass, M. (1996). Considering the electronic participant: Some polemical observations on the ethics of on-line research. *The Information Society, 12*(2), 129–139.

Wiles, R., Coffey, A., Robinson, J., & Heath, S. (2012). Anonymisation and visual images: Issues of respect, "voice" and protection. *International Journal of Social Research Methodology, 15*(1), 41–53. doi: 10.1080/13645579.2011.564423

Wiles, R., Crow, G., Heath, S., & Charles, V. (2004). Informed consent in social research: A literature review. *National Centre for Research Methods Paper Series.* Retrieved August 15, 2011, from http://www.sociology.soton.ac.uk/Proj/Informed_Consent/Resources.htm

Wiles, R., Crow, G., Heath, S., & Charles, V. (2008). The management of confidentiality and anonymity in social research. *International Journal of Social Research Methodology, 11*(5), 417–428. doi: 10.1080/13645570701622231

Young, A., & Andrews, E. (2001). Parents' experience of universal neonatal hearing screening: A critical review of the literature and its implications for the implementation of new UNHS programs. *Journal of Deaf Studies and Deaf Education, 6*(3), 149–160. doi: 10.1093/deafed/6.3.14

Young, A., Skipp, A., Carr, G., Tattersall, H., Hunt, R., & McCracken, W. (2006). Informed choice and deaf children: Underpinning concepts and enduring challenges. *Journal of Deaf Studies and Deaf Education, 11*(3), 322–336. doi: 10.1093/deafed/enj041

Young, A. M., Jones, D., Starmer, C., & Sutherland, H. (2005). Issues and dilemmas in the production of standard information for parents of young deaf children—Parents' view. *Deafness & Education International, 7*(2), 63–76.

5

Populations and Sampling

Any research study will necessitate choices about who and/or what is included and therefore inevitably about who and/or what becomes excluded. Defining the boundaries of the population(s) to be studied and the basis on which a sample is taken is important for the relevance as well as the strength of findings. Good research design requires us to be transparent about the grounds on which we might define a population or the basis on which we might sample. In this chapter, we will review some of the common issues, problems, and consequences that arise in population definitions and sampling approaches in studies which involve d/Deaf people. We will not be presenting a review or summary of theories and techniques of sampling; such are available elsewhere (Bryman, 2012; Dingwall, Murphy, Watson, Greatbatch, & Parker, 1998). Rather, we will be exploring *how specific conditions associated with carrying out research with, by, and among d/Deaf people intersect with key principles and practices of sampling and population definition*. We begin by examining the notion of heterogeneity in relation to d/Deaf people from a variety of perspectives because it will underpin much of the later discussion.

HETEROGENEITY

As Chapter 2 illustrates, the vast heterogeneity of experience and identity subsumed under the word "deaf" has led to a concern to demarcate and differentiate between the many ways in which it is possible to *be* d/Deaf. It would seem, therefore, at first glance to make sense for research studies to be clear about whom they are referring to when designing a study which involves d/Deaf people. This issue is often framed as distinguishing between culturally Deaf people and those who are not. However, as the preceding chapters illustrate, identity is something that is fluid, situated, and contextual. Therefore, boundaries between different populations need to be treated with more caution than first might be apparent. For example, culturally Deaf people and older deafened people who have lost their hearing as a result of the ageing process might seem to be two clearly different populations, but it depends on perspective. If the study concerns an aspect of audiological measurement, the differentiation is less clear cut. Establishing hearing thresholds is not dependent on cultural identity.

However, heterogeneity is not just a fundamental condition in research among d/Deaf people because there are many different individuals, groups, communities, or populations who might be termed "deaf." It is a fundamental consideration because there is vast heterogeneity *within* populations. As Hoiting and Loncke (1990) famously remark, deaf children acquire language in "typically atypical" circumstances. They are surrounded by conversational partners with vastly differing abilities to use spoken and/or signed languages in ways best suited to deaf children's language acquisition needs. Deaf children have differing levels of access to knowledge and social resources in the wider environment. Consequently, how, when, from whom, and to what extent a deaf child might acquire one or several languages is hugely variable. It is not necessarily predictable by such characteristics as level of deafness or hearing status of parents. Their observation that the diversity *within* a population (deaf children) might be of greater consequence than *between* populations (deaf and hearing children) has been borne out by many subsequent studies in a variety of disciplinary areas (Atkinson, Gleeson, Cromwell, & O'Rourke, 2007; Cawthon, 2011; Marschark & Hauser, 2008; Miller & Vernon, 2002; Moeller et al., 2007; Thoutenhoofd, 2010).

Psychologists, for example, have become interested in the ways in which significant variations in deaf children's earliest linguistic, familial, and social experiences have consequences for how individual deaf children learn (Marschark, 1993, 2003). The variability in deaf children's cognitive strengths and differences *from each other* as well as in comparison with hearing children thus becomes a focus of research in its own right. As Marschark, Rhoten, and Fabich (2007) conclude:

> In essence, we now realize that deaf children can be different from hearing children without being deficient...deaf and hearing individuals can vary in their cognitive functioning and have different knowledge organized in different ways without assuming that such differences are either good or bad. This perspective has led us to examine variability among deaf individuals and between deaf and hearing populations as a means of better understanding the intellectual development of deaf children and ways to optimize their early experiences. (p. 53)

Variability within any population of developing children is, of course, only to be expected. However, an increasing number of studies are beginning to demonstrate that the extent of within population variability among deaf children is significantly greater than one would usually expect among hearing children in some domains, such as language acquisition and development. For example, a study comparing the spoken language development of early identified deaf infants with age-matched hearing infants at 10–16 months revealed larger *individual differences* in the deaf group than in the hearing group (Moeller et al., 2007).

From a medical perspective, the variable etiologies of deafness also create a wide spectrum of potential differences between deaf children. Fifty percent of congenital deafness is known to have a genetic cause and of those 30% are syndromic (Hereditary Hearing Loss, 2012; Morton & Nance, 2006). That is to say deafness is one component of a condition that might create a wide variety of cognitive, linguistic, and developmental challenges. Around 10% of infants identified as deaf through universal newborn hearing screening programs have audiological characteristics consistent with a diagnosis of Auditory Neuropathy Spectrum Disorder (ANSD) (Northern, 2008; Uus, Young, & Day, 2012). However, ANSD as a fundamentally neurological developmental condition has several manifestations, including one in which the condition partially or fully "resolves" (the child becomes hearing) (Uus et al., 2012). Speech perception is highly variable and typically poorer than would be predicted from the behavioral audiogram (Rance & Barker, 2009; Rance, Cone-Wesson, & Dowell, 2002).

From a different perspective, acknowledging and understanding heterogeneity among d/Deaf people is important because there is a long history of stereotypes associated with d/Deaf people which rely, in part, on the denial or minimization of heterogeneity. Stereotypes both emphasize the "sameness" of a group based on a shared characteristic and then imbue that sameness with explanatory power. For example, it used to be quite common in the psychiatric literature to refer to a "deaf personality" (Myklebust, 1960). Clinicians had identified a cluster of behavioral traits seen among the d/Deaf patients they encountered such as impulsivity, rigidity, egocentricity, and aggressiveness (Levine, 1956). However, what might have begun as an identified correlation transmuted into a causal inference. It was not just that among d/Deaf patients one might frequently observe the cluster of traits, but that to be d/Deaf implied that an individual would have these "typical" personality characteristics. It became labeled "surdophrenia" (Basilier, 1964). The minimization of intragroup difference and the interpretation of an individual's actions in terms of a group's apparent "same" characteristic enabled the maintenance of the stereotype.

By examining whether intragroup differences are influential within any given population, it is possible to refute or confirm conclusions which might appear stereotypical. For example, in the 1950s/1960s it was quite common to equate deafness with "mental retardation." However, Vernon (1968/2005), by focusing on a different kind of heterogeneity—the etiology of deafness—was able to disprove the link. He demonstrated, through a series of landmark studies and what we would now term an evidence review, that etiology had important consequences for understanding some of the variability in intelligence within deaf child populations. He showed that some etiologies of deafness were also responsible for some neurological impairments and in so doing fundamentally challenged a common assumption of the time—that deafness and mental retardation were *causally* related:

> it is apparent that many of the etiologies of profound hearing loss are also responsible for other neurological impairment which frequently results in lower intelligence. The point to be made is that the relationship, if any, between mental retardation and deafness is not causal. (2005, p. 229)

Thus far, we have discussed the fundamental condition of heterogeneity in research with d/Deaf people in terms of:

- a broad appreciation that the term "deaf" refers to distinctly different groups of people, some of whom would seek to distinguish themselves from others;
- that variation within populations is important and arguably of greater significance than between d/Deaf and hearing populations;
- and that attention to heterogeneity is important in avoiding explanatory errors associated with the creation and maintenance of stereotypes.

However, there is a difficult paradox at the heart of all discussion which highlights the heterogeneity of d/Deaf populations. Deaf people, as groups or individuals, are people(s) who are routinely "othered" and the processes of distinguishing within, between, and about populations we might term "deaf" can reinforce that othered state.

Othering refers to practices, including the use of language, which whether deliberately or not mark out someone as different from the mainstream or oneself (Johnson et al., 2004). As we discuss in Chapter 2, d/Deaf people, whether from a biological or cultural perspective, are usually defined as *not being something else* (i.e., hearing). Even when distinctions are made that begin to acknowledge diversity, they are commonly made in terms of variations in the characteristic which is at the heart of the othering, for example, "deaf with speech," "deaf without speech," "deafened," "partially hearing," "CI user," "Deafblind," "culturally Deaf," and so forth. The acknowledgment of within-group differences becomes of itself a means of reinforcing the othered status and the imbalance of power it implies:

> By talking about individuals or groups as *other*, one magnifies and enforces projections of apparent difference from oneself. Othering practices can, albeit sometimes unintentionally, serve to reinforce and reproduce positions of domination and subordination (Fine, 1994). Consequently, persons who are treated as other often experience

marginalization, decreased opportunities, and exclusion. (Johnson et al., 2004)

For Ladd (2003) a clear example of this dynamic process is the ways in which deaf children for educational purposes are routinely divided into categories such as "profound," "severe," or "partial." In his terms, the categorization atomizes the population of deaf children and creates imposed divisions of identity which are internalized by the children themselves. He argues that this process serves to reinforce the dominance of an approach to deaf children based on how far or near they are to being "hearing normals" rather than an approach that might be based on Deaf values, in which the amount someone hears is not of primary relevance—identity, language, and culture are.

Heterogeneity among d/Deaf populations, however, is not just about issues of identity and representation that cluster around what we might mean by deaf and/or Deaf. Like all people, d/Deaf people are diverse for multiple reasons, including sexuality, gender, ethnicity, and disability. A range of studies have sought to describe and expose this diversity with a focus, for example, on studies of cultural diversity in deaf education (Parasnis, 1996), hidden narratives and histories within Deaf communities such as those of Deaf and gay or lesbian people (Luczak, 1993), and social conditions and divisions such as those concerned with class (Ladd, 2003). Others have sought to challenge the normative assumptions that lie behind dominant representations of Deaf identity and which, whether intentionally or not, suppress its inherent diversity. Myers and Fernandes (2010) argue that "Deaf" is de facto a proxy for being a White, male American Sign Language user; Bienvenu (2008) argues that it implies a baseline of heterosexuality; and Krentz (2009) argues that it circumscribes the experiences of Deaf people from Deaf families to the exclusion of others (see Chapters 2 and 3 for a more detailed discussion of issues of identity and representation).

While this exposure of hidden or marginalized diversities is important in its own right, what does it actually mean for the everyday lives of d/Deaf people and how multiple identity claims might intersect in d/Deaf people's life experience? A few empirical studies have explored this question. For example, Ahmad, Atkin, and Jones (2002) involved 70 young people in an exploration of "being deaf and being other things" that uncovered how they negotiated in everyday life the various identities associated with being Asian, Muslim, Deaf, and a young person in the United Kingdom. Its results queried the privileging of one identity over another and provided concrete examples of the *socially constructed nature of Deaf identity in specific contexts.* For example, for some participants' parents in this study, Deaf culture was perceived as a White, Christian identity and therefore not one to be actively encouraged.

From a culturally "insider" perspective, Deaf anthropologists are beginning to document the tension between claims for a transnational Deaf community, founded on a shared Deaf cultural-linguistic identity, and the local and contextualized Deaf identity that emerges in specific national and cultural contexts (De Clerck, 2011; Kusters, 2009). Their work asserts Deaf culture and Deaf identity while simultaneously exposing its diversity and questioning its universalism. The dominant narrative of being Deaf can serve to exclude and marginalize if the relationship between that which can be claimed as common and that which should be explored as contextual is not examined. This tension is one recognizable in the natural development of other minoritized groups and movements. Early feminists, for example, privileged gender above all else in the analysis of power and marginalization until the initial conceptual ground had been won and it became possible to explore diversity in being women while still being feminist (Collins, 1999). As this extended discussion has demonstrated, appreciating the fundamental heterogeneity of d/Deaf populations requires consideration from several perspectives:

1. Heterogeneity as recognition that being "deaf" implies several distinctly different populations
2. d/Deaf populations exhibit large degrees of within-population heterogeneity.
3. d/Deaf populations exhibit heterogeneity for reasons other than being d/Deaf.
4. Normative assumptions about what it is to be d/Deaf exist which deny heterogeneity and serve to privilege one kind of Deaf identity over another's d/Deaf experience
5. Heterogeneity can be expressed not as distinctions but as tensions, such as that between claims to Deaf universalism and contextualized Deaf localism.
6. A focus on heterogeneity may inadvertently contribute to the othering of d/Deaf people and reinforce power imbalances between those who are othered and those who do the othering.

In the rest of this chapter, we explore the implications of heterogeneity for population definition and sampling by addressing the typical and the atypical; representative samples; partially described samples; cohort effects; and context-specific influences. While we address each topic in turn, illustrative examples used for one issue have salience for another.

THE TYPICAL AND THE ATYPICAL

The significant heterogeneity of d/Deaf populations, and its varied origins, creates an interesting problem in seeking to establish what might be typical or atypical. Some of the difficulty is a question of perspective. For example, for the vast majority of research which concerns deaf people, there is no conundrum. It is perfectly obvious that to be hearing is to be typical and to be deaf is to be atypical. Phrases such as "normally hearing children" are perfectly acceptable descriptions in numerous research texts. Hearing loss is an apt description for those for whom to be fully hearing is a usual expectation of a human being. It matters little whether we regard norm as the median (the most frequently occurring state) or norm as the prevailing hegemony (to hear is the normative expectation), being deaf sets one apart from the majority and renders one atypical.

But what if researchers were to begin from a diversity-derived perspective, as is the case in much of the Deaf cultural discourse? To be Deaf is to be normal, that is, like others who are of the same culture and share a language. Beginning from this starting point, establishing atypical variations requires the identification of what might be usual variability *within* a signing Deaf population and not in comparison to others (hearing people). For example, in order to develop a screen for early signs of dementia among signing Deaf people, the parameters of healthy ageing from a cognitive and linguistic perspective in this group have first to be established (Denmark et al., 2012). Only then might it be possible to identify that which is atypical for that population.

However, even if a study begins from a position of rejecting the absolute distinction of d/Deaf as atypical and embraces the necessity of charting variation within a population in order to establish typical/atypical parameters, there are many complexities. For example, a common distinction made in many research studies is between "native signers" and "nonnative signers." But who is a native signer? Is it someone who grew up with sign language used in his family regardless of whether he is Deaf or hearing? Does it encompass a Deaf person who acquired a signed language early on in her life but who grew up in a home where only spoken language was used?

The ambiguity surrounding the definition of "native" is seen in the increasingly common use in British Sign Language (BSL) of a sign for native in this context that is more akin to "from the gut" rather than a sign for native which indicates "origin" or "first." In other words, a socially constructed, interpretative definition of native which indicates personal, cultural, and political affiliation to a signed language as preferred (if not first) language. Such a definition makes sense in a context where very few Deaf people will grow up with Deaf parents (Mitchell & Karchmer, 2004) and Deaf identity is often something acquired later and in parallel with sign language use (Leigh, 2009; Valentine & Skelton, 2007).

However, from a more pragmatic perspective, does the decoupling of the description "native sign language user" from age of acquisition or language of family of origin actually matter? The population of fluent sign language users in any given country will inevitably consist of the minority who acquired their first (sign) language from their family of origin and the majority who did not. This reality creates an interesting paradox for any study which might be interested in describing normative features of a sign language–using population or in establishing baselines from which variations from the typical might be identified.

For example, Herman, Holmes, and Woll (1999), in developing the BSL receptive language test for children aged 3 to 11 years old, derived the developmental norms from a mixed sample of children acquiring BSL as their first and native language within Deaf families ($n = 78$) and nonnative signers from hearing families ($n = 57$). This choice reflects the population and normative variation within it. It avoids "native sign language acquisition" being used as a simple proxy for typical developmental norms while being able to reflect the extent and variation in how deaf children develop sign language. Consequently, it is possible to plot where any specific child's sign language development might be within or outside the normative range.

A subsequent study of specific language impairment among deaf children in an elementary school also took a relative definition of typical development. It did not use native sign language acquisition as exemplified by Deaf children from Deaf families as its baseline against which atypical developmental trajectories could be identified. Instead, it looked at individual children's sign language development in comparison with those with similar exposure to sign language within the school environment over a similar period of time. As the authors (Mason et al., 2010) explain:

> investigating the causes of language impairment in signing deaf children [are] more complex...due to the fact that poor language skills may be explained by sign language being offered late...and exposure to poor models of sign language, as most parents and teachers are non-native signers. (p. 35)

Investigating and understanding the atypical in d/Deaf populations is also a matter of concern for interpretative and constructivist epistemologies (see Chapter 3). Diverse individuals will vary in what they experience of the world. The meaning of that experience to the individual and how its meaning is conveyed and understood to others is a matter of interpretation. Reality is contingent, not fixed. For example, Atkinson et al. (2007) investigated the seemingly counterintuitive phenomenon of d/Deaf people with schizophrenia "hearing voices." They began by a consideration of the inherent diversity within d/Deaf populations but not in terms of the extent to which an individual had access to sound and therefore might reasonably be "hearing voices." Rather they defined diversity in terms of perceptual experience and how that was interpreted by the individual and conveyed to others. Perceptual experience was inherently diverse in this population and might incorporate sound, vision, movement, as well as different kinds of access to language, including hearing, lipreading, and signing. Consequently, how an individual might construe what it is to "hear voices" is likely to be related to the diversity of those perceptual experiences. They state:

> Deaf people are a highly heterogeneous group and this study demonstrates that by using a methodology that exploits variability, the perceptual characteristics of their voice hallucinations are shown to reflect this diversity...When deaf individuals respond "yes" to the question, "Do you hear voices?" the exact nature of their experiences cannot be assumed. Some may literally mean that they have auditory experiences and these should not be dismissed, nor considered surprising since few deaf people have no conception of sound at all. Others will perceive the communicative intent of the voices via a sense of being signed or fingerspelt to, of lipreading speech that they cannot hear, or a sense of knowing what is said without a clear perceptual agent. (pp. 355–356)

They conclude, with regard to diversity within the d/Deaf population studied, that etiological and organic variables were significant not of and for themselves but for how they influence phenomenological heterogeneity.

Thus far we have considered how approaches to whom or what might be typical or atypical intersect with the inherent diversity of d/Deaf populations. We have considered how the typical and the atypical are largely relative and argued for close attention to be paid to that intersection. Nonetheless, it can be very important to establish the extent to which a minority group with a particular characteristic (being deaf) is similar or different from a majority group with a particular characteristic (being able to hear). This is especially the case if one is seeking to compare against an absolute standard to which a society aspires, such as good population health, antipoverty, or social mobility.

In this respect there have been many important studies which have compared the status, outcomes, or achievements of d/Deaf people in comparison with the general population, with little attention to any issues of differentiation of what might be meant by "deaf" or for that matter "general population." For example, the World Health Organization states that in 2004 there were 275 million people globally with "moderate to severe hearing impairment," 80% of whom live in low- to middle-income countries (WHO, 2012). The Centers for Disease Control and Prevention in the United States report that based on data gathered between 2000 and 2006: "Prevalence of fair or poor health status, difficulties with physical functioning, and serious psychological distress increased with degree of hearing loss" (CDC, 2008).

Such large-scale population studies have been influential throughout the world in evidencing health and social inequalities typically experienced by d/Deaf people.

REPRESENTATIVE SAMPLES

The marked heterogeneity within different populations of deaf children and d/Deaf adults raises important questions for researchers about how to define or construct what might be a representative sample. However, what might be meant by a representative sample is itself differently defined depending on the epistemological and methodological basis of study designs.

In broad terms, for studies beginning from positivist epistemologies and using quantitative data collection methods, representativeness is a judgment of the extent to which a sample reflects the wider population to which it relates within its parameters of interest. For example, a sample of people would need to incorporate both men and women but not those living in France if the study was about those living in Scotland. For studies beginning from an interpretative/constructionist epistemology and using qualitative data collection methods, representativeness is concerned much more with judgments made about who is likely to have the most relevant experience and knowledge on which to draw. A study about those living in Scotland might regard someone born and bred there as far more representative than someone who has only recently moved there, or not. It depends on what kind of experience of living in Scotland researchers are seeking to represent.

Representativeness in samples which in different ways will include d/Deaf people is further complicated because of the issues of heterogeneity and variation we have previously highlighted. For example, what are the implications for knowledge construction about deaf children or adults, of the routine sampling out of some kinds of heterogeneity?

Much of the evidence that we readily utilize about "deaf children" is actually evidence derived exclusively from deaf children who do not have cognitive or physical disabilities. Medically related factors affect between 30% and 40% of deaf children (Hauser & Marschark, 2008) with the prevalence of severe multiple disabilities being at least 20% (van Dijk, Nelson, Postma, & van Dijk, 2010). Similarly, evidence about "parents of deaf children" usually means hearing parents of deaf children, who are the vast majority (Mitchell & Karchmer, 2004). However, researchers rarely specify "hearing" when referring to "parents" or "family" in how the evidence is discussed because the norm is assumed. Sometimes even within the sample description the hearing status of the parents is not explicitly mentioned (Hogan, Stokes, & Weller, 2010).

Vernon (1968) refers to the routine sampling-out of particular groups with specific characteristics as basing research on "incomplete" samples. Routine sampling-out of groups with particular characteristics is problematic because of the *cumulative* effect of many studies which make similar exclusions. Their results come to stand for the extent of knowledge about particular groups/ populations such as deaf children or parents of deaf children, when in fact that knowledge and its utility are partial. As Hauser and Marschark (2008) remark with respect to deaf children with learning disabilities and other medically related factors affecting deaf children:

> ...excluding such individuals from research studies and increasing the study's internal validity might reduce variability in data sets and offer clearer theoretical insights, but it also detracts from external validity and the practice utility of the research. (p. 451)

From a qualitative perspective, the heterogeneity of d/Deaf populations should cause us to think very carefully about who and on what basis a research participant might be regarded as representative of an experience of interest. As we remark throughout this book, from an interpretative and constructionist epistemological standpoint there is no singular deaf or Deaf ontology nor epistemology (see Chapters 2 and 3) and no single way, therefore, for an individual to be representative of the many or to take part on behalf of others. But it is entirely possible to seek to understand an experience, to evaluate an intervention, or to explore an event through the eyes of individuals who in their similarities and differences will construct how something is known and what is known. See, for example, Young and Tattersall's (2005) study of hearing parents' experiences of the introduction of newborn hearing screening in England, which was deliberately designed to examine parents' criteria against which they evaluated the new intervention (Young, Tattersall, Uus, Bamford, & McCracken, 2004). Standards, by which researchers might regard those who are sampled and the knowledge generated as "representative," revolve around such issues as the relevance of the participants' characteristics, the authenticity of their experience, the credibility of their perspective, and the contextualization of their narratives (Hammersley, 1990; Murphy, Dingwall, Greatbatch, Parker, & Watson, 1998).

This approach to representativeness and sampling within qualitative work is *not* fundamentally about selecting individuals or groups to "speak" on behalf of a wider group, community, or population of which they might be a member. They are not representative like a politician might be in respect of her constituency. Nonetheless, in the reading/ watching and interpretation of qualitative research findings, questions inevitably arise about the extent to which those findings are applicable or of relevance to other individuals and contexts. For example, if we explore through qualitative approaches hearing parents' experiences of universal newborn hearing screening in England, is that helpful in understanding the implementation of best practice in newborn hearing screening in South Africa? Within qualitative methodologies, such a question is not a particular problem because generalizabiltiy is usually founded on standards such as theoretical relevance (Murphy et al., 1998); that is, the key issues have been identified but their relevance to particular contexts is of itself a matter of further investigation.

However, it still is vital to ask critical questions about *whose* experiences and perspectives become represented within qualitative studies. Even if the researcher is not seeking to assume an individual's experience is representative of a wider constituency of interest, by the choice of who to include the researcher draws boundaries around who and what comes to be seen. As Svalastog and Eriksson (2010) point out: When a relationship between an individual and a group is established by a researcher, it can be used to define or exclude those who are to be understood as members of this group (p. 108).

As we argue throughout this book, what it means to be d/Deaf is highly contested and therefore decisions about who becomes represented within the research literature and how this takes place are not merely methodological decisions but political ones (see Chapter 3).

PARTIALLY AND INACCURATELY DESCRIBED SAMPLES

There are many examples of well-designed studies which are founded on careful definitions of variables and clear inclusion and exclusion criteria. However, as we demonstrate earlier, a key condition associated with populations of deaf children and d/Deaf adults is variability within populations. When a study design fails to recognize this feature, or samples in such a way as to be unable to recognize its influence, then the validity of its results can be contested.

For example, Kennedy et al. (2006) published a highly respected cohort study comparing 57 children whose deafness was confirmed before 9 months of age in districts in England with newborn hearing screening and 63 whose deafness was confirmed after 9 months of age in neighboring districts without newborn hearing screening. They were then matched with 63 controls with "normal hearing." The children were assessed at a mean age of 7.9 years and the primary outcomes were defined as "language compared with non-verbal ability" and speech expressed as z scores ("the number of standard deviations by which the score differed from the mean score among 63 age-matched children with normal hearing" p. 2131). Although 16 of the 120 deaf children were described as "used only sign language," none of the test material is described as being available in sign language versions nor normed on deaf children who were sign language users. In the case of *none* of these children was an expressive language score recorded. In fact, in 9 out of the 16 no assessments took place at all. They were in effect present in the sample but excluded from its calculations. Nonetheless, the conclusions appear to relate to all deaf children in the sample, yet the potential abilities of these children, be it in a different language, are not considered.

A further 97 children were described as "used oral +/- sign language" with some variability between expressive and receptive preferred use. No information is given about the children's abilities in sign language, whether they come from signing homes, whether they are growing up bilingually with both signed and spoken language, or whether "sign language" actually refers to modality (some signing to support speech) rather than language (a sign language). While measuring "language," the assessments were in reality assessing oral language abilities but allowed for the use of "gesture" and other nonverbal supports.

The paper refers throughout to its conclusions about language and speech, but it does not acknowledge that its definition of "language" is singular (oral language). Potentially its conclusions are confounded by mixing up deaf children developing monolingually with those developing bilingually. Bilingual deaf children typically experience a range of linguistic advantages/disadvantages and characteristically different language acquisition trajectories in their languages in comparison with monolingual children (Knoors & Marschark, 2012). These will affect their developmental scores on whichever language is measured. In interpreting the results of measurements on one language, one is not comparing like with like in comparing the results of monolingual and bilingual children at key points in the early language acquisition process. In this case, it is not simply that a factor had not been fully taken into account (the children's sign language ability had not been measured) but that the description of the sample is incorrect in the first place. It fails to address key within-group differences among deaf children's language development and presents the findings as uniform; that is, referring to language and speech.

On a more basic level, even seemingly simple descriptive questions that might be used to characterize a sample can be fraught with difficulty. Consider the question: "What is your preferred means of communication?" followed by a series of alternatives from which one is instructed to "tick one." The alternatives given are as follows: "speech; speech with sign; British Sign Language; other, please specify." The first problem is the confusion between "means of communication" and language. BSL is a language; speech is a means of communication but could relate to any spoken language (e.g., speech Spanish, speech Hindi, speech Polish, etc.). The second problem is the universal nature of preferred communication implied by the question; namely, that the same means are used in all situations with all people. In fact, the opposite is more commonly the case. Deaf children are particularly adroit at matching their chosen communication method and complexity of communication to their interlocutor, for example, signing with other Deaf friends, speaking and signing at home, and speaking only in the classroom (Sutherland & Young, 2007). Deaf professionals regularly report the accommodations they have to make for the communication limitations of those around them (Young, Ackerman, & Kyle, 1998).

Thirdly, such a question fails to distinguish between expressive language and receptive language. A deaf person may speak well but be a poor lip-reader, for example. An older deaf person may indeed prefer speech but to tick that box says little about how her preference poorly reflects how much she actually understands of what is spoken to her.

Large population-level data sets are also notoriously problematic for any studies which seek to extract d/Deaf-related population data, because of problems with the description of populations in the first place. In the United Kingdom, for example, some official statistics still use the distinction "deaf with speech" or, "deaf without speech" as a means of classification. It is a distinction that originates in the National Assistance Act (1948). Not only does it presume a mutually exclusive binary distinction, in its construction it reinforces speech as the normative standard. Would researchers feel comfortable using the distinction "hearing with English" and "hearing without English" to describe the difference between English people and French people?

In some instances, definitions used to characterize a population are created for a particular purpose but prove unhelpful if data are reused or needed for a different purpose. Schroedel (1984), writing specifically about survey data collection methods, contrasts how the apparent simplicity in categorizing respondents by an audiological metric is of little use to a social scientist seeking an adequate description of the full range of d/Deaf people for purposes of social policy or service planning. Whether someone is, for example, a member of a Deaf community, or whether she or he is pre- or post-vocationally deaf, cannot be discerned.

Even when such problems are recognized, attempts at a solution can result in greater confusion. In the United Kingdom, the Office of National Statistics Harmonisation Group has recently carried out a piece of work specifically associated with disability data collection within UK surveys (White, 2011). One of their concluding recommendations is as follows:

> revise the response categories to better represent service needs and policy requirements; that is, split blindness, deafness and communication into separate categories, using the terms vision, speech and communication impairment, with illustrative categories such as blind or partial sight, deaf or partial hearing. (p. 16)

Where would that leave, for example, a BSL user with good spoken English? Or a deafened adult who is a good cochlear implant user and experiences few problems in everyday conversations?

Commonly, official data sets often collect information based on disability and ethnicity, usually by self-report. From a culturally Deaf perspective, a research participant is unlikely to tick a category marked "disabled" but might tick an ethnicity category labeled "other" (that is, Deaf). Indeed, it could be argued that good practice would dictate that Deaf as an ethnic descriptor (see Chapter 2) should be offered when engaging in research that might include Deaf people. However, doing so would not enable any easy comparisons to be made with larger national data sets where such a category would be unrecognized. A metareview of all major UK surveys/data sets concerning disabled people with respect to equality does not record or acknowledge any distinction between Deaf people who may be sign language users from all those with "hearing impairments" (Purdam, Afkhami, Olson, & Thornton, 2008). At the same time, this review draws attention to differences found with respect to disabled people from minority ethnic groups, but it saw no contradiction.

In some instances, population descriptions are partial or inaccurate for far more straightforward reasons, simply that nobody knows because the population cannot be or is yet to be accurately defined or counted. In many developing world contexts, the numbers of d/Deaf people are unknown. For example, best estimates of congenital and early-onset permanent childhood deafness in countries of the developing world suggest no fewer than 6 per 1,000 live births (Olusanya & Newton, 2007), but individual country estimates vary (Leigh, Newall, & Newall, 2010). In other instances, the languages used by Deaf people are simply unrecorded or are yet to be adequately described (Zeshan & Dikyuva, in press).

COHORT EFFECTS

Being d/Deaf in the early 21st century and being d/Deaf in the mid 20th century are barely comparable experiences in developed world contexts. The pace of change has been rapid from many perspectives. Technological advances in hearing aids and cochlear implants have transformed access to sound and speech. Signed languages have become formally identified as full, grammatically complex languages in their own right. Legislation in some countries has conferred new citizenship rights of access, anti-discrimination, and cultural identity for Deaf people(s). Inward investment in health, education, and social care has increased opportunity and raised expectations for d/Deaf people. Fashions have come and gone in deaf education, founded on differing ideological standpoints, research evidence, and policy imperatives.

All of these changes have transformed in a myriad of different ways the socioeconomic position of d/Deaf people while simultaneously serving to identify what has altered little despite significant technological and social revolutions; literacy in the written word for example (Mayer, 2007).

The scale and pace of change in such a relatively short period of time is an important consideration in sampling in studies involving d/Deaf people. Cohorts of d/Deaf research participants, even separated by as little as 10 years, will have been subject to significantly different social, educational, and technological influences. While "generation effects" are hardly a consideration unique to studies involving d/Deaf people, it is the intensity and scope of change that presents significant challenges. For example, when comparing the educational outcomes of deaf young people in the 1990s with those of today, how would a research design account for not only changes in the educational environment but social changes such as greater public acceptance of sign language on television and medical changes such as easier access to cochlear implantation at a young age? As Thoutenhoofd (2010) writing about attainment research with respect to deaf education remarked, "Deaf learners do not form a homogeneous or stable research population" (p. 216).

Cohort effects should also give us pause for thought about whether the research evidence derived from one generation or at one point in history concerning deaf children and adults remains valid. For example, from the 1950s onward the average age of confirmation of deafness in children in the developed world remained relatively stable at an average of 26 months old (Davis et al., 1997). The range, however, was vast with many instances of children not being identified until well into their third or fourth year. Family intervention services, audiological management, and language acquisition support were well developed in many countries around the world. Consequently, a large number of research studies had been carried out comparing support strategies, outcomes, and maternal or family effects on deaf children's later development.

However, the validity of this body of evidence became questionable with the introduction of universal newborn hearing screening (UNHS). UNHS delivers early identification of deaf children before 3 months of age and supports a process of rapid language development and early intervention (Jont Commission on Infant Hearing, 2007; Yoshinaga-Itano, 2003). Consequently, practitioners had to rethink their skills and approaches, because they were now working with babies in the first few months of life. The evidence base of that practice was also to a large extent redundant. Studies which had identified variables most effecting optimal outcomes for deaf children and their families were based on what we now term "late" intervention. The extent to which their findings still held true or require revision has itself become a focus of research (see for example, Hintermair, 2006, with regard to family stress).

Cohort effects also excerpt influence in terms of cultural histories. Many studies from within a range of populations have demonstrated how the historical landscape from within a minority or minoritized culture often bears little resemblance to that of the dominant or majority culture. These alternative histories are often obscured or written out by the majority world historical narrative. For example, Virago Press from the 1970s onward has done much to publish and publicize not just women's histories, which have been unseen, but history through women's eyes, expressed in literature. Through women's narratives the same events might be differently experienced and signified than through dominant narratives which implicitly have been male. The works of Maya Angelou are well-known examples of this effect, documenting for instance women within, and perspectives on, the Black civil rights movement in the United States (Angelou, 1986). Deaf histories, not only in terms of events but in terms of perspective and significance, are being similarly recognized. For example, consider Bragg's (2001) historical reader from Deaf perspectives, the documentation of Deaf-specific histories (Atherton, Russell, & Turner, 2001; Lang, 2000; Van Cleve, 1999; van Cleve & Crouch, 1989), and Deaf folklore and narrative cultural history (Rutherford, 1993; Sutton-Spence, 2011). The documentation of history, historical narratives, and previously hidden perspectives are important in their own right (see Chapter 6). But more generally, they raise the question of the extent to which *any* study is sensitive to the historical location and context of those it might engage within research.

Studies of older Deaf people, for example, might need to be sensitive to older styles of sign languages when carrying out interviews. In BSL the sign for television, for instance, used to be the turning of knobs on a screen in front using both hands because that is the action needed to tune a television. Many older Deaf people still use that sign. Therefore, ensuring an interview question or prompt tunes into the historical allusion and/or the contemporary usage within data collection and analysis would be important. The Deaf community's time lines of significant historical events might not follow those of the hearing world, or they might only intersect at certain points but not others. For example, while World War II might be a shared historical touchstone for older Deaf and hearing people in Europe, would the day a particular Deaf school was destroyed by a bomb evoke the same degree of significance?

Cohort effects can make many approaches to research design and data collection challenging, including population definition and sampling. Building in some means of controlling for, taking account of, or simply documenting the temporal- and situation- specific influences on participants is vital. The intense technological, social, and cultural changes in d/Deaf people's lives, particularly in the latter part of the 20th century/early part of the 21st century, should cause us to consider:

- the extent to which previous research evidence remains valid;
- when comparing cohorts of d/Deaf people, the basis on which it could be claimed that one is comparing like with like; and
- the influence that the situated histories of d/Deaf participants exerts on how we carry out research practice.

CONTEXT

Qualitative research, in particular, pays attention to the influence of context in making sampling decisions. Whether from interpretative or constructionist traditions, qualitative studies are concerned with the generation of data that acknowledge the contextualized nature of experience, expression, and understanding. Findings are contingent on the context(s) in which they are generated. The context both defines *who* is likely to know and *how* they are likely to know (and be known). Whether sampling uses a purposive, theoretical, or convenience approach, those sampled are to a large extent contextually identified. For example, consider those mothers whose children have undergone universal newborn hearing screening (Young & Tattersall, 2005); members of the Cameroonian Deaf community (De Clerck, 2011); or family members living with "hearing impairment" (Morgan-Jones, 2001). The point is that the sample definition is usually dependent on experience-in-context, in comparison with sample definitions which are dependent on characteristics which may be acontextual for purposes of sample definition, for example, deaf adults with a hearing loss equal or greater than 65 dB nHL.

However, context in combination with the inherent heterogeneity of d/Deaf populations can have powerful effects on sampling even in studies unconcerned with situated epistemologies and contextual inferences normally associated with qualitative designs. A recent study of the contribution of the GJB2 mutation to childhood deafness in Northern Cameroon (Trotta et al., 2011) is a good example of a study whose results were unexpectedly influenced by a socially constructed sampling effect which was not part of the sampling decisions that had been made in the design of the study. It was an artifact of the context in which the study took place.

This research was concerned with testing out the relative contributions of genetic and environmental influences on the prevalence of early childhood deafness. It set out to discover whether GJB2 mutations which account for more than half of all cases of "prelingual non-syndromic recessive deafness" in Caucasians in the industrialized world were as influential in accounting for the incidence of deafness in

Northern Cameroon; a sub-Saharan African context where one might expect environmental rather than genetic factors to be more influential in the etiology of deafness. Using a genetic screening approach on a comparative population of 70 "deaf children" and 67 "unaffected controls" (p. 133), the study concluded that environmental factors were more relevant than genetic factors.

However, the strength of this conclusion was challenged by the study's realization that the definition of deaf children was, in the Northern Cameroon context, a socially constructed one, which in effect excluded deaf children with mild or moderate hearing loss which might have a genetic origin. This had not been apparent when the study was designed. The authors comment that the sample they analyzed might not have been representative of Cameroon's deaf population because of:

> the selection criteria of patients, *which were based on a different social perception of deafness*; the high percentage of severely deaf subjects seen in the Maroua deafness care centre suggests that only deaf children not able to develop spontaneous verbal language are recognized as patients having hearing impairment. (p. 137, emphasis ours)

Our point is that even if context is not an explicit influence on sampling choices or population definition in research studies, it is nonetheless influential. The extent to which it is recognized and accounted for is important in any study, not just those of a qualitative design.

CONCLUDING THOUGHTS

In Chapter 2 we stress the significance of the definitions used in research for what is produced, that is, for findings. We suggest that what is produced during research is affected by our starting point. We would also like to point the reader to Chapter 3, where we argue that there are other goods than "the truth" from which to evaluate research, for example, ethics and politics. In particular, we refer to the importance of evaluating the whole methodological and epistemological edifice upon which research is built, that is, being reflexive. This present chapter is concerned with the importance of such reflexivity about how being d/Deaf is defined and the multiple ways in which the heterogeneity that characterizes d/Deaf populations intersects with key issues in population definition and sampling. We do not set out to cover all approaches to sampling within research designs whether from qualitative or quantitative perspectives. We identify additional considerations that might underpin sampling practice when studies involve d/Deaf people and their influence on research design and ultimately the validity of the inferences that might be drawn from the results of research. We suggest that neglecting to pay attention to the diversity of d/Deaf experiences may make for questionable research. However, we also note the significance of sometimes using categories such as d/Deaf. Where researchers start from (sampling) affects what they are able to say from their research (generalization). Moreover, there are consequences in defining someone as "other" or as "us." We spell out some of these in Chapter 4.

REFERENCES

Ahmad, W. I., Atkin, K., & Jones, L. (2002). Being deaf and being other things: Young Asian people negotiating identities. *Social Science & Medicine*, 55(10), 1757–1769. doi: 10.1016/S0277-9536(01)00308-2

Angelou, M. (1986). *All God's children need travelling shoes.* New York, NY: Random House.

Atherton, M., Russell, D., & Turner, G. H. (2001). *Deaf united: A history of football in the British Deaf community.* Coleford, UK: Douglas McLean.

Atkinson, J. R., Gleeson, K., Cromwell, J., & O'Rourke, S. (2007). Exploring the perceptual characteristics of voice hallucinations in deaf people. *Cognitive Neuorpsychiatry*, 12(4), 339–361. doi: 10.1080/13546800701238229

Basilier, T. (1964). SURDOPHRENIA. The psychic consequences of congenital or early acquired deafness: Some theoretical and clinical considerations. *Acta Psychiatrica Scandinavica*, 39, 363–372. doi: 10.1111/j.1600-0447.1964.tb04948.x

Bienvenu, M. (2008). Queer as Deaf: Intersections. In H. D. L. Bauman (Ed.), *Open your eyes: Deaf studies talking* (pp. 264–276). Minneapolis: University of Minnesota Press.

Bragg, L. (Ed.). (2001). *Deaf World—a historical reader.* New York, NY: New York University Press.

Bryman, A. (2012). *Social reseach methods* (4th ed.). Oxford, UK: Oxford University Press.

Cawthon, S. W. (2011). Making decisions about assessment practices for students who are deaf or hard of hearing. *Remedial and Special Education*, 32(1), 4–21. doi: 10.1177/0741932509355950

CDC. Centers for Disease Control (2008). Health status and routine physical activities in adults by hearing status. Retrieved January 28, 2013, from http://www.cdc.gov/features/dshearing-disparities/

Collins, P. H. (1999). *Black feminist thought.* London: Routledge.

Davis, A., Bamford, J., Wilson, I., Ramkalawan, T., Forshaw, M., & Wright, S. (1997). A critical review of the role of neonatal screening in the detection of congenital hearing impairment. *Health Technology Assessment* (Vol. 1, pp. 1–177).

De Clerck, G. A. (2011). Fostering Deaf people's empowerment: The Cameroonian deaf community and epistemological equity. *Third World Quarterly*, 32(8), 1419–1435. doi: 10.1080/01436597.2011.604516

Denmark, T., Atkinson, J., Woll, B., Marshall, J., Young, A., Ferguson-Coleman, E., Rogers, K., Geall, R., Keady, J., & Burns, A. (2012). *Identifying cognitive disorder and dementia in users of sign languages—moving away from spoken language tests.* Paper presented at the Experimental Psychology Society's workshop, UCL, London.

Fine, M. (1994). Working the hyphens: Reinventing self and other in qualitative research. In N. K. Denzin & Y. S. Lincoln (Eds.), *Handbook of qualitative research* (pp. 70–82). London: Sage.

Hammersley, M. (1990). *Reading ethnographic research: A critical guide.* Essex, UK Addison-Wesley.

Hauser, P. C., & Marschark, M. (2008). What we know and what we don't know about cognition and deaf learners. In M. Marschark & P. C. Hauser (Eds.), *Deaf cognition: Foundations and outcomes* (pp. 439–455). New York, NY: Oxford University Press.

Hereditary Hearing Loss. (2012) Retrieved January 23, 2013, from http:// hereditaryhearingloss.org

Herman, R., Holmes, S., & Woll, B. (1999). *Assessing British Sign Language development: Receptive skills test.* Gloucestershire, UK: Forest Books.

Hintermair, M. (2006). Parental resources, parental stress, and socioemotional development of deaf and hard of hearing children. *Journal of Deaf Studies and Deaf Education, 11*(4), 493–513. doi: 10.1093/deafed/enl005

Hogan, S., Stokes, J., & Weller, I. (2010). Language outcomes for children of low-income families enrolled in auditory verbal therapy. *Deafness & Education International, 12*(4), 204–216. doi: 10.1179/1557069X10Y.0000000003

Hoiting, N., & Loncke, F. (1990). Models of acquisition and processing of multilingual and multiodal information. In T. Prillwitz & T. Vollhaber (Eds.), *Current trends in European sign language research.* Hamburg, UK: Signum.

JCIH. Joint Committee on Infant Hearing (2007). Year 2007 position statement: Principles and guidelines for early hearing detection and intervention programs. *Pediatrics, 120*(4), 898–921. doi: 10.1542/peds.2007-2333

Johnson, J. L., Bottorff, J. L., Browne, A. J., Grewal, S., Hilton, B. A., & Clarke, H. (2004). Othering and being othered in the context of health care services. *Health Communication, 16*(2), 255–271. doi: 10.1207/S15327027HC1602_7

Kennedy, C., McCann, D., Campbell, M., Law, C., Mullee, M., Petrou, S., Watkin, P., Worsfold, S., Yuen, H., & Stevenson, J. (2006). Language ability after early detection of permanent childhood hearing impairment. *New England Journal of Medicine, 354*(20), 2131–2141.

Knoors, H., & Marschark, M. (2012). Language planning for the 21st century: Revisiting bilingual language policy for deaf children *Journal of Deaf Studies and Deaf Education, 17*(3), 291–305. doi: 10.1093/deafed/ens018

Krentz, C. (2009). Open your eyes: Deaf studies talking (review). *Sign Language Studies, 10*(1), 110–132. doi: 10.1353/sls.0.0032

Kusters, A. (2009). Deaf on the lifeline of Mumbai. *Sign Language Studies, 10*(1), 36–68. doi: 10.1353/sls.0.0035

Ladd, P. (2003). *Understanding Deaf culture: In search of Deafhood.* Clevedon, UK: Multilingual Matters.

Lang, G. (2000). *A phone of our own: The Deaf insurrection against Ma Bell.* Washington, DC: Gallaudet University Press.

Leigh, G., Newall, J. P., & Newall, A. T. (2010). Newborn hearing screening and earlier intervention with deaf children: Issues for the developing world. In M. Marschark & E. Spencer (Eds.), *The Oxford handbook of deaf studies, language, and education* (Vol. 2, pp. 345–359). New York, NY: Oxford University Press.

Leigh, I. W. (2009). *A lens on deaf identities.* New York, NY: Oxford University Press.

Levine, E. (1956). *Youth in a soundless world.* New York, NY: New York University Press.

Luczak, R. (Ed.). (1993). *Eyes of desire: A Deaf gay and lesbian reader.* New York, NY: Alyson Books.

Marschark, M. (1993). Origins and interactions in language, cognitive, and social development of deaf children. In M. Marschark & D. Clark (Eds.), *Psychological perspectives on deafness* (pp. 7–26). Hillsdale, NJ: Lawrence Erlbaum.

Marschark, M. (2003). Cognitive functioning in deaf adults and children. In M. Marschark & P. E. Spencer (Eds.), *Oxford handbook of deaf studies, language, and education* (Vol. 1, pp. 464–477). New York, NY: Oxford University Press.

Marschark, M., & Hauser, P. C. (2008). Cognitive underpinning of learning by deaf and hard-of-hearing students: Differences, diversity and directions. In M. Marschark & P. C. Hauser (Eds.), *Deaf cognition: Foundations and outcomes* (pp. 3–23). New York, NY: Oxford University Press.

Marschark, M., Rhoten, C., & Fabich, M. (2007). On ethics and deafness: Research, pedagogy and politics. *Deafness & Education International, 9*(1), 45–61. doi: 10.1179/146431507790560057

Mason, K., Rowley, K., Marshall, C. R., Atkinson, J. R., Herman, R., Woll, B., & Morgan, G. (2010). Identifying specific language impairment in deaf children acquiring British Sign Language: Implications for theory and practice. *British Journal of Developmental Psychology, 28*(1), 33–49. doi: 10.1348/026151009X484190

Mayer, C. (2007). What really matters in the early literacy development of deaf children. *Journal of Deaf Studies and Deaf Education, 12*(4), 411–431. doi: 10.1093/deafed/enm020

Miller, K. R., & Vernon, M. (2002). Assessing linguistic diversity in deaf criminal suspects. *Sign Language Studies, 2*(4), 380–390. doi: 10.1353/sls.2002.0021

Mitchell, R. E., & Karchmer, M. A. (2004). Chasing the mythical ten percent: Parental hearing status of deaf and hard of hearing students in the United States. *Sign Language Studies, 4*, 231–244. doi: 10.1353/sls.2004.0005

Moeller, M. P., Hoover, B., Putman, C., Arbataitis, K., Bohnenkamp, G., Peterson, B. Lewis, D., Estee, S., Pittman, A., & Stelmachowicz, P. (2007). Vocalizations of infants with hearing loss compared with infants with normal hearing: Part II—transition to words. *Ear & Hearing, 28*, (5), 628–642.

Morgan-Jones, R. (2001). *Hearing differently: The impact of hearing impairment on family life*. London: Whurr.

Morton, C. C., & Nance, W. E. (2006). Newborn hearing screening: A silent revolution. *New England Journal of Medicine, 354*, 2151–2164.

Murphy, E., Dingwall, R., Greatbatch, D., Parker, S., & Watson, P. (1998). Qualitative research methods in health technology assessment: A review of the literature. *Health Technology Assessment, 2*(16), iii.

Myers, S. S., & Fernandes, J. K. (2010). Deaf studies: A critique of the predominant U.S. theoretical direction. *Journal of Deaf Studies and Deaf Education, 15*(1). doi: 10.1093/deafed/enp017

Myklebust, H. (1960). *The psychology of deafness: Sensory deprivation, learning and adjustment*. New York, NY: Grune and Stratton Inc.

National Assistance Act (1948). Retrieved March 16, 2013, from http:// http:// www.legislation.gov.uk/ukpga/Geo6/11-12/29/contents

Northern, J. (2008). Guidelines for identification and management of infants and children with auditory neuropathy spectrum disorder. Aurora, CO: The Children's Hospital.

Olusanya, B. O., & Newton, V. (2007). Global burden of childhood hearing impairment and disease control priorities. *The Lancet, 369* (9569), 1314–1317. doi: 10.1016/S0140-6736(07)60602-3

Parasnis, I. (Ed.). (1996). *Cultural and language diversity and the deaf experience.* New York, NY: Cambridge University Press.

Purdam, K., Afkhami, R., Olson, W., & Thornton, P. (2008). Disability in the UK: Measuring equality. *Disability & Society, 23*(1), 53–65. doi: 10.1080/09687590701725658

Rance, G., & Barker, E. J. (2009). Speech and language outcomes in children with auditory neuropathy/dys-synchrony managed by either cochlear implants or hearing aids. *International Journal of Audiology, 48*, 313–320. doi: 10.1080/14992020802665959

Rance G., Cone-Wesson B., J., W., & Dowell, R. (2002). Speech perception and cortical event related potentials in children with auditory neuropathy. *Ear and Hearing, 23*, 239–253.

Rutherford, S. (1993). *A study of American Deaf folklore.* Burtonsville, MD: Linstok Press.

Schroedel, J. G. (1984). Analyzing surveys on deaf adults: Implications for survey research on persons with disabilities. *Social Science & Medicine, 19*(6), 619–627. doi: 10.1016/0277-9536(84)90228-4

Sutherland, H., & Young, A. (2007). "Hate English! Why?..." Signs and English from deaf children's perception. Results from a preliminary study of deaf children's experience of sign bilingual education. *Deafness & Education International, 9*(4), 197–213. doi: 10.1179/146431507790559914

Sutton-Spence, R. (2011). Sign language narratives for Deaf children—Identity, culture and language. *Journal of Folklore Research, 47*(3), 265–305.

Svalastog, A. L., & Eriksson, S. (2010). You can use my name: You don't have to steal my story—a critique of anonymity in indigenous studies. *Developing World Bioethics, 10*(2), 104–110. doi: 10.1111/j.1471-8847.2010.00276.x

Thoutenhoofd, E. (2010). Acting with attainment technologies in Deaf education: Reinventing monitoring as an intervention collaboratory. *Sign Language Studies, 10*(2), 214–230. doi: 10.1353/sls.0.0040

Trotta, L., Iacona, E., Primignani, P., Castorina, P., Radaelli, C., Del Bo, L., Coviello, D., & Ambrosetti, U. (2011). GJB2 and MTRNR1 contributions in children with hearing impairment from Northern Cameroon. *International Journal of Audiology, 50*(2), 133–138. doi: 10.3109/14992027.2010.537377

Uus, K., Young, A., & Day, M. (2012). *Auditory neuropathy spectrum disorder: From parents to parents.* London: National Deaf Children's Society.

Valentine, G., & Skelton, T. (2007). Re-defining norms: D/deaf young people's transitions to independence. *The Sociological Review, 55*(1), 104–123. doi: 10.1111/j.1467-954X.2007.00684.x

Van Cleve, J. V. (1999). *Deaf history unveiled: Interpretations from the new scholarship.* Washington, DC: Gallaudet University Press.

van Cleve, J. V., & Crouch, B. A. (1989). *A place of their own: Creating the deaf community in America.* Washington, DC: Gallaudet University Press.

van Dijk, R., Nelson, C., Postma, A., & van Dijk, J. (2010). Deaf children with severe multiple disabilities: Etiologies, intevention, and assessment. In M. Marschark & E. Spencer (Eds.), *The Oxford handbook of deaf studies, language, and education.* (Vol. 2, pp. 172–191). New York, NY: Oxford.

Vernon, M. (1968). Fifty years of research on the intelligence of the deaf and hard of hearing. *Journal of Rehabilitation of the Deaf, 1*(1), 1–11.

White, C. (2011). Update on the harmonisation of disability data collection in UK surveys (Part 1). *Health Statistics Quarterly* (Vol. 51). London: Office of National Statistics.

Yoshinaga-Itano, C. (2003). From screening to early identification and intervention: Discovering predictors to successful outcomes for children with significant hearing loss. *Journal of Deaf Studies and Deaf Education, 8*(1), 11–30.

Young, A., Ackerman, J., & Kyle, J. G. (1998). *Looking on: Deaf people and the organisation of services.* Bristol, UK: The Policy Press.

Young, A. M., Tattersall, H., Uus, K., Bamford, J., McCracken, W. (2004). To what extent do the characteristics of the object of evaluation influence the choice of epistemological framework? The case of newborn hearing screening. *Qualitative Health Research, 14*(6), 866–874. doi: 10.1177/1049732304265971

Young, A., & Tattersall, H. (2005). Parents' of deaf children evaluative accounts of the process and practice of universal newborn hearing screening. *Journal of Deaf Studies and Deaf Education, 10*(2), 134–145. doi: 10.1093/deafed/eni014

Zeshan, U., & Dikyuva, H. (in press). Documentation of endangered sign languages: The case of Mardin Sign Language. In M. Jones & S. Ogilvie (Eds.), *Keeping languages alive: Documentation, pedagogy and revitalization* (Chapter 3). Cambridge, UK: Cambridge University Press.

6

Narrative, Epistemology, and Language

Throughout this book we argue that how we define, understand, and represent what it is to be d/Deaf is central to the methodological decisions we make about how to carry out a piece of research. We emphasize that choices made about who to include in research and how to carry out that research are also choices about who can participate in the production of knowledge. This may mean that some perspectives are excluded and therefore such decisions inevitably have ethical and political dimensions. Furthermore, we contend that researchers construct realities rather than straightforwardly reflect them in research.

In this chapter we pull together these arguments specifically in relation to narrative and focus on narrative analysis. We begin with a broad consideration of different kinds of narratives in association with d/Deaf people and use this as a means of beginning to define varieties of narrative before moving on to consider the epistemological claims made from narrative research and how narratives might be analyzed in theory and in practice. We then go on to look at whether d/Deaf narratives differ and ask what the consequences might be of treating the experience of being deaf or Deaf as the central consideration within narrative analysis. Finally we question whether the construction of narratives as d/Deaf narratives is to miss the significance of other aspects of identity

NARRATIVES AND d/DEAF PEOPLE

Researchers are increasingly choosing to see their data as narratives. However, social research literature on narrative and that produced by researchers working in the d/Deaf field specifically remain largely separate. In both, terms such as narrative, story, life history, oral history, discourse, and biography are frequently used without definition and distinction. Roberts (2002) provides a useful guide through the differing and sometimes overlapping use of these terms. In this chapter, we engage with the work of researchers who use a variety of terms to describe what we define as narrative in order to be able to benefit from the range of ideas available.

How narratives are analyzed and how researchers see the status of the narratives they collect, as well as those they make during research, varies according to disciplinary perspective, theoretical stance, and epistemology (see, for example, Baker, 2005; Elliott, 2005; Frank, 1995; Gubrium & Holstein, 2009; Riessman, 2008; Roberts, 2002 for overviews of different narrative approaches within social research). They all view narratives as in some way involving a telling, that is a representation of self and/or others for a purpose, within a context, structure, and medium, be it words or signs. Each of these elements, as well as the sum of their parts, is open to analysis and interpretation. In this chapter we follow Riessman and Quinney (2005), who define narrative as a form of discourse that "interrogates language—how and why events are storied, not simply the content to which language refers" (p. 102). This is a long way from the highly restrictive definition of some sociolinguistics, where narrative refers to a discrete unit of discourse (Riessman, 2008, p. 5). Interrogation of narratives, therefore, involves close attention to context, which encompasses the relationship between participants, including the audience/reader and narrator, and particularly "the institutional constraints, power relations and cultural discourses that contextualize all narrative" (Riessman, 2008).

For example, a perspective on deafness as pathology, impairment, a problem, or something unexpected has generated a range of narratives about coping and in some cases overcoming deafness. These are very much in the tradition of other kinds of pathography associated with illness (Frank, 1995). Common examples include hearing parents' narratives about reactions to their child being deaf and a struggle for normality (Spradley & Spradley, 1979) and adults' stories of recognition of and coming to terms with hearing loss (Morgan-Jones, 2001). While the content of the narratives is of importance—what did the parent, child, or deafened person do, find out, or decide?—so too is the presentation of the structure of the story. Is this a heroic tale of the struggle to overcome adversity? Or is it a journey related in the present moment with few predesigned assumptions of the likely end? We are interested in the shape of the narrative, not just its material, because that shape gives clues to attitudes and assumptions and ways of knowing, in this case about what it is to be deaf (we return to this later).

West (2012), for example, engages hearing parents with deaf children in telling stories of family life. These families were seeking to bring up their children as sign-bilinguals. The analysis of their narratives over time led her to the development of new ways of seeing Deaf/hearing family life, constructed around such concepts as "strong together." These were not hearing families with a deaf child; these were families whose narratives attested to the transformation of their self-concept into being Deaf/hearing families.

From a more instrumental perspective, Young and Tattersall (2007) engage hearing parents of early identified deaf children in talk about their expectations of their children's language development as they grew up. The analysis of these narratives suggested assumptions and expectations which parents tied to the fact that their children were early identified, not just that they were deaf. The findings were used to help sensitize professionals to parents' informational and emotional needs (Young & Tattersall, 2007). Similarly, Engelund (2006) focuses on how people losing their hearing recognized change. She identifies the tipping points which led them to seek help with the aim of better targeting of intervention and support. She does so in part by considering the expressions participants used to describe their experiences and the presentation of their (hearing) self within their narratives (Engelund, 2006).

Narratives therefore are not just data to be generated in research. They form part of everyday life. From within a cultural understanding of being Deaf, narratives are prized as evidence of the nature of that culture, and narrative analysis is pursued as a form of cultural archeology to uncover and display. Common examples include biographical and historical narratives of being Deaf in a variety of contexts and at historical moments. For example, consider Christiansen and Barnartt's (1995) work on the Deaf President Now protests at Gallaudet University and Carmel's (2006) "oral history," in American Sign Language (ASL), of Deaf Holocaust survivors, which forms part of the permanent collection of the US Holocaust Memorial Museum. From an individualized perspective, personal narratives of discovering sign language and making an identity transition from being an oral deaf person to being Deaf are repeated in countries throughout the world (Dodds, 2003; Oliva, 2007). The child's self-discovery that she or he is deaf is also a commonly recurring and shared narrative. Sutton-Spence (2011) argues that:

> Just as members of a gay community will have personal "coming out" stories, all the Deaf people I have ever asked can relate the moment they first realized they were deaf… These narratives are often shared with other members of the community, particularly new members, because they represent shared experiences with which other Deaf people can identify. (p. 274)

Deaf communities share a rich history of narrative and are regarded as storytelling cultures (Ladd, 2003; Peters, 2000; Rutherford, 1993; Sutton-Spence & Napoli, 2012). In common with other "oral" (that is, nonwritten) traditions, cultural knowledge and know-how are passed intergenerationally through shared stories (Sutton-Spence, 2011). The difference is that few Deaf people have Deaf parents (Mitchell & Karchmer, 2004); therefore, the intergenerational significance of narrative is a largely collective, rather than family-based one, transcending blood ties but serving as the glue of kinship. Through the sharing of stories, Deaf adults maintain a shared sense of identity and children are brought into the culture of Deaf world knowledge (Sutton-Spence & Napoli, 2012). Such story-sharing kinship is international in scale, as many of the same kinds of narratives on similar themes are found in diverse countries. For example:

> A large number of "Deaf" narratives, especially narratives of personal experiences, have recurrent themes of protagonists being caught, shut in or locked out behind doors. Conflicts arise because of the opaqueness of doors, which make them inaccessible transporters of visual elements and language modalities...Windows are permeable...As conveyors of light, windows are conveyors of visual communication...In terms of communication permeability, doors are to hearing people what windows are to deaf people. (Bahan, 2011, p. 14)

However, the capturing of signed narratives and their dissemination and recognition as cultural narratives of significance has been, until recently, severely constrained by their visual rather than written or spoken form. As Bahan (2011, p. 22) reflects: "So many generations of signers have been handcuffed in a society intoxicated by the ideology that speech is language and vice versa." We return to the significance of information and communication technologies for the redress of power imbalances between the written and the signed text in Chapter 8. Suffice it to say at this point, that signed narratives are not new. It is only the relative newness of means for their recording and sharing, first through video and then later information and communication technologies (ICTs), that has created this impression.

Narratives also exist as stories *about* being d/Deaf. Until recently, these have largely been written by hearing people. They have tended to portray d/Deaf people in stereotypical, one-dimensional and often negative ways (Atherton, Russell, & Turner, 2001; McDonald, 2010). McDonald (2010) defines being deaf not as a loss but as *the experience of* "a state of hearingness that is substantially less than what is understood to be normal hearing" (p. 464). She argues that "deaf" people (referring both to those who sign and those who do not) have rarely been allowed to take their place in literature, often being used to represent alienation "or serving as a source of special knowledge, laden with stereotypical constructs of pity and crude assumptions about deafness" (p. 465). See, for example, the portrayal of a deaf school girl in Jeffrey Deaver's (1995) popular thriller *A Maiden's Grave* (a lip-reading pun on "amazing grace"). McDonald (2010) notes in relation to memoir, biography, and fiction that to date published narratives by deaf people are still small in number. Notable examples include Cyrus, Katz, Cheyney, and Parsons (2006) and Wright (1969). She argues that if assumptions about deaf people are to be shattered, this must be by deaf people themselves: "hearing people cannot take on the task, missionary-like, on their behalf" (2012, p. 168). Importantly, she locates herself within her discussion as "deaf" and states (using her terminology) that she is not a member of any deaf community, upper or lower case, and cautions against assuming that deaf identity is the only significant identity or of limiting deaf history to the history of the signing deaf community (McDonald, 2012).

Alternative ways of seeing, experiencing, and telling have the potential to change fundamental definitions of reality and their social and political consequences (Bamberg & Andrews, 2004). For disabled, deaf, and Deaf people alike, narrative potentially, therefore, has a crucial function in challenging perspectives, assumptions, and hegemonies through the generation of counternarratives. Consider the implications of statements such as "Deafness is not an illness," "She is a hearing person trapped in a deaf body," or "I'm disabled, not deaf." These narrative constructions, be they in different ways, all present counternarratives to dominant discourses. One of the most famous counternarratives is Groce's (1985) description of life at Martha's Vineyard, where there had been a high incidence of hereditary deafness for over 200 years. The context where everyone "spoke" sign language challenged the view that people who are Deaf are handicapped. As no one perceived being Deaf as a problem, but rather as indicative of a language use which was shared among those who were hearing, then deafness as a handicap is shown to be socially constructed (see also Levy, 2002).

Narrative analysis in its various forms is, therefore, fertile territory from which to understand a vast range of human experience; to explore, document, and appreciate that which is new or hidden; through which to identify factors relevant to specific intents; and as a result of which to challenge, protest, and reconstruct. As such, narrative analysis has increasingly obtained a significant epistemological authority but on what grounds is such authority claimed and can it be unquestioningly justified?

EPISTEMOLOGICAL CLAIMS OF NARRATIVE RESEARCHERS

There is disagreement about the status of knowledge claims made in narrative research. For some, the personal account is authentic because it is reality as perceived by the individual who recounts it; her world, her understanding, her expression should stand and be assessed in no other terms than those which the narrator has chosen. It has epistemic authority because it derives from someone recognized as possessing the "lived experience" which is of interest. This authority is commonly contrasted with those who might talk *about* an experience as an outsider (and see Chapter 3 for problems with trying to specify insider or outsider).

However, as we argue earlier, narratives are to a large extent constructed accounts which are situated in time and place and have a purpose. This is not necessarily a self-conscious purpose; it may be an artifact of how time and experience have changed what a narrative means for the individual. Young and Greally (2003) asked 1,028 parents of deaf children (969 of whom were hearing and 59 d/Deaf) to express what it was they would now say, based on their experience, to parents of newly diagnosed deaf children. They then analyzed how parents had constructed and presented their experiences to the unknown other. They found, for example, differences between parents who represented time as a "healer" and those who represented it as a "revealer" (pp. 72–75). For those who saw it as a healer, getting used to having a deaf child meant that things did not seem so difficult, the initial sense of loss disappeared, and family life continued in ways that had seemed initially impossible. For those who saw it as revealer, time having a deaf child had meant the opening up of new experiences, new abilities in themselves and their child in ways they could not have imagined and were thankful for. For some parents it was both at different times.

In asking parents to "speak" to unknown new parents from within their experience, the researchers had both endorsed that experience as endowing authority and invited a public narrative by signaling that it would be used for a deliberate purpose involving others. These conditions obviously influenced the narratives produced. The circumstances of narrative production are influential, not neutral. West (1990) in comparing two studies of parents' accounts of having a disabled child explores how differences in a researcher's behavior are likely to lead to more or less "private" or "public" accounts by parents. He reminds us, after Emerson (1983), that "there is no absolute 'truth' against which an account may be compared; there are only other accounts" (West, 1990, p. 1230). As we indicate in Chapter 3, this opens up other criteria for assessing research, including narratives collected within research as well as those researchers produce themselves.

Many sociologists, as well as researchers from other disciplines, therefore argue for looking beyond the notion that narratives are unchallengeable accounts of personal experience. An analysis of narrative grounded in social and historical context enables new facets of the way they are understood that may go beyond or in some cases challenge that of the narrator. A good example here is the writing of the social researcher Atkinson (2009) in which he challenges researchers working on illness narratives on their presentation of medical narratives. He contrasts the portrayal of narratives of medical practice as decontextualized and impersonal with lay narratives as personal and experiential and unquestioning holders of truth (see also Riessman, 2008; Roberts, 2008). These writers argue that some narrative researchers are privileging narratives, and sometimes narratives by particular people, over other kinds of research data. Their arguments relate to the impossibility of reading off meaning directly from language. Narratives are rhetorical in nature and there can be many versions of what a narrator "meant." Understanding narratives therefore involves understanding how narrators use language and for what intent. Are they showing themselves as survivors rather than victims? Is deafness portrayed as a tragedy to be overcome or the beginning of an identity to be discovered?

Consequently, there are problems in trying to adjudicate between narratives according to their pedigree. As we argue in Chapter 3, there are dangers in attaching epistemological privilege to narratives from particular sources. Lay narratives are not a priori nearer "the truth" than medical narratives. However, some narratives are more powerful as they are the means by which some social groups express their relative power to endorse one version of reality rather than another (West, 1990). As Lane, Hoffmeister, and Bahan (1996) argue at length, dominant social narratives about what it is to be deaf founded on disability, impairment, and what they refer to as hearing people's assumptions of "subtraction" (from what is "normal") usurp the equally grand narrative of Deaf people's identity as a cultural-linguistic and ethnic group who have not "lost" anything (see Chapter 2). These differences are expressed in the everyday narratives of how society conducts its business, privileging one discourse over another. For example, in England, the Equality Act (2010) makes no specific reference to Deaf people's use of British Sign Language (BSL) but addresses deafness as disability. As we point out in Chapter 2 and throughout this book, research too reflects and co-creates the narratives about what it is to be d/Deaf and the status of these are themselves open to scrutiny. The example of the Equality Act (2010) indicates that government documents and policies can also be viewed as narrative constructions which can be challenged.

However, as is the case generally within social research, many academics working with narratives about being d/Deaf do not discuss the status of their work with regard to its knowledge claims. Exceptions include Ladd (2003); Rathmann, Mann, and Morgan (2007); Hole (2007a, 2007b); and Sutton-Spence (2010). We point here to the writing of Hole (2007a, 2007b), who draws on social constructionism and postmodern feminist work to argue that cultural representations and language are tools by which we construct lived reality. She examines the role of sign language narratives in developing Deaf identity in children and gives examples of the importance of language in the performances of stories. We give other examples in Chapter 3 of research with people who are Deaf which are based on epistemologies which challenge the possibility of presenting research as objective gathering of data.

ANALYZING NARRATIVES

We note earlier how narratives in social research are variously defined according to disciplinary perspective, theoretical stance, and epistemology. Findings are also analyzed in different ways (see, for example, Baker, 2005; Frank, 1995; Gubrium & Holstein, 2009; and Riessman, 2008, as examples of how researchers have analyzed narratives). We have chosen to use Riessman (2008) to discuss narrative analysis because she gives detailed examples of different kinds of narrative analysis and her work is one of the few narrative texts that takes seriously the view that language constructs rather than reflects reality in relation to *cross-language* narratives. This is in contrast to many narrative researchers who highlight the significance of language in their discussion of narrative yet ignore the elephant in the room when they look at narratives using languages other than their own, usually English, language. For example, while Gubrium and Holstein (2009) give examples of research from all over the world, there is no mention of how to approach cross-language narratives. We discuss later how narrative structures can vary across languages and how ironing out structural differences to conform to an English language baseline can result in power inequalities in the representation of people who use different languages, signed, spoken, or written.

When analyzing narratives, some researchers are solely interested in content or what Riessman (2008) calls thematic analysis. The decision to focus on content may be influenced by the aim of the research. For example, researchers interested in challenging oralist narratives of the lives of d/Deaf people may decide to collect narratives that challenge deafness as deficit and focus on what it means to be "deaf" (McDonald, 2010) or Deaf (Ladd, 2003). Ladd (2003) defines oralism as "an all-encompassing set of policies and discourses aimed at preventing them [deaf children and their parents] from learning or using sign languages to communicate" (2003, p. 7). For this purpose content alone may suffice to challenge established narratives. Other examples are Groce (1985); Christiansen and Barnartt (1995); Dodds (2003); and Kittel, Kittel, and Kittel (2003). Researchers looking at content may use "codes" to designate themes in their research. This involves going through interviews and marking chunks of text according to what the researcher believes they are "about," for example, views about attendance at Deaf associations, about being d/Deaf, or treatment by hearing people. These codes may then be traced through interviews in much the same way as researchers working with questionnaires code replies to questions. Qualitative researchers may also use codes to group data. Examples of quotes from themes that they find significant may then be chosen. For example, Sheridan (2000) codes themes around images of self and others in a study of the stories of children using ASL or simultaneous communication.

Content analysis using coding may be used on its own or in combination with more structural/performance analyses (see later). Coding need not be the preserve of positivists. De Clerck's (2007) use of

thematic coding in her research with Flemish Deaf leaders is an interesting example. She carried out ethnographic interviews and writes of
themes "that emerged from the data and categorization of the data"
(p. 8). The latter part of this statement suggests a recognition that reality does not lie in the data but that researchers produce realities, in this
case via the construction of codes. She contrasts the rhetorical claims
of Deaf people in terms of sign language, Deaf culture, and a "can-do"
rhetoric with the rhetoric of oralism, maintaining an explicit acknowledgment of the constructed nature of this rhetoric. De Clerck's (2007)
research is situated within its cultural and historic context with her own
perspective laid out at the onset. Arguably, this is an example of coding
of content being used with a performance analysis rather than as a way
of picking out and describing themes that exist independently of the
researcher (see here also McIlroy & Storbeck, 2011, on Deaf identity).

Social researchers have argued that examining structure, variously
defined, is also an important aspect of narrative analysis. They analyze,
for example, the lexicon used or the way the narrator works with plot or
humor to compare narratives, arguing that narratives are rhetorically produced (Atkinson, 2009; Riessman, 2008; Roberts, 2008) and that narrative
analysts should not take narrative content as objectively true but examine *how* narratives are put together. For example, how is language used
to persuade, how are people described, in what ways are some events
privileged over others? In other words, these writers recognize that narratives have configurational as well as episodic dimensions (Ricoeur, 1988).
Looking at content alone in narratives may not allow one to pick up on
how people have been presented and their narratives evaluated.

Furthermore, we allude earlier to research which shows that structures considered appropriate for narratives in one language may not
be considered appropriate for others, resulting in the dismissal of
alternative ways of narrating. We return to this in Chapter 7, where
we examine the writing of social researchers who argue that interpreta-
tion/translation often involves the silencing of alternative views. This
occurs, they contend, because interpreted/translated narratives are
judged according to the expected structure of the target language, and
the content is dismissed as inauthentic if not presented in this form. In
relation to signed languages, written narratives are often judged by criteria for assessing the written narratives of hearing people. For example,
Kuntze (2008, p. 146) argues that literacy has largely been defined using
an "audiocentric framework" (see also Wang, 2012). Kuntze (2008) uses
research on visual literacy to show language is more than writing, and
he redefines literacy to include the ability to reconstruct experiences
through visual information in a meaningful way. Languages are not
equal, in that they are not necessarily afforded equal status. An exploration of their varying structures within narrative productions may help
to discuss cross-cultural narratives in a less imperialistic way.

Narratives that are signed have been shown to have different structures from spoken narratives (Bahan, 2008; Bishop & Hicks, 2005; Burch, Jaafar, West, & Bauer, 2008; Sutton-Spence, 2010). This is not just about the particular grammatical features and structures of signed languages in comparison with spoken languages. It is also about the scope, flexibility, and resources for narrative representations, narrative development, character, plot, and action which spoken languages do not produce or possess in the same way. For example, signed languages incorporate grammatical features such as footing or role shift (Monikowski & Winston, 2003) whereby the narrator becomes the characters within her story or indicates who is signing/speaking by bodily movements such as changing the orientation of the character's body from left to right, her gaze from straight on to sideways (Bahan, 2011), or the actual shape of how she looks, for example, hunched or tall. In so doing, the narrator incorporates many more features of the character *simultaneously* than a more straightforward "he said...then she mentioned..." linear kind of structure might do. We learn the direction from which a character might enter a scene, her impression on the narrator, and her bearing as an individual. The style of the signing as each character, portrayed wordlessly, provides more information—is this the staccato signing of someone anxious and distressed or the languorous signing of someone taking events as they come? All such features happen in a multilayered fusion and are graspable as deliberately meaningful quite separately from what a character might then be portrayed as "saying"—the content of her utterance. Features such as role shift, eye gaze, and many more are intrinsic to the grammar of signed languages and enable narrative and storytelling in ways that differ from those put together by hearing people using spoken language (Bahan, 2006; Emmorey & Falgier, 1996; Mather & Winston, 1998; Morgan, 1999; Rayman, 1999). This is not just dramatic embellishment; it is language.

An interesting example of how understanding is filtered not only through the perspective chosen but also the linguistic resources available is provided by Rayman (1999). She used the work of Berman and Slobin (1994) and Slobin (1996a, 1996b) to study stories produced by five adult native ASL users and five adult native English language users about a silent cartoon of one of Aesop's fables (the tortoise and the hare). She found that Deaf storytellers used role shift to represent characters' personalities and behaviors through facial expressions, attitudes, and body movements. However, hearing storytellers rarely used facial expressions or the equivalent of role shift, since as Rayman states, "it is not a practice readily available in their language system" (p. 78). She also discusses how ASL users relied heavily on space to represent concepts rather than using features of tense and gender that are prevalent in English. For example, she notes how ASL relies on spatial relationships to represent time, usually "locating the past behind the signer and the future in front of the signer" (p. 63). She concludes that the processes and resources involved in the visual-gestural modality differ from those of the aural/oral modality, shaping not just *how* a story is told *but also what is told/included*.

The structure of *written* narratives by people who use sign language has also been shown to differ from those of hearing writers (Koutsoubou, Herman, & Woll, 2006; Maxwell, 1990). For example, Maxwell (1990) describes findings from a variety of sources, including written samples collected from both deaf children who sign and children who rely on oral communication. She suggests that some children write using visual-centered narrative structures. Reporting on research where hearing adults and Deaf ASL signers were asked to read the responses of signing children to questions such as: "What's your favorite movie"? or "What's the most exciting thing that you have seen in real life or on TV?," Maxwell shows how the former see the texts as incomplete attempts at English while the latter see the written words as "keys to what the child has seen" (p. 225). However, Maxwell goes on to show that nonsigning children also organize their writing visually and suggests that "visual-centered narratives may be structures which start with a biological condition and develop culturally into a complex linguistic discourse form" (p. 213). In other words, being deaf in a physiological sense produces a more visual orientation, but it is only through exposure to visual language that the orientation becomes developed as a linguistic resource.

Therefore, in studying how different resources between languages are deployed researchers may find different narrative structures. This different kind of structuring has been linked to different ways in which deaf children think (cognitively) and the insight has gone on to be applied to concerns about the most appropriate ways to teach deaf children (Kuntze, 2008; Marschark & Hauser, 2008). As Marschark and Hauser (2008) show, deaf children are not just children who cannot hear; they are children whose visual orientation and exposure, in some cases, to signed language, has forged different cognitive strengths and preferences. In their overview of research in the United States concerned with the teaching of science to deaf, "hard of hearing," and hearing students, they show that there are cognitive differences between deaf and hearing students at a variety of levels, including visual perception, memory, and problem solving. However, they emphasize that there are more similarities than differences but conclude that relatively small differences in knowledge or approaches to learning can have significant effects that may be cumulative over time (Marschark & Hauser, 2008, p. 17).

We hint earlier that some writers suggest that narrative analysis needs to go further than exploring structural similarities and differences, for example, when discussing the work of De Clerck (2007).

Riessman (2008) suggests the significance of both content and structure in narrative analysis. However, she argues that interrogation of narratives involves an additional focus: If thematic and structural analysis involves "what" and "how," dialogic/performance analysis refers to "when" and "why," that is, who the narrator is, the intended audience, and the context and purpose of the narrative. Ladd (2003), for example, includes his own life story to situate his perspective on his research and his views on the role of hearing researchers. Hole (2007b) describes her approach as poststructural narrative analysis and discusses Butler's *Gender Trouble* (1990) and *Bodies That Matter* (1993) to help her describe discourses of normalcy, difference, passing, and Deaf culture. She states specifically that her focus is not on the content but how meanings are constructed and how women drew on ideas, images, representations, and discourses to construct their identities. She also asks how the kind of analysis she has undertaken can add to political debates rather than trying to establish the truth claims of narratives.

In a similar way, Ohna (2004) specifically builds on the work of Riessman to explore the narratives of 22 "deaf people" in Norway (used to include both deaf and Deaf people). He discusses the use of personal pronouns (I, they, we) and the mechanisms participants used to ensure cohesion in their narratives, such as sentence coupling. He also focuses on the links between the individual narrative and the narrator's community and positions himself as a hearing son of sign lingual, deaf parents. Sutton-Spence's (2010) narrative analysis of interviews with British Deaf teachers and other Deaf adults as well as stories told by children using BSL are situated in the socio-historical context of BSL narratives and analyzed as "performances" (p. 287).

Structural or performance elements of narratives can be analyzed in different ways (Riessman, 2008). Riessman suggests that narratives analyzed in terms of structure or performance tend to take a "case-centered" approach (p. 74) rather than involving coding across cases. Neither structural nor performance analysis would necessarily involve, although they may include, coding chunks of interviews. Forms of narrative analysis are not exclusionary. Moreover, narratives are not always analyzed using qualitative methods. Peterson and Slaughter (2006) carry out a quantitative analysis of storytelling in late-signing deaf children and use the traditional tools of quantitative analysis such as t-tests and multiple regression. Van Beijsterveldt and Van Hell (2009) examine the written Dutch narratives of deaf children who are proficient in Sign Language of the Netherlands (SLN), deaf children who are "low-proficient" in SLN, and hearing monolingual and bilingual children. They use statistics to produce their findings. As we note in Chapter 3, not all analysts who use quantitative methods are positivist. Quantitative researchers also produce narratives, that is, referring back to Riessman and Quinney's (2005, p. 394) definition of narrative as a form of discourse that interrogates language, social researchers have interrogated quantitative research to look at how it is produced and interpreted (Elliott, 2005; Law, 2009; Temple, 1999, 2005). This is not to say that quantitative narratives are the same as qualitative ones. Elliott (2005), for example, argues that the collection of "event history data" in quantitative surveys does not allow respondents to provide fully formed narratives as their own evaluative element of narrative is missing.

EMBODYING NARRATIVE

In our discussion to date we may have given the impression that social researchers have limited themselves to analyzing what can be said or written down. This is not the case. Many have been arguing for the significance of the body as a site of knowledge, including Goffman (1961), Connell (1995), Frank (1995), Valentine (2001), Shilling (2003), Young (2005), Sparkes (1996), and Menary (2008). Researchers working with people with disabilities also argue for the reinstatement of the body within disability research, and we discuss this in Chapter 2. Building on this work, there is, therefore, interest in examining and presenting as research ways of looking at the world that are normally associated with the arts, such as plays, poems, paintings, and photographs.

Roberts (2008) provides a useful overview of this move to "performative social science" and the issues involved in introducing "a more 'complete' portrait of the individual as an active, communicative and sensual being" (p. 1). For example, he discusses movement and dance and suggests that a performative social science is interested in the body as "communicative"—not merely through activities such as dance but in everyday activities. More specifically, it is interested in how people act and relate to others "by complex means via the body—by gesture, touch, sound, smell, etc.—which provides the bases for both contemporary interaction and the evocative elements of memory" (p. 22). The term "performative" here is used to describe "the collection, organisation and dissemination of research which moves beyond traditional modes, such as the text-based journal article or overhead presentation" (p. 3).

However, as Rose (2006) points out, while hearing poets and visual artists have begun to turn to more literally performative ways, "the body and space are not problematized in sign language literature; the body and space make up the text itself" (p. 131). Reviewing the reasons for the increased interest in sign language poetry, Sutton-Spence (2005) suggests that it is "the 'ultimate' form of aesthetic signing, in which the form of language used is as important as—or even more important than—the message" (p. 14) and that signed poems have strong narrative features. Focusing on the poems of Dorothy Miles, she argues that they can be used to empower Deaf people by using creativity to explore who they are. Researchers have, therefore, used poetic representations to research and present Deaf narratives. For example, West (2011) presents the poetic narratives of two hearing and one "deaf" mother of both deaf and hearing children. West uses "deaf" to include both deaf and Deaf mothers and children to indicate its ambiguity. She does not, however, define her use of the term "narrative" or explain how re-presenting stories as written poetic texts can "bridge the gap between 'oral' narrative and the written (translated) word" (p. 732). Sutton-Spence (2005) acknowledges that using written English to present sign language poetry is problematic and uses both sign language glosses and illustrations to convey the signed poems she writes about. We discuss the problems of using glosses in Chapter 7 and return later to issues in representing Deaf identities in writing.

Menary's (2008) claim that "Narrative arises from a sequence of bodily experiences, perceptions and actions" (p. 75) could be turned around to suggest that bodily experiences *are* narrative. McCleary (2003) proposes using the term "*corporality*" rather than "orality" "to remind us of the essentially embodied nature of the interaction through which we construct our worlds" (p. 112). He notes how children learning to read touch the book, trace letters with their fingers, pronounce words out loud, and accompany words with gestures. These "bodily supports" (p. 113) are gradually suppressed as the child acquires more silent control of language, but McCleary suggests that they are always there. This can be seen when people come across difficult words when it appears that language is stored not only in the mind but in the body (p. 113). Sign language literally embodies the narrative (Davis, 1995).

Mohay's (2000) research with deaf children suggests another example of McCleary's bodily supports (see also Harris & Mohay, 1997, and authors in Spencer, Erting, and Marschark, 2000). Her comparison of the strategies that mothers of deaf and hearing children use to get their children's attention suggests that deaf children rely heavily on vision to make sense of their environment and communication that takes place in it. Hearing children can observe objects and events while listening simultaneously to the words used to describe them. Mohay argues that for deaf children the links between language and meaning may be less obvious because they have to divide their attention between the mother and the object being discussed; they need to see the mother's words or signs. Mothers use strategies to get their attention which involve contact, such as touching, pointing, and movement of the hands and body, before communicating something linguistic. They also trace the child's attention back to the object, having provided the word/sign for it in order to reinforce the relationship between the signifier and the signified.

Visual Narratives

Some social researchers have focused specifically on visual narratives (Banks, 2008; Hill, 2008; Riessman, 2008; Rose, 2000) as ways of "re-embodying" narrative and moving away from a reliance on written and oral texts. For example, Stanley (1992) and Harrison (2002) discuss the analysis of photographs. However, these writers are concerned with the status of the visual in research and not specifically with the *status of visual language*. We discuss in Chapter 3 claims that Deaf epistemologies are centered on the visual *and* on visual language. Here we point to the significance of the status of embodiment generally and the visual specifically in such debates about Deaf ways of being and knowing. For example, research into iconicity suggests that the visual nature of sign languages results in many direct iconic, visual-to-visual mappings. For example, the BSL sign for "cry" visually depicts the path of tears falling down the face (Perniss, Thompson, & Vigliocco, 2010). However, Perniss, Thompson, and Vigliocco (2010) also argue that once we move from a Euro-centric perspective to look at spoken languages such as those in sub-Saharan Africa, Australian Aboriginal languages, Japanese, Korean, Southeast Asian languages, indigenous languages of South America, and Balto-Finnic languages, iconicity is also prevalent in spoken languages. Readers should therefore refer to our discussion in Chapter 3 of essentializing what it means to be Deaf by limiting discussion to the visual and signed languages. Our discussion in Chapter 7 on interpretation, transcription, and translation also supports the argument that it matters *which* languages are involved in research.

Does it matter that social researchers have generally not been interested in visual languages and that the foundational writings of researchers working with people who sign are generally little recognized? What can researchers learn about language and narrative if they take on board the points made by researchers working with signed narratives? We give examples of some of this body of work in Chapter 7, including Stokoe's work (2001, 2005), in challenging the assumption that language is synonymous with speech (see also Armstrong & Karchmer, 2009). In the following section we argue that as sign languages are visually based, language reproducing a signed narrative involves issues of identity and representation. In writing down spoken French narratives, for example, researchers have the option of translating into written French; but there is no agreed-upon, written version of a sign language and there are structurally inherent problems in attempting to create one (see Chapter 7). Benvenuto (2005) describes sign language as "a minority language unlike all others" (p. 12). Sacks (1989) points out that the difference between the most diverse spoken languages is small compared to the difference between speech and sign (pp. 73–74). He suggests that sign differs in its "biological mode" and that "this...may determine, or at least modify, the thought processes of those who sign, and give them a unique and untranslatable, hypervisual cognitive style" (pp. 73–74). Moreover, he points out that sign language is the embodiment of personal and cultural identity (1989, p. 123). Therefore, using speech or writing down signed languages may have ontological and epistemological consequences; that is, it may undermine a signer's identity as well as his or her knowledge claims (we discuss this issue again in relation to information and communication technologies in Chapter 8).

Harmon (2007), looking at ASL, argues that writing in English (or any other print language) displaces "a cultural identity grounded in a visual-spatial language (p. 200)." She notes the problems of trying to sequence information on a page that would be perceived in a simultaneous rather than linear fashion by signers. She argues, therefore, that the conventions of printed English embody the hearing and not the Deaf world. She goes on to ask: Is there a subaltern sensibility emerging in the texts of Deaf writers? She shows how some Deaf writers are resisting "norming" in their use of gloss, italics, and fingerspelling, for example, to make English strange or foreign to a hearing reader and to make the reader *look.* "Glossing" involves using the nearest equivalent in printed text. For example, Harmon (2007) in her story of a gay couple discussing one of them leaving to go with another man to New York uses sentences formed as they would be in ASL, not in written English, for example, writing "Himself Gay?" We return to some of the issues in using gloss in Chapter 7.

However, some researchers caution against ascribing visually centered narratives to signing. Maxwell (1990) discusses previous research on group narratives of children who are deaf and ASL poetry. She describes how the Star Wars story is expressed by a child who is deaf using the topic-comment structure of sentences and focusing on visual scenes and images. She argues that not everything deaf children do in communication is derived from ASL. She states that "Some of what they do, like the nonsigning children's visual-centered discourse, may be because they are deaf" (pp. 227–228). She also points out that there are other cultures that have developed visual-centered narrative structures. In a similar way, Rée (1999) reminds readers that vision does not "have a monopoly in spatial apprehension: distances are perceived by touch as well as vision, and they can also be explored by the sense of hearing" (p. 324). He goes on to describe the idea that "there is a metaphysical gulf dividing communication by visible gestures from communication by audible words" as a fantasy or hallucination (see also Nelson, 2006).

Thoutenhoofd's (1998) discussion of "Deaf visuality" is useful here in exploring the link between epistemology, modality/language choice, and ontology. Thoutenhoofd used two parallel texts, photographic and written, cross-referenced by hyperlinks. He undertook three photographic projects: a documentary one based on his photographs of

Deaf volunteers in a Deaf club taking part in social events; an auto-biographical project where students who were deaf and hearing were given cameras to take photos of events to compare the results; and a critical review of photos used in magazines aimed at deaf audiences. His premise is that signing is "played out through and on the body." Visual expression is central to cultural identity for those Deaf people who use sign language. His analysis is subtle and challenges positivist assumptions about reality, identity, and the visual. He cautions against the assumption that photographs, a visual modality, reflect reality but does not dismiss them as a tool for research. He warns of the reduction of sociological investigation to the cataloguing of "the visual as (differ-ent) experience." Nevertheless, as Thoutenhoofd asserts, visual materi-als can broaden the field of Deaf research as they may be less based on hearing loss to the exclusion of other sensory experience. For example, Sutherland and Young (2013) developed a set of "deaf centered and child centered" data collection tools in a study of deaf children's expe-riences of sign bilingual education. Their visuality played to the per-ceptual strengths of the children while not imposing any assumptions about the kind of language (spoken, signed, or both) deaf children might use in engaging with them.

We argue earlier that people who use sign languages have differ-ent resources at hand to express who they are and that there may be ontological and epistemological consequences to this. However, this does not mean that who we are is determined by the language we use. Moreover, most of the research we discuss earlier involves people who sign and not, for example, those deafened in later life and those who use hearing aids or have cochlear implants and use spoken language only. The role of visual language for these people may not differ from that of hearing narrators.

This limited overview of narrative analysis signals ongoing debate about the status and significance of rhetoric and language in produc-ing narratives. A study of signed language narratives draws atten-tion to the neglected role of the inherent structuring and grammatical resources of particular languages, which of themselves enable narra-tive in ways which other languages and their structures might not. In terms of narrative analysis generally, this feature, while noted, has not been considered in depth, with a few exceptions discussed in the following chapter. Although narrative researchers generally nod in the direction of the significance of the structure of narratives, they rarely take on board such concerns in cross-language narrative research. Research with Deaf people highlights as unavoidable the examination of linguistic resources and structures and provides sig-nificant insights into why such examination involves exploring issues of identity and power in research generally, that is, why performance analysis is needed.

DIFFERENTLY d/DEAF AND NOT JUST DEAF

McCleary's (2003) notes the varied circumstances of deafness, people's varying beliefs, and the resulting "almost infinite number of relations among oral language, written language, and sign language" (p. 106). The focus in this chapter has been on differences in the narratives of people who sign and people who speak/hear. However, there are other influences acting on research with d/Deaf people that have had relatively little attention, partly for strategic reasons around the need to establish recognition for Deaf culture and signed languages. We discuss in Chapter 3 some of the different ways in which researchers have approached identity and interaction. One approach we mention is that of "intersectionality." Parasnis (2012) uses this approach to help understand the ways diversity in Deaf communities creates complex Deaf identities. She suggests that analyses of Deaf culture generally ignore how being Deaf interacts with other identities such as race, ethnicity, gender, or sexuality (see also De Clerck, 2012). She cautions against treating such identities as "separate additive factors" (p. 68) and missing connections and intersections. She advocates the advancement of new political goals that "respect the full complexity of Deaf identity" (p. 69).

The research we discuss in this chapter suggests a complex picture in which researchers have found differences between the narratives of d/Deaf and hearing people for example, in rhythm and spatial characteristics as well as content and performance. However, many of these writers also note the similarities between d/Deaf and hearing narrators and the significance of factors other being deaf, Deaf, or hearing on narrative formation, for example, the age at which children who are deaf are exposed to language (Courtin, 2000; Marschark & Hauser, 2008). They also recognize cultural and social influences not directly connected to being d/Deaf. There is a growing interest in cultural diversity in research with people who are deaf/D, which indicates the layers of complexity around examining culture and its links with language use and structure (De Clerck, 2012; Lucas, 1996; Mather, Rodriguez-Fraticelli, Andrews, & Rodriquez, 2006; Metzger, 2000; Parasnis, 1996, 2012; Zheng & Goldin-Meadow, 2002). Sutton-Spence and Woll (1999) discuss differences in BSL use, for example, documenting differences in the sign language used across generations and differences of dialect.

In an exploratory piece of research on "linguistically isolated" children who are deaf, Van Deusen-Phillips, Goldin-Meadow, and Miller (2001) observed and videotaped interactions between eight children who are deaf and have hearing parents in two cultures, four European-American and four from Taiwan. They describe narratives as "multi-modal performances" and refer to "culturally embedded ways of moving and engaging the body in interaction" (p. 313) which are learned in childhood. They analyze children's narratives in terms of the components developed by Labov and Waletzky (1967), such as complication, and conclude that all the children had invented gesture systems to communicate and their gestured stories were of the same types and structures as those told by hearing children. However, *the narratives were still culturally specific*. They suggest that "these particular messages are so central to the culture as to be instantiated in nonverbal as well as verbal practices" (p. 311). For example, they discuss how each of the Chinese families produced narratives of transgression in which the child was portrayed as having violated a social or moral rule. In contrast, when an American child's misdeed was framed in a story, the message was directed towards maintaining the positive value of the child (p. 329).

Moreover, the narratives of people who have lost their hearing later in life and who do not sign are arguably still underresearched (see also Parasnis, 2012). Morgan-Jones (2001) suggests that this is puzzling, given that the number of people with acquired hearing loss greatly outstrips the numbers who are prelingually deaf. She documents the ways in which hearing loss affects all aspects of life and may cause identity confusion. The lack of research with older people who have lost their hearing mirrors the situation in clinical research, where McMurdo, Witham, and Gillespie (2005) argue that there is serious bias against older people and "a yawning chasm between patients in the real world and patients who participate in clinical studies" (p. 1036).

In this section we draw attention to the importance of linking the fluid, situational, and contextual nature of identity/ies (Chapter 2) with narrative analysis because not everything is about being d/Deaf. We discuss some identity theories presented by social researchers in Chapter 3 and suggest that identities interact so that researchers can no longer use one identity, such as being gay, a woman, or d/Deaf as the single organizing condition for analysis or primary perspective in all cases.

CONCLUDING THOUGHTS

Narratives do not give access to unadulterated experience or truth. Language is the medium used to produce narratives, and in this chapter we present language as a resource and not a neutral tool for the transfer of meaning. We discuss some of the possible ways of analyzing narratives based on Riessman's (2008) framework of content (thematic), structure, and performance. A focus on content has helped to challenge grand narratives which exclude and homogenize d/Deaf populations. A structural analysis can help to deconstruct how these grand narratives have been put together. However, an analysis which includes exploration of the performance nature of narrative enables readers to fully engage with the power dynamics within research narratives.

That is, it involves asking who put the narrative together and for what purpose as well as moving beyond presentation of research as written text. This removes the shield of objectivity from researchers and opens up issues such as: How does the attempt to write down what was signed change the nature of knowledge produced and does it write out Deaf identities? We suggest that changing modality/language within research is not just a technical maneuver but has possible ontological and epistemological significance. Questions of how we write about visual languages and how we represent people when we research across languages and modalities are not minor interests but central to issues of power in the research process.

We argue that narratives produced through signing use different language resources and *may* produce *different knowledge and different realities*. We note in Chapter 3 that "good" research for us involves an explication of a researcher's epistemological position. This implies that narrative analysis needs to include performance aspects. In practice, content, structure, and performance analysis are intertwined in research. Discussing what has been told in narratives often includes how it has been told and by whom. Audiences will take these into account when evaluating narratives. Which kind of analysis researchers choose to use depends on what they are looking to achieve. What they decide to analyze will itself be the subject of debate. For example, we discuss earlier the dangers of assuming different languages have the same structures. Does it matter if a researcher abandons any interest in the structure of a narrative and chooses to present findings in the form of a poem in the target language? How readers view this will depend on whether the abandonment is seen to involve significant loss in how narrators' lives and identities are represented. This is a matter of judgement which cannot be made without knowledge of the researcher's views, that is, his or her positionality and epistemology. Participants' language use and their identity(ies) must also be considered; see Chapter 7.

We finish this chapter with a note of caution. We return briefly to the argument presented in Chapters 2 and 3 about the dangers of essentializing what it means to be d/Deaf and hearing. Much of the research we refer to concerns Deaf people who sign. Many deaf people do not sign, and some signers are not deaf but may be Deaf. Moreover, there is little research on the significance of hearing loss on older deaf people's sense of who they are, for example, or on the experiences of deafblind people. Researchers also need to establish the significance of their own identities on their research as well as those of taking part in research rather than assuming at the outset that any identity always takes precedence over others. Throughout this chapter we point to different aspects of identity, language, and narrative in social research which would benefit from the insights of researchers exploring d/Deaf identities, sign languages, and narratives. However, in relation to the influence of identity on research, there is an abundance of literature on the dangers of building hierarchies of identities; these texts are important to explore and could usefully contribute to these debates. In the following chapter we explore further how d/Deaf people are represented in research and how changes in language and modality are dealt with in practice. We suggest, for example, that choices about how to interpret, transcribe, and translate research are also choices about how to represent d/Deaf identities. We point to the challenges for social researchers interested in cross-language research of taking on board research into transcription, interpretation, and translation of signed languages. We also point to the value of expanding analysis beyond influences other than hearing/d/Deaf.

REFERENCES

Armstrong, D., & Karchmer, M. (2009). William C. Stokoe and the study of signed languages. *Sign Language Studies, 9*(4), 389–397. doi: 10.1353/sls.0.0027

Atherton, M., Russell, D., & Turner, G. H. (2001). *Deaf united: A history of football in the British Deaf Community.* Coleford, UK: Douglas McLean.

Atkinson, P. (2009). Illness narratives revisited: The failure of narrative reductionism. *Sociological Research Online, 14*(5), Article 16, 1–22. doi: 10.5153/sro.2030

Bahan, B. (2006). Face-to-face tradition in the American deaf community: Dynamics of the teller, the tale, and the audience. In H. D. L. Bauman, J. Nelson, & H. Rose (Eds.), *Signing the body poetic: Essays on American Sign Language literature* (pp. 21–50). Berkeley, CA: University of California Press.

Bahan, B. (2008). Upon the formation of a visual variety of the human race. In H. D. L. Bauman (Ed.), *Open your eyes: Deaf studies talking* (pp. 83–99). Minneapolis: University of Minnesota Press.

Bahan, B. (2011). Memoir upon the formation of a visual variety of the human race. Retrieved January 8, 2013, from http://deafspace.files.wordpress.com/2012/03/bahan-2011.pdf

Baker, M. (2005). Narratives in and of translation. *SASE Journal of Translation and Interpretation, 1*, 4–13.

Bamberg, M., & Andrews, M. (Eds.). (2004). *Considering counter-narratives: Narrating, resisting and making sense.* Philadelphia, PA: John Benjamins Publishing Company.

Banks, M. (2008). *Using visual data in qualitative research.* London: Sage.

Benvenuto, A. (2005). Bernard Mottez and the sociology of the deaf. *Sign Language Studies, 6*(1), 4–16. doi: 10.1353/sls.2006.001

Berman, R., & Slobin, D. (1994). *Relating events in narrative: A crosslinguistic developmental study.* Hillsdale, NJ: Lawrence Erlbaum.

Bishop, M., & Hicks, S. (2005). Orange eyes: Bimodal bilingualism in hearing adults from deaf families. *Sign Language Studies, 5*, 188–230.

Burch, M., Jaafar, A., West, T. & Bauer, P. (2008). Autobiographical narratives of deaf and hearing adults: An examination of narrative coherence and the use of internal states. *Memory, 16*, 517–529.

Butler, J. (1990). *Gender trouble: Feminism and the subversion of identity.* New York, NY: Routledge.

Butler, J. (1993). *Bodies that matter: On the discursive limits of "sex."* New York, NY: Routledge.

Carmel, S. (2006). Oral history interview with Simon Carmel. Retrieved January 1, 2013, from http://collections.ushmm.org/search/catalog/irn39659

Christiansen, J., & Barnartt, S. (1995). *Deaf president now! The 1988 revolution at Gallaudet University.* Washington, DC: Gallaudet University Press.

Connell, R. (1995). *Masculinites.* Cambridge, MA: Polity Press.

Courtin, C. (2000). The impact of sign language on the cognitive development of deaf children. *Journal of Deaf Studies and Deaf Education, 5*(3), 266–276. doi: 10.1093/deafed/5.3.266

Cyrus, B., Katz, E., Cheyney, C., & Parsons, F. (2006). *Deaf women's lives: Three self-portraits.* Washington, DC: Gallaudet University Press.

Davis, L. (1995). *Enforcing normalcy: Disability, deafness and the body.* London: Verso.

De Clerck, G. A. (2007). Meeting global deaf peers, visiting ideal deaf places: Deaf ways of education leading to empowerment, an exploratory case study. *American Annals of the Deaf, 152*(1), 5–19. doi: 10.1353/aad.2007.0009

De Clerck, G. (2012). Valuing deaf indigenous knowledge in research through partnership: The Cameroonian deaf community and the challenge of "serious" scholarship. In P. Paul & D. Moores (Eds.), *Deaf epistemologies: Multiple perspectives on the acquisition of knowledge* (pp. 81–104). Washington, DC: Gallaudet University Press.

Deaver, J. (1995). *A maiden's grave.* London: Hodder and Stoughton.

Dodds, J. (2003). Being deaf and proud. In G. Taylor & A. Darby (Eds.), *Deaf identities* (pp. 22–31). Colefield, Gloucestershire, UK: Douglas McLean.

Elliott, J. (2005). *Using narrative in social research: Qualitative and quantitative approaches.* London: Sage Publications.

Emerson, R. M. (Ed.). (1983). *Contemporary field research: A collection of readings.* Boston, MA: Little, Brown & Company.

Emmorey, K., & Falgier, B. (1996). Talking about space within space: Describing environments in ASL. In E. Winston (Ed.), *Storytelling and conversation: Discourses in Deaf communities* (pp. 3–26). Washington, DC: Gallaudet University Press.

Engelund, G. (2006). *Time for hearing: Recognising process for the individual.* PhD thesis, University of Copenhagen, Copenhagen. Retrieved January 1, 2013, from http://www.eriksholm.com/~asset/cache.ashx?id=14933&type=14&format=web

Equality Act (2010). Retrieved March 15, 2013, from http://www.legislation.gov.uk/ukpga/2010/15/contents

Frank, A. (1995). *The wounded storyteller: Body, illness and ethics.* Chicago, IL: The University of Chicago Press.

Goffman, E. (1961). *Encounters: Two studies in the sociology of interaction.* New York, NY: The Bobbs-Merrill Company.

Groce, N. (1985). *Everyone here spoke sign language: Hereditary deafness on Martha's Vineyard.* Cambridge, MA: Harvard University Press.

Gubrium, J., & Holstein, J. (2009). *Analyzing narrative reality.* London: Sage.

Harmon, K. (2007). Writing deaf: Textualizing deaf literature. *Sign Language Studies, 7*(2), 200–207. doi: 10.1353/sls.2007.0002

Harris, M., & Mohay, H. (1997). Learning to look in the right place: A comparison of attentional behavior in deaf children with deaf and hearing mothers. *Journal of Deaf Studies and Deaf Education, 2*(2), 95–103.

Harrison, B. (2002). Photographic visions and narrative inquiry. *Narrative Inquiry, 12,* 87–111. doi: 10.1075/ni.12.1.14har

Hill, A. (2008). Writing the visual (pp. 1–17). Centre for Research on Socio-Cultural Change. Paper Number 51, CRESC, Open University. Retrieved March 17, 2012, from http://www.cresc.ac.uk.

Hole, R. (2007a). Working between languages and cultures: Issues of representation, voice, and authority intensified. *Qualitative Inquiry, 13*(5), 696–710. doi: 10.1177/1077800407301186

Hole, R. (2007b). Narratives of identity: A poststructural analysis of three deaf women's life stories. *Narrative Inquiry, 17*(2), 259–278.

Kittel, C., Kittel, P., & Kittel, R. (2003). Cochlear implant: A family's experience. In G. Taylor & A. Darby (Eds.), *Deaf identities* (pp. 51–66). Coleford, Gloucestershire, UK: Douglas McLean.

Koutsoubou, M., Herman, R., & Woll, B. (2006). Bilingual language profiles of deaf students: An analysis of the written narratives of three deaf writers with different language proficiencies. *Deafness & Education International, 8*(3), 144–168. doi: 10.1002/dei.195

Kuntze, M. (2008). Turning literacy inside out. In H. D. L. Bauman (Ed.), *Open your eyes: Deaf studies talking* (pp. 146–157). Minneapolis: University of Minnesota Press.

Labov, W., & Waletzky, J. (1967). Narrative analysis: Oral versions of personal experience. In J. Helm (Ed.), *Essays on the verbal and visual arts* (pp. 12–44). Seattle, WA: American Ethnological Society/University of Washington Press.

Ladd, P. (2003). *Understanding Deaf culture: In search of Deafhood.* Clevedon, UK: Multilingual Matters.

Lane, H., Hoffmeister, B., & Bahan, B. (1996). *A journey into the Deaf world.* San Diego, CA: Dawn Sign Press.

Law, J. (2009). Seeing like a survey. *Cultural Sociology, 3*(2), 239–256. doi: 10.1177/1749975509105533

Levy, N. (2002). Deafness, culture, and choice. *Journal of Medical Ethics, 28*(5), 284–285.

Lucas, C. (1996). *Multicultural aspects of sociolinguistics in Deaf communities.* Washington, DC: Gallaudet University Press.

Marschark, M., & Hauser, P. C. (2008). Cognitive underpinning of learning by deaf and hard-of-hearing students: Differences, diversity and directions. In M. Marschark & P. C. Hauser (Eds.), *Deaf cognition: Foundations and outcomes* (pp. 3–23). New York, NY: Oxford University Press.

Mather, S., Rodriguez-Fraticelli, Y., Andrews, J., & Rodriquez, J. (2006). Establishing and maintaining sight triangles: Conversations between deaf parents and hearing toddlers in Puerto Rico. In C. Lucas (Ed.), *Multiculturalism and sign languages: From the Great Plains to Australia* (pp. 159–251). Washington, DC: Gallaudet University Press.

Mather, S., & Winston, E. (1998). Spatial mapping and involvement in ASL storytelling. In C. Lucas (Ed.), *Pinky extension and eye gaze: Language use in Deaf communities* (pp. 183–210). Washington, DC: Gallaudet University Press.

Maxwell, M. (1990). Visual-centered narratives of the deaf. *Linguistics and Education, 2*(3), 213–229.

McCleary, L. (2003). Technologies of language and the embodied history of the deaf. *Sign Language Studies, 3*(2), 104–124. doi: 10.1353/sls.2003.0002

McDonald, D. M. (2010). Not silent, invisible: Literature's chance encounters with deaf heroes and heroines. *American Annals of the Deaf, 154*(5), 435–446. doi: 10.1353/aad.0.0114

McDonald, D. M. (2012). Toward an understanding of epistemology and deafness. In P. Paul & D. Moores (Eds.), *Deaf epistemologies: Multiple perspectives on the acquisition of knowledge* (pp. 158–175). Washington, DC: Gallaudet University Press.

McIlroy, G., & Storbeck, C. (2011). Development of Deaf identity: An ethnographic study. *Journal of Deaf Studies and Deaf Education, 16*(4), 494–511. doi: 10.1093/deafed/enr017

McMurdo, M., Witham, M., & Gillespie, N. D. (2005). Including older people in clinical research: Benefits shown in trials in younger people may not apply to older people. *British Medical Journal, 331*, 1036–1037. doi: 10.1136/bmj.331.7524.103

Menary, R. (2008). Embodied narratives. *Journal of Consciousness Studies, 15*(6), 63–84.

Metzger, M. (2000). *Sign language interpreting: Deconstructing the myth of neutrality*. Washington, DC: Gallaudet University Press.

Mitchell, R. E., & Karchmer, M. A. (2004). Chasing the mythical ten percent: Parental hearing status of deaf and hard of hearing students in the United States. *Sign Language Studies, 4*(2), 138–163. doi: 10.1353/sls.2004.0005

Mohay, H. (2000). Language in sight: Mothers' strategies for making language visually accessible. In P. Spencer, C. Erting, & M. Marschark (Eds.), *The deaf child in the family and at school* (pp. 151–166). Mahwah, NJ: Lawrence Erlbaum.

Monikowski, C., & Winston, E. (2003). Interpreters and interpreter education. In M. Marschark & P. Spencer (Eds.), *Oxford handbook of deaf studies, language, and education* (pp. 347–360). New York, NY: Oxford University Press.

Morgan-Jones, R. (2001). *Hearing differently: The impact of hearing impairment on family life*. London: Whurr.

Morgan, G. (1999). Event packaging in British Sign Language discourse. In E. Winston (Ed.), *Storytelling and conversation: Discourses in deaf communities* (pp. 27–58). Washington, DC: Gallaudet University Press.

Nelson, J. (2006). Textual bodies, bodily texts. In H. D. L. Bauman, J. Nelson, & H. Rose (Eds.), *Signing the body poetic: Essays on American Sign Language literature* (pp. 118–129). Berkeley LA : University of California Press.

Ohna, S. (2004). Deaf in my own way: Identity, learning and narratives. *Deafness and Education International, 6*, 1, 20–38.

Oliva, G. (2007). A selection from *Alone in the mainstream: A deaf woman remembers public school. Sign Language Studies, 7*(2), 212–219. doi: 10.1353/sls.2007.0011

Parasnis, I. (1996). *Cultural and language diversity and the deaf experience*. Cambridge, UK: Cambridge University Press.

Parasnis, I. (2012). Diversity and deaf identity: Implications for personal epistemologies in deaf education. In P. Paul & D. Moores (Eds.), *Deaf epistemologies: Multiple perspectives on the acquisition of knowledge* (pp. 63–80). Washington, DC: Gallaudet University Press.

Perniss, P., Thompson, R., & Vigliocco, G. (2010). Iconicity as a general property of language: Evidence from spoken and signed languages. *Frontiers in*

Language Sciences, Psychology, 1(31, December), Art. 227, 1–15. doi: 10.3389/fpsyg.2010.00227

Peters, C. (2000). *Deaf American literature: From carnival to the canon.* Washington, DC: Gallaudet University Press.

Peterson, C., & Slaughter, V. (2006). Telling the story of theory of mind: Deaf and hearing children's narratives and mental state understandings. *British Journal of Developmental Psychlogy, 24*(1), 151–179. doi: 10.1348/026151005X60022

Rathmann, C., Mann, W., & Morgan, G. (2007). Narrative structure and narrative development in deaf children. *Deafness & Education International, 9*(4), 187–196. doi: 10.1002/dei.228

Rayman, J. (1999). Storytelling in the visual mode: A comparison of ASL and English. In E. Winston (Ed.), *Storytelling and conversation: Discourses in deaf communities* (pp. 59–82). Washington, DC: Gallaudet University Press.

Rée, J. (1999). *I see a voice.* London: Harper Collins.

Ricoeur, P. (1988). *Time and narrative,* vol. 3. Chicago: University of Chicago Press.

Riessman, C. (2008). *Narrative methods for the human sciences.* London: Sage Publications.

Riessman, C. K., & Quinney, L. (2005). Narrative in social work: A critical review. *Qualitative Social Work, 4*(4), 391–412. doi: 10.1177/1473325005058643

Roberts, B. (2002). *Biographical research.* Buckingham, UK: Open University Press.

Roberts, B. (2008). Performative social science: A consideration of skills, purpose and context. *Forum: Qualitative Social Research, 9*(2), Art. 58, 1–72.

Rose, H. (2000). *Visual methodologies: An introduction to interpreting visual materials.* London: Sage.

Rose, H. (2006). The poet in the poem in the performance: The relation of body, self, and text in ASL literature. In H. D. L. Bauman, J. Nelson, & H. Rose (Eds.), *Signing the body poetic: Essays on American Sign Language literature* (pp. 130–146). Berkeley, LA: University of California Press.

Rutherford, S. (1993). *A study of American Deaf folklore.* Burtonsville, MD: Linstok Press.

Sacks, O. W. (1989). *Seeing voices: A journey into the deaf world.* Berkeley: University of California Press.

Sheridan, M. (2000). Images of self and others: Stories from the children. In P. Spencer, C. Erting, & M. Marschark (Eds.), *The deaf child in the family and the school: Essays in honor of Kathryn P. Meadow-Orlans* (pp. 5–17). Mahwah, NJ: Lawrence Erlbaum.

Shilling, C. (2003). *The body and social theory.* London: Sage.

Slobin, D. (1996a). From "thought and language" to "thinking for speaking." In J. Gumperz & S. Levinson (Eds.), *Rethinking linguistic relativity* (pp. 70–90). Cambridge, UK: Cambridge University Press.

Slobin, D. (1996b). Two ways to travel: Verbs of motion in English and Spanish. In M. Shibatani & S. Thompson (Eds.), *Grammatical constructions: Their form and meaning* (pp. 195–220). New York, NY: Oxford University Press.

Sparkes, A. (1996). The fatal flaw: A narrative of the fragile body-self. *Qualitative Inquiry, 2*(4), 463–494. doi: 10.1177/107780049600200405

Spencer, P., Erting, C., & Marschark, M. (Eds.). (2000). *The deaf child in the family and the school: Essays in Honor of Kathryn P. Meadow-Orlans.* Mahwah, NJ: Lawrence Erlbaum.

Spradley, J., & Spradley, T. (1979). *Deaf like me.* New York City, NY: Random House.

Stanley, L. (1992). *The auto/biographical I: The theory and practice of feminist auto/biography*. Manchester, UK: Manchester University Press.

Stokoe, W. (2001). *Language in hand: Why sign came before speech*. Washington, DC: Gallaudet University Press.

Stokoe, W. (2005). Visible verbs become spoken. *Sign Language Studies, 5*(2), 152–169. doi: 10.1353/sls.2005.0006

Sutherland, H., & Young, A. (2013). Research with deaf children, not on them: A study of method and process. *Children and Society*, 1–14.

Sutton-Spence, R. (2005). *Analysing sign language poetry*. Basingstoke, Hampshire, UK: Palgrave Macmillan.

Sutton-Spence, R. (2010). The role of sign language narratives in developing identity for deaf children. *Journal of Folklore Research, 47*(3), 265–305.

Sutton-Spence, R., & Napoli, D. J. (2012). Deaf jokes and sign language humour. *International Journal of Humour Research, 3*, 311–338.

Sutton-Spence, R., & Woll, B. (1999). *The linguistics of British Sign Language: An introduction*. Cambridge, UK: Cambridge University Press.

Temple, B. (1999). *Household strategies and types: The construction of social phenomena*. PhD thesis, University of Manchester, Manchester, UK.

Temple, B. (2005). Nice and tidy: Translation and representation. *Sociological Research Online, 10*(2), 1–19. http://www.socresonline.org.uk/10/2/temple.html

Thoutenhoofd, E. (1998). Method in a photographic enquiry of being deaf. *Sociological Research Online, 3*(2), 1–18. http://www.socresonline.org.uk/3/2/2.htm

Valentine, G. (2001). *Social geographies: Space and society*. London: Prentice Hall.

Van Beijsterveldt, L., & Van Hell, J. (2009). Evaluative expression in deaf children's written narratives. *International Journal of Language & Communication Disorders, 44*(5), 675–692. doi: 10.1080/13682820802301498

Van Deusen-Phillips, S., Goldin-Meadow, S., & Miller, P. (2001). Enacting stories, seeing worlds: Similarities and differences in the cross-cultural narrative development of linguistically isolated deaf children. *Human Development, 44*(6), 311–336. doi: 10.1159/000046153

West, D. (2011). Deaf-hearing family life: Three mothers' poetic voices of resistance. *Qualitative Inquiry, 17*, 732–740. doi: 10.1177/1077800411420974

West, D. (2012). *Signs of hope: Deaf/hearing family life*. Cambridge, UK: Cambridge Scholars Publishing.

West, P. (1990). The status and validity of accounts obtained at interview: A contrast between two studies of families with a disabled child. *Social Science & Medicine, 30*, 1229–1239. doi: 10.1016/0277-9536(90)90263-R

Wang, Y. (2012). Educators without borders: A metaparadigm for literacy instruction in bilingual-bicultural education. In P. Paul & D. Moores (Eds.), *Deaf epistemologies: Multiple perspectives on the acquisition of knowledge* (pp. 199–217). Washington, DC: Gallaudet University Press.

Wright, D. (1969). *Deafness a personal account*. London: Allen Lane.

Young, A., & Greally, A. (2003). Parenting and deaf children—report of the needs assessment study London: National Deaf Children's Society.

Young, A., & Tattersall, H. (2007). Universal newborn hearing screening and early identification of deafness: Parents' responses to knowing early and their expectations of child communication development. *Journal of Deaf Studies and Deaf Education, 12*(2), 209–220. doi: 10.1093/deafed/en1033

Young, I. (2005). *On female body experience: "Throwing like a girl" and other essays.* New York, NY: Oxford University Press.

Zheng, M., & Goldin-Meadow, S. (2002). Thought before language: How deaf and hearing children express motion events across cultures. *Cognition, 85,* 145–175.

7

Interpretation, Transcription, and Translation: Representation in Research

Interpreting without a thorough grounding and appreciation of the cultural implications is like trying to hang pictures in a house without walls. Without building a cultural framework that holds the house together, the pictures—words and signs—will crash to the floor.

—*Mindess*, 2006, p. 16

Interpretation, transcription, and translation are everyday practices in social research. Interpretation enables communication generated in one language to be conveyed in another; transcription allows us to shift between modalities such as the spoken to the written for another purpose, for example, data analysis; translation ensures that knowledge and understanding are equally salient in one context as another. Yet to present the trio of interpretation, transcription, and translation in this way is largely to miss the point. They are not just tools at the disposal of researchers to be deployed to ensure valid data capture, analysis, and dissemination. They are *processes* which mediate how we as researchers use language to represent others. Moreover, as will become evident when reading the chapter, defining and demarcating the terms themselves is not straightforward. The choices and decisions we make, connected with interpretation, transcription, and translation, are epistemological ones because fundamentally they mediate what is known, how it is known, and who is seen to tell.

We propose that by focusing on the trio specifically within research which involves d/Deaf people, we are able to explore avenues and implications more easily because of specific conditions associated with this field of research. We begin with a discussion which locates the practices of interpretation, transcription, and translation within an epistemological framework before considering the argument that all three involve situating language as cultural praxis; that is, they are all ethnographic enterprises.

Having established this broader field, we turn to how debates about interpretation, transcription, and translation intersect with those concerning research with d/Deaf people. In particular, we address issues of modality shift that routinely occur in studies involving sign language.

We examine whether and how the bilingual and/or bicultural biographies of researchers and participants influence the generation of data and the acquisition of knowledge. We question how interpretation, transcription, and translation, of themselves, can construct and extinguish some readings of reality. Through these debates we argue for the centrality of the reflexive researcher in all aspects of the research process, including how the researcher wields the tools of interpretation, transcription, and translation.

EPISTEMOLOGY AND LANGUAGE WITHIN RESEARCH

Researchers treat language within research in a variety of ways, ranging from a complete indifference to how language can shape a research narrative, as in the case of Barak and Sadovsky (2008), to recognition of its central position in adopting a reflexive view of the research process, as in the work of Jones and Boyle (2011). Researchers using positivist epistemologies (see Chapter 3) treat language as a neutral medium through which meaning can be conveyed without problem across languages. Those who do not reflect on their approach to moving across languages are implicitly, if unintentionally, working within these epistemologies. Typical assumptions include "accurate" interpretation possible only by professional interpreters, "verbatim" transcription, and "correct" translation using back translation. These are often presented as evidence to support the validity of work because care has been taken to get these issues of language right. But there is no right (in the singular).

For example, what is verbatim transcription? Every word, or also the pauses and hesitations an interviewee might make and the style of delivery she or he adopts? Is body language to be noted in spoken interviews, and how are signs to be conveyed in writing? What about humor or irony? Treating transcription solely as it relates to lexical content is not enough to be able to compile the one correct representation. In relation to translation, "back translation" involves taking the translated version in the target language and translating back into the source language until the two versions are judged to be equivalent (Brislin, 1970). However as Rogers, Young, Evans, and Lovell (2013) argue, a presumed literal forward translation may show equivalence of meaning when translated back into the source language but still may be a very poor translation in terms of cultural equivalence. They use an example provided by El-Rufaie and Absood (1987) of the translation and back translation from English to Arabic of the phrase "butterflies in the stomach" from the Hospital Anxiety and Depression Scale. Once the translation was empirically tested, it was found that there is no equivalent phrase in Arabic or for the terms "anxiety" or "depression." Back translation cannot provide the "correct" solution to equivalence, only possibilities for consideration and testing.

Researchers who adopt epistemologies other than those concerned with trying objectively to capture reality view language as helping to create as well as to describe social worlds. For example, Wierzbicka (1997) looks at cultures through their keywords and shows close links between the life of a culture and the lexicon of the language. She notes that words for particular foods can tell you something about the eating habits of a culture. It matters which words and concepts are used and that they may have different meanings. She describes the differences in possible meanings of words for friendship and freedom, for example, in different languages. In a similar way, Ladd (2000) asks why cultures privilege particular concepts. He gives the example of British Sign Language (BSL), which has a sign for "mind your own business" that appears to lack American Sign Language (ASL) equivalents and has to be conveyed by several signs. Looking at ASL and English, Rayman (1999) uses the work of Slobin (1996a, 1996b) and Berman and Slobin (1994) to argue that language provides a range of resources but does not determine or limit thought. She suggests, in her comparison of ASL and English storytelling, that "encoding events into language is filtered through the perspective chosen and the linguistic resources available within a particular language" (p. 60). She goes on to argue that linguistic resources do not determine thought but that they do shape how we think and live through language (Cooper, 2012).

These examples illustrate well how language use is something to be understood *contextually*. This is a very different perspective from a search for a correct interpretation, transcription, or translation. It requires the researcher to adopt a reflexive stance toward language and how it is manipulated. Referring to the wider use of the term "interpretation" to refer to how researchers explain meaning, Alvesson and Skoldberg (2009) define *reflexive interpretation* as "a demand for reflection in research in conjunction with an interpretation at several levels: contact with the empirical material, awareness of the interpretative act, clarification of political-ideological contexts, and the handling of the question of representation and authority" (2009, p. 263). We suggest that reflexive research which considers language is of necessity ethnographic because ethnography, while consisting of many diverse approaches, is nonetheless "grounded in a commitment to firsthand experience and exploration of a particular social and cultural setting on the basis of (though not exclusively) participant observation" (Atkinson, Coffey, Delamont, Lofland, & Lofland, 2001, p. 4). In particular, the concept of "linguistic ethnography" (Creese, 2008; Leung, Harris, & Rampton, 1997) recognizes that we cannot understand the way language is used without situating it within its context.

It matters therefore who uses what kind of language, to whom. Language can be endlessly modified, manipulated, played with, and hidden for a host of deliberate and nondeliberate purposes. Jepson

(1991a, 1991b), using the work of Hymes (1974), argues that language must be studied in its social context and function and that "the divorce of language structure from language use enables linguistics to build models of grammar but not of language" (Jepson, 1991b, p. 37). Based on fieldwork in India which involved observation and interviews, she compares Indian urban and rural sign language and shows how both enable efficient communication but have developed differently in response to different environments.

An ethnographic approach to language use extends beyond an interest in the social, economic, historic, and cultural worlds of participants. It encompasses the effects of the material, including the technological environment. Researchers working with d/Deaf people have long recognized the significance of their physical surroundings for communication. The layout of a room may influence how well people can communicate visually in that they need to see each other. The material composition of a room can increase the accessibility of spoken communication depending on whether surfaces absorb or reverberate sound. For example, using the work of sociolinguists, Mather's (2005) research establishes the significance of the interpreter's physical location for students who are "deaf" (not defined) in that it can affect their ability to participate in classroom activity or answer questions posed by teachers. She gives as an example the benefits reported by a student when the interpreter is moved to the side of the classroom in a group discussion and the student's chair turned to face the entire class so that she could see who was talking, who the next speaker was, and whom the speaker was addressing (and see Balch & Mertens, 1999; Jones & Boyle, 2011; Kroll, Barbour, & Harris, 2007; Mindess, 2006 for other examples).

The significance of "practicalities" such as the positioning of chairs or the use of technological aids stretches beyond the ability of participants to communicate with each other and with the researcher. We note in Chapter 8 that new technologies help to challenge what counts as data and knowledge, and we argue here that they change the nature of the ethnographic project. Noting the influences of technological developments, Thoutenhoofd (2007) suggests that a "digital humanities ethnography" is beneficial for the study of sign language corpora (see also Tchalaov, 2004). He defines this as "the inclusive study of dynamic interaction between people, their heritage, institutions, and new technology" (see also Chapter 8). This approach resonates with social researchers who use Actor Network Theory (ANT), where the links between social and material worlds, not just technology, and identities have long been a central concern (Carter, Jordan, & Watson, 2008; Du Gay, 2008; Redman, 2008; and for a critique and alternative framework, see Thoutenhoofd, 2007).

Proponents of ANT argue that social worlds are not only constructed through human actions and meaning but that they are "the outcome of various mechanisms by which, not only people, but also people and things are connected or assembled into specific relations or networks that are multiple and persist over time" (Redman, 2008, p. 12). For example, the term "couch potato" is used to describe someone who gets little exercise and spends most of her or his time sitting, usually watching TV. The couch and the TV in this instance help to make the person who she or he is.

However, most social researchers view the physical surroundings and material objects used to produce findings as mere backdrops to research to make participants feel comfortable and to enable them to communicate. What are usually seen as "practicalities" in research may have both epistemological and ontological significance; that is, they may affect the kind and quality of data that can be produced, how researchers and participants present themselves, and how they interact. "Practical" arrangements and material objects are fundamental to *participation* in knowledge production and, in a quite literal way, to use of language within that process.

THE LANGUAGE BIOGRAPHIES OF RESEARCHERS AND RESEARCH PARTICIPANTS

In the previous section we put forward our position that reflexivity in research entails an exploration of language and that this is by definition an ethnographic endeavor. We suggest here that part of this reflexivity includes the need to ask *who* is going to do the research, *what* her or his language affiliations and experiences are, and *how* this affects the research process.

Both within social research generally and research with d/Deaf people specifically, whether researcher and participants have adequate language to communicate with each other is often as far as any exploration of language goes. Yet researchers who work across languages have complex decisions to make about whether to use their own bilingual/ multilingual skills or employ interpreters and translators and whether participants understand concepts in the same way as researchers. They have to decide who is going to carry out the research and the extent to which they will be involved at different stages, be it data collection, data analysis, or dissemination of findings to varied audiences. Decisions made about the extent of involvement and by whom have consequences for the kind of findings produced in studies. We address many of these in the following sections on interpretation, transcription, and translation. At this stage, by way of introduction, we introduce some preliminary considerations about researchers' language biographies. We also note the significance of taking on board possibly different understandings by participants resulting from different language biographies.

Being able to speak, read, or sign does not automatically make you an insider among those who do likewise (see Chapter 3). Rampton (2003) points out that we should "inspect each 'native speaker's' credentials" and "not assume that nationality and ethnicity are the same as language ability and language allegiance" (2003, p. 111). Some sociolinguists and sociologists argue that we should consider issues such as language expertise, perceived language prestige and authority, the context of language acquisition, the age of acquisition of languages, language inheritance, and language affiliation as people experience and use languages differently (Edwards, Alexander, & Temple, 2006; Leung, Harris, & Rampton, 1997; Pavlenko, 2005, 2006; Temple, 2006). Bilingual researchers may view themselves and others through different and multiple language lenses, which vary according to their different experiences.

Just as we have emphasized throughout the book that there are many ways to be d/Deaf, there are also many ways in which to be d/Deaf and bilingual, including across modalities. Deaf bilingual people may be bilingual in that they can sign and read and write English but not speak it; use voice, sign, and read and write English; be bilingual in multiple signed languages (ASL and BSL, for example); and so forth. The case of CODAs (Children of Deaf Adults) exemplifies some of the complexities of language biographies.

Bishop and Hicks (2005) argue that "Codas" (here defined as hearing people with parents who are Deaf and who were raised in the Deaf community regardless of whether they have an affiliation with the CODA organization) find it difficult to separate their Deaf identity from ASL and their hearing identity from English, and they may produce a third language system. They discuss code blending in which aspects of both a signed and a spoken language are combined as well as code switching, which involves moving back and forth between sign language and English. They show how bimodal/bilingual Codas have an additional dimension to their bilingualism in that they can blend modalities.

Their study (Bishop & Hicks, 2005) analyzes e-mails taken from a forum on the Internet for hearing people with Deaf parents. They note that unlike single modality bilinguals, a bimodal bilingual does not have to stop one language before beginning another and that this expands the field of bilingualism and the role of code blending as a cultural identifier. They identify "a strong tendency to use English to 'describe' an ASL sign" (p. 188). For example, the phrase "My father fork-in-throat" in the context they were analyzing means "stuck." What is of interest is that the Coda chose to use a visual description of a sign instead of the lexical equivalent in English. They argue for a separate identity called "Coda" and state that Codas "bring their own 'aural imprints,' visual memories, and childhood experiences to their languages" (p. 221). This suggests that their narratives may be concerned with different themes and structured differently (and see Chapter 6 for discussion of the possible significance of different language structures).

Discussing the psycholinguistics and neurolinguistics of bilingualism, Grosjean (1996) notes that a bilingual person is not two monolinguals in one but "a unique speaker-hearer" (p. 25) using languages according to context. He describes (1996, 2008, 2010) the similarities and differences between Deaf bilinguals and hearing bilinguals. Bilingualism in Deaf communities, he notes, is a form of minority language bilingualism in which people acquire and use both the minority language (sign language) and the majority language in its written and sometimes spoken or signed form. He discusses similarities between Deaf and hearing bilinguals: Both are very diverse; they often do not judge themselves to be bilingual; they use their languages for different purposes, in different domains of life, with different people and may code switch between languages. However, he notes that there are differences between them: There has been little recognition until recently of Deaf people's bilingual status; Deaf bilinguals will remain so throughout their lives; the use of majority language skills may never be fully acquired by some Deaf people; Deaf bilinguals rarely find themselves at the monolingual signing end of the language mode continuum; patterns of language knowledge and use appear to differ and may be more complex for Deaf bilinguals than for spoken language bilinguals.

Grosjean (2010) also points to evidence that bilingual speakers who are fluent in a sign language and a spoken language rarely code switch, that is, stop talking and switch to signing (Hauser, 2000). Most code blend, that is, they produce signs simultaneously with English words. Hakuta and Feldman Mostafapour (1996) note that one of the most obvious differences between oral and Deaf bilinguals is that there is no written counterpart for signed languages (we return to this later).

This chapter begins with a reference to the significance of cultural competence. Grosjean (2008) stresses that bilingual Deaf people are also bicultural and points to the lack of coextensiveness between bilingualism and biculturalism. He argues that what really matters is communicative competence rather than grammatical competence. Bilingual people can identify with either culture or with both. He argues that they may not be equally proficient in both their languages in all domains of their life. For example, bilingual researchers may be able to communicate adequately in a spoken or signed language in everyday conversation but may not be proficient enough to be able to express themselves in other domains such as academic life. Equally participants may be bilingual in some areas but struggle more in others.

Much linguistic research, Grosjean (2008) argues, treats bilingual people as if they are the sum of two monolingual people rather than individuals who have unique linguistic competences. Grosjean draws out the implications for research when he notes that the kind of bilingualism used is important in sampling and in understanding results. Bilingual people are "speaker-hearers" in their own right and will not give the same results as monolinguals. In any research involving bilinguals there will be differences. For example, some will be dominant in one language and some in another; some will be fluent in spoken/signed languages, some in written languages. The ways in which people are bilingual will affect how they express themselves in research. Grosjean's research explores *research participants'* bilingual status. It is rare to take on board the nature of the bilingual status of researchers themselves in social research; it is also rare to do so with respect to research participants. As we note earlier, the assumption is often made that participants can be included in research if they speak or sign any language "well enough."

The point we are making is that domain-specific competence may impact on the kind of data produced. This point has relevance in research: Researchers who include people in their sample or assume that they themselves can speak or sign "well enough" just because they can use a language are implying that understanding comes merely from the act of communicating at any level (see Chapter 5, Populations and Sampling). We are also making another point which has been well rehearsed in literature concerned with doing research with Deaf people. Grosjean's body of work suggests that being able to communicate is not the same as being *culturally competent*. Selecting bilingual researchers according to level of perceived sign language competence is not enough. We return to this later in our discussion of the significance of community ties.

However, as Parasnis (2012) points out, Grosjean's work "only addresses peripherally the sociocultural issues related to power and oppression" (p. 70) for Deaf people from racial/ethnic minorities who are bilingual/bicultural. The issue of who is chosen to do research is one involving power relationships between people, modalities, and languages (Temple & Young, 2004). We discuss in Chapter 6 the argument that the act of writing literally writes out (excludes) the identity of Deaf people who use sign languages and we present the arguments around insider/outsider research in Chapter 3. Representing others is always a political act in which language is used to construct self and other (for example, Alcoff, 1991; Blommaert, 2001). In relation to sign languages, issues of power have been well documented (Bishop & Hicks, 2005; Keating & Mirus, 2003; McCleary, 2003; Temple & Young, 2004). The lack of recognition of signed languages as distinctive languages, the predominance within academia of written accounts, and the assumption that sign languages are just spoken languages signed are some of the factors that result in power asymmetries.

For example, Keating and Mirus (2003) describe their research in Texas using observations and video recordings of school children who are "deaf" and hearing and remind us that sign and voice are different modalities but that they are also different bases of power and authority in societies. In this study the authors note that they use "small 'deaf'" (p. 132) because they are discussing deaf children of hearing parents who are not yet culturally Deaf. They show how children who are deaf are skilled in using a variety of resources to communicate with hearing children but that hearing children interpret deaf children's participation in the hearing world "not as extraskillful, but as not fully competent and hearing children do not exploit their own visual resources to advantage" (2003, p. 118). They point out that communication between children who are deaf and children who can hear is influenced by different abilities to see and hear the other's language. However, it is also affected by interactional or sociolinguistic practices specific to each modality. Factors particular to communicating across these two modalities influence these children's lack of successful interactions with each other. Eye gaze, visual monitoring, scanning, turn-taking, and listening behavior are resources used differently in the two modalities (2003, p. 130).

We are arguing that the different ways in which it is possible to be bilingual mean that language proficiency does not necessarily make a researcher an "insider" in terms of culture. How bilinguals use language within research will vary, as will how they relate to communities they are working with and how those communities respond to them. We also note here that there is no automatic preference by participants for language "insiders" (see later) and that the knowledge produced by them, or by anyone else, is not epistemologically privileged (see Chapter 3). We now move on to discuss issues of representation within interpretation, transcription, and translation; that is, how do researchers portray others in these processes?

INTERPRETATION

In studies involving Deaf sign language users, where the field has been and continues to be dominated by hearing people who are not native sign language users, interpreters have taken center stage in research production. Typically the researcher with little or no sign language competence is put in a position where she or he relies on an interpreter to facilitate communication in data collection, for example, in conducting an interview, a focus group, an experiment, or an observation. The significance of the interpreter in the conduct of research and the construction of research knowledge is the topic to which we now turn.

It is common for researchers who do not sign to treat the role of an interpreter as unproblematic. A largely conduit model of interpreting is employed based on the view that language carries messages in a neutral way and interpreters only need to find the one correct version of a statement in another language (Mindess, 2006). The presence of an interpreter can mean that researchers cease to consider a whole raft of influences on a study that might emanate from themselves as well as from working with an interpreter, their views on language, and assumed relationships between language and methodology.

For example, in an article making recommendations on how to carry out focus groups with d/Deaf people, the necessity of a board-certified ASL interpreter is mentioned for those who are sign language users (Greenabaum, 2000). However, in so doing the author implicitly assumes that the researcher must be a hearing person who does not sign and will need such an interpreter. A Deaf researcher would not, but that circumstance is not considered. A recommendation presented as good practice embodies an assumed norm which reinforces a power differential, be it implicitly, between who carries out research on whom.

The status of participants as producers of knowledge can also be affected through research when an interpreter enters the scene. In a study designed to improve a questionnaire on sexual behavior and HIV/AIDS in Brazil, focus groups were carried out with Deaf and hearing young people (Bisol, Sperb, & Moreno-Black, 2008). In the direct quotations used in the reporting of the data, those taken from the Deaf groups feature the "investigator" and the "interpreter." In those taken from the hearing groups, they feature the "investigator" and "participant," variously identified as participant 1, 2, or 3. No comment is made about this difference in which both the presence and the individuality of Deaf people who took part disappears behind the identity of those who interpreted. The hearing participants remain identified individuals, not a represented group. Also at no point do the authors comment on their own status, presuming that the reader will understand that they are hearing because an interpreter was used when they facilitated groups with Deaf people. Finally, no comment is made on the potential differences between hearing groups of participants commenting on the wording of a questionnaire in a language they share, and Deaf groups commenting on the wording of a questionnaire which they only access through an interpreted version of each question. The responses of both groups are treated as of equivalent saliency.

Another example of the lack of engagement with interpretation as process is Barak and Sadovsky's (2008) comparison of the influence of the Internet on the sense of well-being of both d/Deaf and hearing people using questionnaires in schools in Israel. They argue that it is only in cyberspace that people who are d/Deaf (in their terms hearing impaired) can avoid being identified as handicapped and "quickly feel similar to normal people" (p. 1803). In reaching this conclusion, they comment, almost as an aside, that a few participants did not understand specific terms in the questionnaire "and these were communicated to them in sign language" using an interpreter (p. 1087). The interpreter's presence is seen as solving any problems that arise in data collection. They do not examine the implications for their conclusions of having to use an interpreter for participants whose first or preferred language is not a written/spoken one. The difference disappears. They subsume all of the sample under the term "hearing impaired," which implies not hearing and having, as they put it, "voice communication difficulties— such as stuttering or muteness" (p. 1803). The links between epistemology (there is one view of well-being based on hearing perspectives), ontology (people who are d/Deaf experience the world in terms of lack of hearing, are not normal, and can only approach being normal when in cyberspace), and methodology (questionnaires that have not been built on any investigation of the views of people who are deaf or Deaf) are obvious. As Leigh (2009) argues, technology offers the ability to control presentations of who we are. However, this does not entail Deaf people basing their self-worth on standards of what is "normal" for hearing people.

These kind of built-in assumptions display a lack of awareness of possible language difference which can have serious epistemological consequences because of how they privilege one kind of knowing over another. The implications of using one language as the baseline for other languages is acknowledged within social research across spoken languages, and numerous researchers have critiqued this process (Blommaert, 2001; Temple, 2005; Venuti, 1998).

In introducing an interpreter within research processes, there are, therefore, difficulties when it is assumed that the presence of an interpreter is enough to ensure understanding. The lack of any indication of *who* an interpreter might be is problematic. By "who," we mean such issues as their language affiliation and the range of considerations we discuss earlier about the different ways in which it is possible to be bilingual; whether they are trained in research methods and concepts; their connections with communities of Deaf people; and other possible considerations such as gender, class, and ethnicity. Social researchers have shown how issues of identity, contextual knowledge, and social location influence how interpreters work (Sheppard, 2011; Temple, 2006).

Jones and Boyle (2011) argue that cultural competence in a Deaf community would include an understanding of the controversies surrounding deafness as a physical disability or a unique culture. They go on to suggest that in planning a study with the Deaf community, researchers should be cautious in selecting a translator with a cochlear implant. However, as we have argued in Chapters 2, 3, and 6, there are dangers in assuming that one social characteristic always takes precedence in someone's life whether in terms of her or his identity or in how others might represent it.

Mindess (2006) provides some evidence that Deaf people value the "humanness" of interpreters most and that the term "PROFESSIONAL" in the Deaf world may have negative elitist connotations. They note the significance of "good attitude" and "humanness" with values such as sensitivity to cultural norms, rapport, and honesty about interpreting skills. Social researchers have also questioned presumptions about what people who need interpreters want and argue, for example, that trust rather than professional qualifications may sometimes be valued more highly (Alexander et al., 2004; Edwards et al., 2006).

In citing this work, our intention is to challenge any taxonomy of appropriate interpreter characteristics that omits the views of people who need to use them. It is also to point out the likely influence of the *social identities* of the interpreter on the research: Participants may be prepared to talk about different issues according to how they perceive interpreters, not just how they might perceive researchers. Furthermore, the perception of interpreters is not confined to a perception of their linguistic competence.

Who the interpreter is, her or his characteristics, skills, knowledge, experience, and identity/identities are of particular importance if interpreting is understood in terms of a "communicator facilitator model" (Mindess, 2006). In this model interpreters manage and negotiate communication as bicultural mediators (see also Napier, 2002; Roy, 2000). Therefore, one of the major challenges they face is not in finding equivalent words and phrases but in presenting them in a familiar structure and form. This model is closer to the view of language in terms of ethnographic encounters we discussed at the start of the chapter. It is based on epistemologies such as social constructionism which challenge the possibility of a single truth about social reality (see Chapter 3). It also acknowledges that identity/ies are performed within social interactions. Consequently, the interpreter is charged with making sense and conveying those performances, not simply the content of what someone might have communicated.

In this respect, many researchers working with people who use sign languages cite Wadensjö's (1998) *Interpreting as interaction* (Metzger, 1999, 2000; Metzger, Fleetwood, & Collins, 2004; Napier, 2002; Napier & Barker, 2004). She notes Goffman's (1961) valuable insight that people can display different social identities by their appearance and language use, for example, by their use of dialect. She argues that:

> In conversations, an individual's social identities are brought to the fore in different proportions as interaction progresses. In Goffman's terms, co-interlocuters understand each other as *multiple-role-performers* rather than as persons with one single all-dominating identity. (1998, p. 82, emphasis original)

If we understand an interpreter's role within a research process as encompassing the co-construction of knowledge, then the need to interrogate the choice of interpreter and investigate how she or he works within a study becomes clear. It is a far cry from the research we discuss earlier which regards the interpreter's presence as a self-evident functional necessity.

Social researchers have approached the issue of how to investigate the influence of the interpreter in different ways (for example, Edwards, 1998; Temple, 2002). They aim to explore the influence of all involved in research, including participants, researchers, and interpreters and translators if they are needed. They explore language ties, skills, and affiliations and their impact on findings. Adopting an epistemology such as social constructionism means acknowledging the possibility that different researchers may elicit different narratives from participants and may themselves produce different research narratives. Such approaches also often involve training researchers in the aims of the research and on the research methods used as well as de-briefing sessions during research and after its completion so that they can engage in debate about the research process, including concept choice when interviewing, for example, and decisions about how to interpret, transcribe, and translate. They also often transcribe/translate in ways that show where there were choices to be made about how to present what was said in interviews. We return to this later in our discussion of translation.

TRANSCRIPTION OF RESEARCH DATA

Many researchers who use qualitative methods use transcription as a means of transforming data into a more manageable medium for purposes of data analysis. Typically this involves a shift from the verbal to the written. Spoken interviews that have been recorded become fixed in print so that they can more easily be studied and considered. Many approaches to qualitative inquiry require the immersion of the researcher in the data (Alvesson & Skoldberg, 2009) and while theoretically this can be achieved through listening again or watching again (see later), more commonly it is achieved through reading and re-reading. There are standard conventions, used by conversation analysts and others in social research, for writing down spoken words. Sometimes researchers use these conventions to note pauses, for example, which may denote hesitation (Riessman, 2008). Other researchers use their own methods to mark factors that are not easily transferable to written texts but which may be important in understanding the interview, for example, silence, laughter, or irony. The written text is amenable to segmentation and rearrangement into thematic categories or close structural analysis (see Chapter 6 on narrative). Elements from one interview are easily combined with another and new and varied connections made between what has been said by many.

When writing down what participants have said, researchers make decisions that can influence meaning, for example, about where sentences begin and end, or how to transcribe half-finished sentences or hesitations. It is impossible for researchers literally to write down "verbatim" what participants have said in interviews (Ross, 2010). However, few researchers discuss how they transcribe in their research, present authors included. In research with d/Deaf people, Wheeler, Archbold, and Gregory (2007), for example, video record and transcribe "verbatim" interviews with young people who have had cochlear implants. Arndt (2010) explains that she transcribed interviews with people who are Deafblind. None of these authors investigate their own transcription processes nor consider the effects of having transcribed on the construction of the knowledge they produce.

There are various conventions for transcribing signed utterances which have derived largely from the work of linguists and sociolinguists interested in the study of signed languages. Sutton-Spence and Woll (1999) provide an example of a widely used process for representing signs on paper. Although they do not use the term "transcription" themselves, they provide a good example of a technique used by many researchers working with Deaf populations: glossing. They use glossing to describe BSL signs. They define the gloss of a sign as writing its meaning using an English word or words, but they point out that when using a gloss "we are referring to the BSL sign and not to the English word used to write it down" (p. xi). Glosses are usually written in capital letters. Sutton-Spence and Woll (1999) also describe different ways of noting face and hand movements and handshapes (see also Hole, 2007a; Metzger et al., 2004; Montoya et al., 2004; Napier & Barker, 2004, for further discussion of the complexities of transcribing signs).

There are, however, problems in attempting to represent signed utterances in two-dimensional space (on paper) when in reality they occur in four dimensions (see Chapter 2). Some researchers have used conventions which, while retaining a gloss, also indicate some of the qualitative features of the "way" something is signed which cannot easily be read from "what" was signed as represented on paper. For example, Metzger et al. (2004) use a musical score format in order to maintain the temporal relationship between participants' utterances. It is interesting, because it uses space, be it two-dimensional space, to echo the spatial relationships between sign language users which are vital to conversational flow between people (both literally and figuratively). In their structure, the interpreter receives two lines within the score of the transcript to allow for overlapping utterances. Stone and West (2012) use sub- and superscript markings to the same end (although they define this as translation).

This kind of convention, while related to the points made by Poland (2003) and others about embellishing spoken language transcripts with additional information, is significantly different. The additional features usually marked are ones intrinsic to the grammatical structure of the signed language. How something might be signed conveys of itself layers of deliberately intended meaning which occur simultaneously. For example, the shape of the window, how high up in a building, the position of the people in the room and the intensity of a movement might all overlay an utterance glossed as "WINDOW. MAN RAN, JUMPED. FIVE PEOPLE WATACHED, SURPRISED."

But do researchers really have to transcribe? This is a question not just about signed languages; it is also a question increasingly asked in qualitative research studies more generally. Wainwright and Russell's (2010) short, thought-provoking article explores "audio-coding," that is, coding audio data directly using a software package such as NVivo 6. The stage of transcription is bypassed because the software enables the sound bites to be rearranged under specific thematic codes in the same way as written data segments might be rearranged from transcribed data. The audio themes can then be listened to in this synchronic configuration, not just in the diachronic structure of the original.

Wainwright and Russell (2010) argue that audio coding, without the stage of transcription, enables the researcher to "think analytically about the data while being immersed in the flow of the recorded interview, attending to utterances, silences, emotions and the interactive dialectic between interviewer and interviewee in ways that are difficult when reading even detailed transcripts" (p. 3). They call for more critical reflection on the centrality of transcripts and the relationship between mode of engagement with data and analytical thought about them. What we read differs from thinking critically and analytically about what we hear.

Advances in sort and retrieve software used for the coding and analysis of qualitative data is now permitting the same kind of one-step coding, without shift in modality, to be used for signed data. Video recorded interviews can be directly uploaded to software packages such as the latest versions of QSR NVivo watched repeatedly in the same way as audio data might be listened to again, and thematic codes applied. Segments of video data pertaining to a code can literally be moved into a different place to be watched alongside other segments which have been coded under the same theme (Belk, 2013; Raistrick, 2013). The segments retain their digital marker for their place within the original interviews and can be easily tracked back to context and rearranged infinitely. Stone (2009) adapted iMovie™ and its thumbnail facility for similar purposes. However, it has been suggested that watching data can take more of a physical toll than listening to data, and early adopters of this software solution suggest that it should be approached with care (Raistrick, 2013). The reader is also cautioned at this point that coding is only one way of analyzing data (see Chapter 6).

Apart from the technical possibilities of being able to avoid transcribing, there are issues to consider in using the term in relation to signed languages. Transcription generally refers to a change in modality, that is, writing down what has been said in the original language. Historically, transcription has been a problem in studies where data have been collected in sign language (Temple & Young, 2004). To transcribe, to fix in a written form, has implicitly involved movement from a signed to a *different* written *language*, although this is not routinely acknowledged. The change in modality is accompanied by a change in language, something that is usually defined as translation and not transcription. There are plenty of examples of researchers who report having collected data in a signed language then write that it was subsequently transcribed.

Some of the issues in transcription and translation, as well as interpretation, overlap, for example, the influence of social/political contexts, the impossibility of neutrality, and the significance of the way research participants are represented. However, the issues for researchers are not identical in interpretation, transcription, and translation (see Cokely, 1992; Metzger, 2000; Metzger, Collins, Dively, & Shaw, 2003 and also Chapter 3 on whether modality matters in research). In some cases, the imperative to make the data manageable by writing it down ("transcription") is regarded as so self-evident that the act of "translation," that is, exploring equivalence across language, which has been required to achieve this end, is not even mentioned. Although the data may now be decoupled from its original language, this is seen as of less importance than the capturing of the semantic content of what is "said".

However, as remarked earlier, to regard language as decontextual and transcription/translation as unproblematic, changes fundamentally the conditions of knowledge production. Within interpretive and constructionist epistemologies it matters how something is said, in which context, and using which choice of language. Language constructs, not just reflects reality.

Written texts are a powerful medium (Grosjean, 2010; Street, Braunack-Mayer, Facey, Ashcroft, & Hiller, 2008). McClearly (2003) argues that most people live in graphocentric cultures which afford more prestige to the written than to the spoken or signed word. Academic cultures are traditionally founded on publication in the written word with strong links between what is regarded as evidence and what can be found and written down (Stone & West, 2012; Young & Ackerman, 2001). Therefore, in writing down signed data is the researcher not complicit in supporting this hierarchy of language and by implication hierarchy of evidence? The language which is the less powerful is made to disappear and by implication so too do the users of that language, the cultural contexts in which it is produced and has meaning. From an ethnographic perspective, the seemingly straightforward and expedient research practice of transcription is akin to epistemological and ontological vandalism.

Arguably, therefore, the examples we give earlier of transcription can be defined as translations. Translation between languages involves significant issues of representation of language (and users of the language). However, we reserve discussion of those for the section on translation later. At this point in addressing "transcription" of signed languages, we end with Slobin's (2008) discussion of "the tyranny of glossing" (p. 121) in which he suggests that there may be significant *epistemological* issues with glossing. He points out that it seems strange and an "almost neocolonialist acceptance that the *spoken* language.... is somehow relevant to a linguistic analysis of the local *signed* language" (p. 122, emphasis original). He goes on to describe an alternative transcription system using a standard notion for representing "meaning components" (p. 123) that is not based on a language structure for spoken languages. He makes the point that there are dangers in analyzing glosses rather than the signs themselves. This debate echoes that around the domestication of translation, which we discuss later. Here we note that if the baseline for "transcription" chosen is that of another language, this has implications for how Deaf people are represented. It also has ethical and political implications if identities based on being Deaf and signing are camouflaged or ignored (see Chapter 6).

TRANSLATION

In social research the term "translation" is generally used to reference the act of turning a written source text into a written target language text. Research involving signed languages challenges and extends this meaning. As there are no agreed-upon written versions of signed languages, we argue earlier that a signed interview, for example, is not transcribed but is translated directly into another language. The problem of delineating transcription from translation can be illustrated using an example.

One of the most complex circumstances in research with people who sign involves the collection of qualitative data through focus groups where the researcher is a Deaf sign language user. There are technical difficulties of seeking to record simultaneously data from several people, even if multiple cameras are used. Consequently, some researchers use an interpreter. The interpreter is not present to facilitate conversation within the group, but to make an audio recording in real time. This is then "transcribed" to form a record of the content of what is said in a group (Crowe, 2003). The researcher then works from the written English text combined with her or his visual memory of the signed group interaction during the process of data analysis. In so doing, the researcher is working between languages but also with two versions of an original set of data, the "transcription" of the live interpreter's version, which is in another language (and therefore should this be translation?), and the researcher's own retrospective memory of the original. The final product of the research, if a written text, involves another transformation depending on the language(s) in which the analysis has been thought about. Data may be thought about in a signed language but then written down (Young & Ackerman, 2001). And finally there is the problem of quotation. Which is the original from which the quote will be taken?

Rather than using "transcription," the term "translation" has therefore been used to signal the movement between a signed language and a different written one, such as when data collected in BSL might be quoted in written English within an academic paper or book. The translation implies *a shift in language* as well as modality. Signed languages exploit to the full the possibilities of vision, space, movement, and the body to produce highly compressed, multilayered, detailed, precise expression. The structure of the language poses significant challenges to renderings in languages built on very different kinds of structures, such as the more linear connections between subject, verb, and object. Ladd (2003) additionally argues that there are cultural features of sign languages which are challenging in trying to render them in written languages. He lists the importance of storytelling, "theatrical re-enactment," repetition, poetics, and the tendency for creation of new signed lexical items as a matter of course, which may be for one-off usage.

Moreover, all translations between languages pose challenges rooted in the differences between linguistic structures, cultural usage, and historical context. Can translations between signed and nonsigned languages lie claim to anything additional, simply because such a translation implies also a modality shift?

Rogers et al. (2013) discuss in detail a range of translation issues that they encountered in moving between written English and BSL in the course of producing a BSL version of the standardized psychological instrument the CORE-OM (Clinical Outcomes Routine Evaluation Outcome Measure) (Barkham et al., 1998). Many were specific to issues of linguistic structure and cultural norms such as those we discuss earlier; however, they argue that some were specifically centered on modality, for example, the implications of modality for pronoun use and direction of signing.

The CORE-OM is a written self-assessment instrument. Usually an individual reads the statements herself, then rates her responses on a scale which specifies increasing frequency. The statements to which an individual responds are formed using the first person, for example, "I have felt despairing or hopeless." However, in translating the instrument into BSL, the terms of engagement between the individual and the assessment change because the modality changes. The individual *watches* each item which is signed on line by someone else and then enters, via computer, her or his rating in response. In piloting the translated version, it became clear that there was significant scope for confusion if the signer on screen continued to use the first person with the direction of the signing referring to himself. The authors remark:

> There is the risk that the participant might think that the statement refers to what *the signer* might be feeling, rather than asking what *they*, the participant, feel. To minimise possible confusion, it was agreed to change the pronoun from "I" to "You," resulting in a change in the direction of the signed item. "I have felt despairing or hopeless" in English becomes "This week, you (with the signer in the video signing towards the camera and respondent) have felt helpless and hopeless" in BSL. In this way it is clear that whoever is watching the video will know that it is asking them to what extent *they* have felt a certain way in the last week. (emphasis original) (p. 292)

Yet a shift from first to third person in translation of a standardized tool is usually anathema. It is the modality, the need to watch another, rather than read to oneself, which created the additional layer of complexity and necessitated a different approach to translation. Other studies working on similar projects have reached the same conclusion about the influence of modality within translation in examples similar to this one (Graybill et al., 2010; Jones, Mallinson, Phillips, & Kang, 2006; Montoya et al., 2004).

The arguments about additional issues associated with modality shift and language shift do not imply that common debates arising from researchers' reflections on how translations have been produced and who does the translation are irrelevant. Social researchers who want to reflect on how their translations of written texts have been produced have used the work of a wide range of writers and disciplines (Bourdieu, 1990; Buzelin, 2007; Derrida, 1976, 1978; Inghilleri, 2005; Venuti, 1998; Wolf, 2007; Wolf & Fukari, 2007). Venuti (1998) writes that translation often involves processes of "domestication" as the translator, in using the conventions of the target language, covers possible differences in worldviews. He argues that texts should indicate issues that were of concern or choices made during the translation process. He sees much translation as a process of domestication in which:

> ...the fact of translation is erased by suppressing the linguistic and cultural differences of the foreign text, assimilating it to dominant values in the target language culture, making it recognizable and therefore seemingly untranslated. With this domestication the translated text passes for the original, an expression of the foreign author's intention. (1998, p. 31)

Deaf researchers who caution against writing down signed languages because Deaf identities are linked to signing and not to written texts would recognize the need not to domesticate language in this way (see Chapter 6).

However, making it clear that a text is a translation in the way Venuti suggests comes with its own dangers in that it can reinforce stereotypes of illiterate "others" when quotes using the grammar of the source language result in a text in which people appear not to be able to express themselves according to expected grammatical conventions (Hale, 2002; McCleary, 2003; Ross, 2010; Standing, 1998; Temple, 2005). Ross (2010) cautions that foreignizing texts may "marginalize a foreign culture as hopelessly different and unreachable, and possibly, in the presence of a colonial impulse, needing intervention" (unpaginated). In relation to Deaf communities, this is a particularly sensitive issue because of persisting stereotypes of Deaf implying dumb, in the sense of stupid, not just without voice. Also the challenges that many d/Deaf people face in written language are still erroneously taken as evidence of deficits in intelligence and ability. "Foreignizing" a translated text into one which appears to be "incorrect" can both reinforce these assumptions for the reader while failing to show off the sophistication of the original (signed) language.

Eco (2003) suggests that all translators make decisions about the extent to which they want to foreignize texts and therefore have to grapple with these issues, whether they specify their strategies of not. Stone and West (2012), writing specifically about signed languages, cite Venuti's writing and describe four approaches to their translations. The first involves ensuring that the English is syntactically appropriate and not exploring issues of possible differences in meaning. The second creates a gloss of BSL and notes other features such as mouthings. The third translation strategy gives some explanation of meaning, and the fourth retains BSL sign order but includes features from the first two strategies. Contrary to Slobin (2008), Stone and West do not dismiss glossing. They argue that glosses can provide a bridge between BSL and the final translation.

Underlying all of these debates by researchers, including those working in signed languages, is the recognition of the translator as *active* in producing texts and not an innocent bystander (Baker, 2005; Rogers et al., 2013; Spivak, 1993; Stone & West, 2012; Temple & Young, 2004). Consequently, the investigation of the influence of the translator on research should also be part of the investigation of the different forms of equivalence (see Jones & Boyle, 2011, for a full discussion of the different types of equivalence in translation in social research). However, community researchers/bilingual researchers often interpret, translate, and transcribe without any investigation of their technical skills in these areas, let alone their language and community affiliations or their social location (see earlier).

As in the case of interpretation, some social researchers have begun to investigate the influence of *who* has translated in terms not only of language proficiency but in all aspects that could affect the validity of translations, such as individual perspectives on concept definition, phrasing, and understanding of the original text. This entails examining the social location of the translator, including gender, sexuality, and class, for example. These possible influences have been explored through an interest in biography and narratives (see earlier and Chapter 6). Researchers use debriefing sessions and biographical interviews with interpreters and translators to explore links between concept definition and perspective. However, although many researchers who work with d/Deaf people recognize the active role that interpreters and translators play in research, it is less common to explore the influence of their *identities* on interpretation/translation outside of whether they are d/Deaf.

For example, Stone's (2009) exploration of the differences between Deaf and hearing translators/interpreters (T/Is) within news broadcasting suggests that there are differences between the two in the use of prosody, blinking, head and body movements, pragmatic shifts, enrichments and impoverishments, and in audience awareness. Hearing T/Is were less likely to modify interpretations in terms of register or "to domesticate the target language in the same way as the Deaf T/Is" (p. 134 and see Venuti earlier). Stone discusses Deaf T/Is, Deaf (hearing) T/Is (audiologically hearing but culturally Deaf), and hearing T/Is and the ways in which they carry out their work. He argues that the primary experience for Deaf T/Is is visual and that the bilingual skills of both Deaf (hearing) and hearing T/Is without this primary visual experience "will necessarily be different from the Deaf T/Is" (p. 30). However, other influences on interpretation/translation such as those discussed by Grosjean (2008, 2010) in relation to bilingual identities and the influence of multiple identities are not explored; Deaf or hearing status is the only aspect considered. The lack of research on factors such as gender or class, for example, is striking both in social research generally with respect to translation and in research with people who use sign languages.

As is the case with interpreters, translators may be differently positioned within communities, and issues of cultural competence may significantly affect the research. *Which* communities and languages are involved in translation matters. Feminists have shown how language is not neutral—it is literally man-made (Spender, 1980)—and that translation is gendered (Simon, 1996). Discussing written translations, Spivak (1993) makes links between language, identity, and writing and points to the power differentials between languages and countries in constructing identities. She argues that when we translate we learn about ourselves and others in the choices we have to make about how "they" differ from "us" and how much we will need to change or explain in our translations. She alerts us to a "politics of translation" (see also Blommaert, 2001).

The nature of the bi- or multilingual status of the researcher exerts a key influence on how and when translation occurs within a study (see earlier). Researchers are only just beginning to explore the significance of such issues as how they might understand data when they do not have linguistic competence in the source language but only through the translated version (Temple, Edwards, & Alexander, 2006) and whether it matters which language research is analyzed and transcribed in (Hole, 2007b; Young & Ackerman, 2001 and see Chapter 6 for a discussion of why it might matter). The implications of the common research practice of choosing not to transcribe in the source language but to translate straight into the target language have been largely ignored. Liamputtong (2010), when discussing spoken languages, unequivocally comes down on the side of always transcribing and analyzing in the source language. She misrepresents Temple (2002) as supporting the view that direct transcription into English carries the possibility of interpreter bias. She does not consider the possibility of "bias" during the transcription process in the original language as well as in later translation (see discussion earlier on transcription). In social research studies generally and in those specifically involving signed languages, there is a wide diversity of practices taking place with little reflection on their consequences.

CONCLUDING THOUGHTS

The process of writing this chapter has made it clear to us that we, as all researchers do, paint a particular version of the three representational processes of interpretation, transcription, and translation. Definitions of the trio vary, as do views about their status within research. Translation can be seen as only the movement between written texts in different languages, its traditional definition. Writing down spoken or signed data can be viewed as transcription, but some researchers prefer to use the term "translation" when different languages are involved. Authors cited in this chapter use terms in differing ways and we use examples which cover all of these meanings. We draw the boundaries in order to present an argument, and our process of knowledge construction is challengeable. As we discuss in Chapter 2, the definitions researchers use influence what and who is included or omitted from research.

However interpretation, transcription, and translation are defined, we argue for reflexivity in relation to language use in terms of both participants and researchers. We suggest that research is an ethnographic enterprise in that it involves reflecting on the influence of context, including who did the research and how the process influenced findings. While there has been much interest focused on participants and researchers when considering interpretation, transcription, and translation in terms of whether they are hearing or d/Deaf, there has been little written about factors such as gender, class, or ethnicity.

In Chapter 3 we discuss research which argues that people cannot be reduced to one identifying characteristic; that particular identities do not necessarily affect research in predetermined ways; and that identities are performed and interact. In relation to our three representational processes, this means that who takes part in research affects the data generated. That is, *who* the researcher is influences what is said/ signed and what we can know from any piece of research. The question of "who" is linked to the nature of language and community ties but not with any in-built presumption that particular kinds of people are always preferable. *Who* the participants are also matters. As in everyday conversation, what we say depends on who we are in conversation with. Someone who is seen as an outsider in terms of not being able to sign, for example, may produce different but valid knowledge. The decision of who to use within research is based on considerations of "goods" (see Chapter 3) such as those of ethics and politics, rather than objective or predetermined criteria.

In addition to the significance of "who" in data generation, we focus on *how* researchers who carry out ethnographies influence *what* we can know about social realities. That is, interpretation, transcription, and translation all raise epistemological as well as ontological issues for all researchers.

We realize that we have given no simple "how-to" guide to help researchers decide how to do research with d/Deaf people. This is not possible. We prefer to give pointers to take into account when deciding how to proceed, with some implications for particular courses of action. It is up to the reader to decide how to proceed within her or his own epistemological, ontological, and ethical framework.

REFERENCES

Alcoff, L. (1991). The problem of speaking for others. *Cultural Critique*, 20(Winter), 5–32.

Alexander, C., Edwards, R., & Temple, B. (2004). Access to services with interpreters: User views. New York, NY: Joseph Rowntree Foundation.

Alvesson, M., & Skoldberg, K. (2009). *Reflexive methodology: New vistas for qualitative research*. London: Sage.

Arndt, K. (2010). Conducting interviews with people who are deaf-blind: Issues in recording and transcription. *Field Methods*, 23, 204–214. doi: 10.1177/1525822X10383395

Atkinson, P., Coffey, A., Delamont, S., Lofland, J., & Lofland, L. (2001). Editorial introduction. In P. Atkinson, A. Coffey, S. Delamont, J. Lofland, & L. Lofland (Eds.), *Handbook of ethnography* (pp. 1–7). London: Sage.

Balch, G., & Mertens, D. M. (1999). Focus group design and group dynamics: Lessons from deaf and hard of hearing participants. *American Journal of Evaluation*, 20(2), 265–277. doi: 10.1177/109821409902000208

Baker, M. (2005). Narratives in and of translation. *SASE Journal of Translation and Interpretation*, 1, 4–13.

Barak, A., & Sadovsky, Y. (2008). Internet use and personal empowerment of hearing-impaired adolescents. *Computers in Human Behavior*, 24, 1802–1815. doi: 10.1016/j.chb.2008.02.007

Barkham, M., Evans, C., Margison, F., McGrath, G., Mellor-Clark, J., Milne, D., & Connell, J. (1998). The rationale for developing and implementing core outcome batteries for routine use in service settings and psychotherapy outcome research. *Journal of Mental Health*, 7(1), 35–47. doi: 10.1080/09638239818328

Belk, R. (2014). *Genetic counselling and terminology in BSL.* PhD thesis, Manchester, UK.

Berman, R., & Slobin, D. (1994). *Relating events in narrative: A crosslinguistic developmental study.* Hillsdale, NJ: Lawrence Erlbaum.

Bishop, M., & Hicks, S. (2005). Orange eyes: Bimodal bilingualism in hearing adults from Deaf families. *Sign Language Studies*, 5(2), 188–230. doi: 10.1353/sls.2005.0001

Bisol, C. A., Sperb, T. M., & Moreno-Black, G. (2008). Focus groups with deaf and hearing youths in Brazil: Improving a questionnaire on sexual behavior and HIV/AIDS. *Qualitative Health Research*, 18(4), 565–578.

Blommaert, J. (2001). Investigating narrative inequality: African asylum seekers' stories in Belgium. *Discourse and Society*, 12(4), 413–449. doi: 10.1177/0957926501012004002

Bourdieu, P. (1990). *In other words: Essays towards a reflexive sociology.* Cambridge, UK: Polity Press.

Brislin, R. W. (1970). Back-translation for cross-cultural research. *Journal of Cross-Cultural Psychology*, 1(3), 185–216. doi: 10.1177/135910457000100301

Buzelin, H. (2007). Translations "in the making." In M. Wolf & A. Fukari (Eds.), *Constructing a sociology of translation* (pp. 135–169). Amsterdam: John Benjamins Publishing Company.

Carter, S., Jordan, T., & Watson, S. (2008). Introduction. In S. Carter, T. Jordan, & S. Watson (Eds.), *Security: Sociology and social worlds* (pp. 1–16). Manchester, UK: Manchester University Press.

Cokely, D. (1992). *Interpretation: A sociolinguistic model.* Burtonsville, MD: Linstok Press.

Creese, A. (2008). Linguistic ethnography. In K. A. King & N. H. Hornberger (Eds.), *Encyclopedia of language and education* (2nd ed., vol. 10): *Research methods in language and education* (pp. 229–241). New York, NY: Springer Science.

Crowe, T. V. (2003). Using focus groups to create culturally appropriate HIV prevention material for the deaf community. *Qualitative Social Work*, 2(3), 289–308. doi: 10.1177/14733250030023005

Derrida, J. (1976). *Of grammatology* (G. Spivak, Trans.). Baltimore, MD: Johns Hopkins University Press.

Derrida, J. (1978). *Writing and difference* (A. Bass, Trans.). Chicago, IL: University of Chicago Press.

Du Gay, P. (2008). Organising conduct, making up people. In L. McFall, P. du Gay, & S. Carter (Eds.), *Conduct: Sociology and social worlds* (pp. 21–53). Manchester, UK: Manchester University Press.

Eco, U. (2003). *Mouse or rat? Translation as negotiation.* London: Weidenfeld & Nicolson.

Edwards, R. (1998). A critical examination of the use of interpreters in the qualitative research process. *Journal of Ethnic and Migration Studies*, 24(1), 97–208. doi: 10.1080/1369183X.1998.9976626

Edwards, R., Alexander, C., & Temple, B. (2006). Interpreting trust: Abstract and personal trust for people who need interpreters to access services.

Sociological Research Online, 11(1), 1–26. http://www.socresonline.org.uk/11/1/edwards.html

El-Rufaie, O. E. F. A., & Absood, G. (1987). Validity study of the Hospital Anxiety and Depression Scale among a group of Saudi patients. *British Journal of Psychiatry, 151*(5), 687–688. doi: 10.1192/bjp.151.5.687

Goffman, E. (1961). *Encounters: Two studies in the sociology of interaction.* New York, NY: The Bobbs-Merrill Company.

Graybill, P., Aggas, J., Dean, R. K., Demers, S., Finigan, E. G., & Pollard, R. Q., Jr. (2010). A community-participatory approach to adapting survey items for deaf individuals and American Sign Language. *Field Methods, 22*(4), 429–448.

Greenabaum, T. (2000). Conducting focus groups with disabled respondents. Retrieved January 21, 2013, from http://www.groupsplus.com/pages/disabled.htm

Grosjean, F. (1996). Living with two languages and two cultures. In I. Parasnis (Ed.), *Cultural and language diversity and the deaf experience* (pp. 20–37). Cambridge, UK: Cambridge University Press.

Grosjean, F. (2008). *Studying bilinguals.* New York, NY: Oxford University Press.

Grosjean, F. (2010). Bilingualism, biculturalism, and deafness. *International Journal of Bilingual Education and Bilingualism, 13*(2), 133–145. doi: 10.1080/13670050903474051

Hakuta, K., & Feldman Mostafapour, E. (1996). Perspectives from the history and politics of bilingualism and bilingual education in the United States. In I. Parasnis (Ed.), *Cultural and language diversity and the deaf experience* (pp. 38–50). Cambridge, UK: Cambridge University Press.

Hale, S. (2002). How faithfully do court interpreters render the style of non-English speaking witnesses" testimonies? A data-based study of Spanish-English bilingual proceedings. *Discourse Studies, 4*(1), 25–47. doi: 10.1177/14614456020040010201

Hauser, P. (2000). An analysis of codeswitching: American Sign Language and cued English. In M. Metzger (Ed.), *Bilingualism and identity in deaf communities* (pp. 43–78). Washington, DC: Gallaudet University Press.

Hole, R. (2007a). Working between languages and cultures: Issues of representation, voice, and authority intensified. *Qualitative Inquiry, 13*(5), 696–710. doi: 10.1177/1077800407301186

Hole, R. (2007b). Narratives of identity: A poststructural analysis of three deaf women's life stories. *Narrative Inquiry, 17, 2,* 259–278.

Hymes, D. (1974). *Foundations of sociolinguistics: An ethnographic approach.* Philadelphia, PA: University of Pennsylvania Press.

Inghilleri, M. (2005). The sociology of Bourdieu and the construction of the object in translation and interpreting studies. *The Translator, 11*(1), 125–145.

Jepson, J. (1991a). Two sign languages in a single village in India. *Sign Language Studies, 70,* 47–59.

Jepson, J. (1991b). Urban and rural sign languages in India. *Language in Society, 20,* 37–57. doi: 10.1017/S0047404500016067

Jones, E., & Boyle, J. (2011). Working with translators and interpreters in research: Lessons learned. *Journal of Transcultural Nursing, 22*(2), 109–115. doi: 10.1177/1043659610395767

Jones, E. G., Mallinson, R. K., Phillips, L., & Kang, Y. (2006). Challenges in language, culture, and modality: Translating English measures into American Sign Language. *Nursing Research, 55*(2), 75–81.

Keating, E., & Mirus, G. (2003). Examining interactions across language modalities: Deaf children and hearing peers at school. *Anthropology & Education Quarterly, 34*(2), 115–135.

Kroll, T., Barbour, R., & Harris, J. (2007). Using focus groups in disability research. *Qualitative Health Research, 17*(5), 690–698. doi: 10.1177/1049732307301488

Ladd, P. (2000). Time to locate the big picture. In A. Baker, B. van den Bogaerde, & O. Crasborn (Eds.), *Cross-linguistic perspectives in sign language research: Selected papers from TISLR* (pp. 3–15). Hamburg, Germany: Signum.

Ladd, P. (2003). *Understanding Deaf culture: In search of Deafhood.* Clevedon, UK: Multilingual Matters.

Leigh, I. (2009). *A lens on deaf identities.* New York, NY: Oxford University Press.

Leung, C., Harris, R., & Rampton, B. (1997). The idealised native speaker, reified ethnicities, and classroom realities. *TESOL Quarterly, 31*(3), 543–560.

Liamputtong, P. (2010). *Performing qualitative cross-cultural research.* New York, NY: Cambridge University Press.

Mather, S. (2005). Ethnographic research on the use of visually based regulators for teachers and interpreters. In M. Metzger & E. Fleetwood (Eds.), *Attitudes, innuendo, and regulators: Challenges of interpretation* (pp. 136–161). Washington, DC: Gallaudet University Press.

McCleary, L. (2003). Technologies of language and the embodied history of the deaf. *Sign Language Studies, 3*(2), 104–124. doi: 10.1353/sls.2003.0002

Metzger, M. (1999). Footing shifts in an interpreted mock interview. In E. Winston (Ed.), *Storytelling and conversation: Discourses in Deaf communities* (pp. 190–213). Washington, DC: Gallaudet University Press.

Metzger, M. (2000). *Sign language interpreting: Deconstructing the myth of neutrality.* Washington, DC: Gallaudet University Press.

Metzger, M., Collins, S., Dively, V., & Shaw, R. (2003). (Eds.) *From topic boundaries to omission: New research on interpretation.* Washington, DC: Gallaudet University Press.

Metzger, M., Fleetwood, E., & Collins, S. (2004). Discourse genre and linguistic mode: Interpreter influences in visual and tactile interpreted interaction. *Sign Language Studies, 4*(2), 118–137. doi: 10.1353/sls.2004.0004

Mindess, A. (2006). *Reading between the signs: Intercultural communication for sign language interpreters* (2nd ed.). Boston, MA: Intercultrual Press.

Montoya, L. A., Egnatovitch, R., Eckhardt, E., Goldstein, M., Goldstein, R. A., & Steinberg, A. G. (2004). Translation challenges and strategies: The ASL translation of a computer-based, psychiatric diagnostic interview. *Sign Language Studies, 4*(4), 314–344. doi: 10.1353/sls.2004.0019

Napier, J. (2002). University interpreting: Linguistic issues for consideration. *Journal of Deaf Studies and Deaf Education, 7*(4), 281–301. doi: 10.1093/deafed/7.4.281

Napier, J., & Barker, R. (2004). Sign language interpreting: The relationship between metalinguistic awareness and the production of interpreting omissions. *Sign Language Studies, 4*(4), 369–393. doi: 10.1353/sls.2004.0020

Parasnis, I. (2012). Diversity and deaf identity: Implications for personal epistemologies in deaf education. In P. Paul & D. Moores (Eds.), *Deaf epistemologies: Multiple perspectives on the acquisition of knowledge* (pp. 63–80). Washington, DC: Gallaudet University Press.

Pavlenko, A. (2005). *Emotions and multilingualism*. Cambridge, UK: Cambridge University Press.

Pavlenko, A. (2006). *Bilingual minds: Emotional experience, expression and representation*. Clevedon, UK: Multilingual Matters.

Poland, B. (2003). Transcription quality. In J. A. Holstein & J. F. Gubrium (Eds.), *Inside interviewing: New lenses, new concerns* (pp. 267–287). London: Sage Publications.

Raistrick, T. (2014). *An evaluation of the BSL Bible Translation Project*. Unpublished PhD thesis, University of Chester, UK.

Rampton, B. (2003). Displacing the "native speaker": Expertise, affiliation and inheritance. In R. Harris & B. Rampton (Eds.), *The language, ethnicity and race reader* (pp. 107–111). London: Routledge.

Rayman, J. (1999). Storytelling in the visual mode: A comparison of ASL and English. In E. Winston (Ed.), *Storytelling and conversation: Discourses in deaf communities* (pp. 59–81). Washington, DC: Gallaudet University Press.

Redman, P. (2008). Introduction. In P. Redman (Ed.), *Attachment: Sociology and social worlds* (pp. 1–18). Manchester, UK: Manchester University Press.

Riessman, C. (2008). *Narrative methods for the human sciences*. London: Sage Publications.

Rogers, K. D., Young, A., Lovell, K., & Evans, C. (2013). The challenges of translating the clinical outcomes in routine evaluation—Outcome measure (CORE-OM) into British Sign Language. *Journal of Deaf Studies and Deaf Education, 18*(3), 287–298.

Ross, J. (2010). Was that infinity or affinity? Applying insights from translation studies to qualitative research transcription. *Forum: Qualitative Social Research, 11*(2), Art 2, 1–16.

Roy, C. (2000). *Interpreting as a discourse process*. New York, NY: Oxford University Press.

Sheppard, K. (2011). Using American Sign Language interpreters to facilitate research among Deaf adults: Lessons learned. *Journal of Transcultural Nursing, 22*(2), 129–134. doi: 10.1177/1043659610395765

Simon, S. (1996). *Gender in translation: Cultural identity and the politics of transmission*. London: Routledge.

Slobin, D. (1996a). From "thought and language" to "thinking for speaking." In J. Gumperz & S. Levinson (Eds.), *Rethinking linguistic relativity* (pp. 70–90). Cambridge, UK: Cambridge University Press.

Slobin, D. (1996b). Two ways to travel: Verbs of motion in English and Spanish. In M. Shibatani & S. Thompson (Eds.), *Grammatical constructions: Their form and meaning* (pp. 195–220). New York, NY: Oxford University Press.

Slobin, D. (2008). Breaking the molds: Signed languages and the nature of human language. *Sign Language Studies, 8*(2), 114–130. doi: 10.1353/sls.2008.004

Spender, D. (1980). *Man made language*. London: Routledge & Kegan Paul Ltd.

Spivak, G. (1993). *Outside in the teaching machine*. London: Routledge.

Standing, K. (1998). Writing the voices of the less powerful: Research on lone mothers. In R. Ribbens & R. Edwards (Eds.), *Feminist dilemmas in qualitative research: Public knowledge and private lives* (pp. 186–202). London: Sage Publications Ltd.

Stone, C. (2009). *Toward a Deaf translation norm.* Washington, DC: Gallaudet University Press.

Stone, C., & West, D. (2012). Translation, representation and the Deaf "voice." *Qualitative Research, 12*(6), 645–665. doi: 10.1177/1468794111433087

Street, J. M., Braunack-Mayer, A. J., Facey, K., Ashcroft, R. E., & Hiller, J. E. (2008). Virtual community consultation? Using the literature and weblogs to link community perspectives and health technology assessment. *Health Expectations: An International Journal of Public Participation in Health Care & Health Policy, 11*(2), 189–200.

Sutton-Spence, R., & Woll, B. (1999). *The linguistics of British Sign Language: An introduction.* Cambridge, UK: Cambridge University Press.

Tchalakov, I. (2004). Language and perception in the coupling between human and nonhuman actors. Available at http://www.ifz.tugraz.at/ias/IAS-STS/Publications/Yearbook-2004

Temple, B. (2002). Crossed wires: Interpreters, translators, and bilingual workers in cross language research. *Qualitative Health Research, 12*(6), 844–854. doi: 10.1177/104973230201200610

Temple, B. (2005). Nice and tidy: Translation and representation. *Sociological Research Online, 10*(2), 1–19. http://www.socresonline.org.uk/10/2/temple.htm

Temple, B. (2006). Being bilingual: Issues for cross language research. *Journal of Research Practice, 2*(1), Article M2, 1–18.

Temple, B., Edwards, R. & Alexander, C. (2006). Grasping at context: Cross language qualitative research as secondary data analysis. *Forum: Qualitative Social Research, 7*(4), Art. 10, 1–13. http/nbn-resolving.de/urn:nbn:de:0114-fqs0604107

Temple, B., & Young, A. (2004). Qualitative research and translation dilemmas. *Qualitative Research, 4*(2), 161–178. doi: 10.1177/1468794104044430

Thoutenhoofd, E. (2007). Sign language corpus creation: A digital humanities ethnography. *Virtual Knowledge Studio for the Humanities & Social Sciences, Royal Netherlands Academy of Arts & Sciences,* 1–15. Retrieved July 25, 2011, from http://www.academia.edu/704459/Sign_language_corpus_creation_A_digital_humanities_ethnography

Venuti, L. (1998). *The scandals of translation: Towards an ethics of difference.* London: Routledge.

Wadensjö, C. (1998). *Interpreting as interaction.* London: Longman.

Wainwright, M., & Russell, A. (2010). Using Nvivo Audio Coding: Practical, sensorial and epistemological considerations. *Social Research Update* (60), 1–4. Retrieved July 25, 2011, from http://sru.soc.surrey.ac.uk/

Wheeler, A., Archbold, S., & Gregory, S. (2007). Cochlear implants: The young people's perspective. *Journal of Deaf Studies and Deaf Education, 12*(3), 303–316. doi: 10.1093/deafed/enm018

Wierzbicka, A. (1997). *Understanding cultures through their key words: English, Russian, Polish, German, and Japanese.* New York, NY: Oxford University Press.

Wolf, M. (2007). The location of the "translation field": Negotiating borderlines between Pierre Bourdieu and Homi Bhabha. In M. Wolf & A. Fukari

(Eds.), *Constructing a sociology of translation* (pp. 109–119). Amsterdam: John Benjamins Publishing Company.

Wolf, M., & Fukari, A. (Eds.). (2007). *Constructing a sociology of translation.* Amsterdam: John Benjamins Publishing Company.

Young, A. M., & Ackerman, J. (2001). Reflections on validity and epistemology in a study of working relations between deaf and hearing professionals. *Qualitative Health Research, 11*(2), 179–189. doi: 10.1177/104973230101100204

8

The Impact of Information and Communication Technologies

Technological innovations have changed forever many previously unquestionable principles of communication. Physical proximity is no longer a prerequisite for face-to-face communication, thanks to Web-based video telephony. Spoken language no longer dominates real-time distance communication since the advent of text messaging. Nonsynchronous forms of communication are no longer slow since e-mail has replaced letter writing. Information and knowledge, whether in written, visual, spoken, or video format is accessible, searchable, modifiable, storable, and portable for the many, not the few. These are living realities for the population in general, not for any special populations, specific cultures, or language-using groups in particular. However, much has been written about the potential of information and communication technologies (ICTs) to unlock opportunities for d/Deaf people, to reduce inequities of access between d/Deaf and hearing people, and to break down communication barriers between those who use spoken language and those who do not (Barak & Sadovsky, 2008; Bowe, 2002; Power & Power, 2004; Power, Power, & Rehling, 2007).

In this chapter on technology, we will consider specifically the implications of this information and communication technology revolution for research studies with, by, and about d/Deaf people. The chapter does not address hearing technologies such as radio aids, hearing aids, or cochlear implants. We will consider the ways in which common uses and new applications of ICTs impact on research designs, the methods of data collection, and approaches to analysis and publishing. However, the influence of information and communication technology goes beyond issues of adaptation and innovation in research process and practice. At an epistemological level, the new technologies have the potential to create *new kinds of knowledge* through addressing *new forms of knowability* and including *new populations of knowers*. This chapter will, therefore, also consider the ways in which the application of new information and communication technologies to research involving d/Deaf people is changing the nature of what and how we know, and from whom.

ASKING NEW QUESTIONS

Deaf People in Society

From a sociological perspective, the advent of new information and communication technologies is causing researchers to ask new kinds of questions about d/Deaf people in society. These are prompted by three key characteristics of the new technologies: their universality; the predominance of nonoral (text-based) communication; and more recently, their integrated visual functionality. Power and Power (2004), for example, have suggested that the universality of technology, allowing d/Deaf and hearing people to communicate without special equipment (e.g., via texting) and to communicate in sign language through online and video telephony, is "disrupting" the historical separateness of Deaf communities. Certainly within living memory, Deaf people required special kinds of equipment to access even the telephone network and struggled to achieve the right to communication through it (Lang, 2000).

However, the idea of a shared platform and means of communication between d/Deaf and hearing people does not of itself imply an assimilation or equivalence between communities. Valentine and Skelton (2008), for example, conclude from an interview study involving a sample of 40 d/Deaf people that:

> Deaf people's ability to participate in mainstream society on-line does not necessarily translate into social inclusion in the off-line hearing community because they are mainly using the internet to communicate with hearing people in ways that do not challenge hearing normatives. In doing so, their use of the internet is contributing to the maintenance and normalisation of hearing hegemony, leaving the discrimination D/deaf people encounter in off-line space unchallenged. (p. 481)

Historically, Deaf culture has, in part, been shaped by the necessity to meet in person in order to communicate. Deaf clubs in terms of physical spaces where people met have always been important. They have enabled the exchange of information, the reinforcing of social bonds, and access and transfer of knowledge throughout the Deaf community by means of in-person interactions (see Chapter 2). Now it is possible to chat, in sign languages online via common media such as Skype and ooVoo; to look up information on the Web that is available in signed as well as written languages; to access interpreters virtually for contact with nonsigning organizations and people such as doctors and teachers.

Consequently, practices that have hitherto seemed indicative of Deaf culture, such as regular attendance at the Deaf club to meet with others, will undergo change. However, whether such changes signal significant cultural shifts is debatable. One could argue that the regularity of meeting in person, while born from a practical necessity (there was no other way to see/communicate), was never really that which defined the cultural value. Rather it was the necessity to sign with another, to see oneself as "same" not "different" in interaction with others, and for culture to be nourished and grow through those interactions. In shifting the medium away from the in-person interaction, is one really shifting a cultural signifier or rather only changing the circumstance in which it is enabled to occur? Is communication over the Internet, through mobile telephony and via online fora, all available in signed languages, really just a 21st-century version of a network of Deaf clubs? Or is there something vitally important about the corporality of meeting in person? Such are the new kinds of questions that ICT is raising with respect to Deaf people. In a similar way, but from a different starting point, more global questions are being raised about whether the ICT revolution has changed how we think, socially relate, and define what is of value (Carr, 2010).

However, the impact of ICT on culture, community, and language with respect to Deaf people(s) also arises indirectly as a result of research practices that are now available. For example, digital recording, editing, and retrieval technologies are now enabling the large-scale collection of signed languages as they are used in real life (McCleary, 2003). These are no longer static collections of lexical items as in the past (Deaf Studies Research Unit [DSRU], 1993) but living language in use. Sign language corpus research projects are under way in a range of countries (Crasborn, 2010). This does not remove the need to examine their epistemological claims as such corpora are still situated within the contexts in which they are produced (Grimes, Thoutenhoofd, & Byrne, 2007). However, beyond the linguistic analyses such corpus research enables, there are indirect effects on the communities from which the signed data derive. For example, the existence, easy accessibility, and visibility of these studies and their data lend a higher social status to the languages, and their users, than previously. It is usually the case in Western and developed world cultures that society has afforded greater prestige to languages that can be "fixed" in print (McCleary, 2003). Through the written word, knowledge can take a substantial form and become indicative of one's cultural identity, historical presence, and enduring evidence of influence. Now signed languages too can be fixed in a medium that also enables their retrieval, rewatching, creative manipulation, and historical archiving.

The new digital video technologies are challenging the graphocentric nature of literacy and historical record through permitting new forms of recordable cultural practice(s). This is a revolution for all, not just for Deaf people, as the inexorable rise of YouTube demonstrates (Burgess, Green, Jenkins, & Hartley, 2009). However, this is also arguably the first major communication-related technological revolution that has not excluded sign language users de facto, nor required special adaptation for their inclusion. As McLeary (2003) remarks:

> For Deaf people...who have missed the impact of telephone conver-sations and realized little benefit from national television in terms of long-distance communication, the rise of video on the Internet brings a condensed version of these technological advances, which have been spread out over several decades for hearing people. For that reason, the online publication of collections of sign language video material may have a greater impact on Deaf communities than may be foreseen. (p. 279)

The technology removes the cloak of invisibility which has surrounded Deaf knowledge and Deaf ways of communicating that knowledge because the platforms used are ones shared within the mainstream. This fact is not just a facilitative practicality; it has epistemological sig-nificance, too. Deaf ways of knowing are placed on an equal footing with those who communicate through sound and the spoken word. The same technological means is shared. The same rights of partici-pation in mass cultural production are afforded. As De Clerck (2010) argues: "Deaf epistemologies...are driven by a desire to have eyes for the hands that sign deaf perspective(s) on social reality" (p. 436). Online digital video technologies are both the medium and the mes-sage (McLuhan, 1964) in their realization of this desire and its exposure.

Technology, however, does not just raise questions of impact on identity, social relationships, and status for those Deaf people who sign. Waskul and Douglass (1996), writing before the advent of embed-ded video technologies, comment the Internet is also a "faceless and non-oral" medium where social relationships typically are created though the written word, not the spoken word, via social networking media and online chat rooms. Within these social spaces, participants are neither seen nor heard and can adopt (and perform) whichever identity/identities they might wish (Gill & Elder, 2012). This phenom-enon can also be regarded as a social advantage to deaf people who might want to hide their deafness or to communicate and participate without others' assumptions and stigmatizing attitudes about being deaf and/or disability getting in the way (Barak & Sadovsky, 2008; Bowker & Tuffin, 2003; Seymore & Lupton, 2004). In social model of disability terms (see Chapter 2) the medium dismantles barriers that create the disability in the first place.

> [The Internet] puts the hearing-impaired in a special situation, one they usually do not experience in their ordinary social contacts: the ability to freely communicate with people—be it via email, forum, instant messaging (IM), chat, or blogs—without revealing their spe-cial health status. This fact not only projects upon their enhanced

communication ability, but also relieves them of regular psychological uneasiness and stress from fearing and being defensive about stereotypic responses toward them. (Barak & Sadovsky, 2008, p. 1803)

However, such a view is firmly grounded in a perception of deafness as a deficit in access to sound and spoken language, and a stigmatized trait within mainstream society (see Chapter 2). How then might one explain studies which evidence how culturally Deaf people might also value the fact that online and text-based communication enables them to conceal their identity (Valentine & Skelton, 2008)? At first glance it seems a curious result because at the heart of Deaf cultural identity is a nondeficit model which actively excludes any notion of seeking to pass as hearing (see Chapter 2).

Valentine and Skelton (2008) suggest that the result can be explained by a desire to avoid misinformation and discrimination by hearing people if their identity were revealed. However, just because identities are not stated, does not mean that they are being hidden. Rather what is at stake is the status of the identity as relevant (or not) to the communicative transaction/knowledge exchange. When I e-mail a travel agent, or when I join an online interest group, would I always make sure that those with whom I interact know I am a woman? Or is it only relevant for some purposes and in some contexts? If I do not reveal my gender, it does not necessarily mean I am hiding it. If Deaf Internet users value the fact that they are not immediately identified by others as Deaf, this does not necessarily infer that the advantage lies in hiding the fact. Instead, it demonstrates that Deaf people are no different from any other Internet users, within nonvisual interfaces, who have the right to exercise choice about what becomes revealed of identity, in which circumstances, and for what purpose. In face-to-face interaction a Deaf person does not have that ability to choose and control when, how, why, and for what reason another recognizes her or him to be Deaf. But then neither does anyone have any such control over any feature of identity that is immediately identifiable within a face-to-face interaction.

Our point in working through this example is to demonstrate, once again, how assumptions we might hold about what it is to *be* d/Deaf fundamentally influence the research process, in this case the interpretation of data. Does the faceless medium of some ICT mean Deaf people can hide their identity because of the negative connotations attributed by some within mainstream society, or does it simply mean Deaf people along with everyone else can make the same sorts of choices about what is revealed when, why, and for what purpose, because to be Deaf is no different from any other kind of identity marker revealed through sight? How we read the data and the connections we make with disability and cultural identity determine which interpretation(s) we might reach.

Technologies Used by d/Deaf People

Societal-level concerns about identity, community, language, and culture are not the only kinds of new questions provoked by the impact of recent communication and information technologies. These technologies are also generating highly specific, quasi-experimental research questions about the technologies themselves as used by d/Deaf people and, conversely, what d/Deaf people's ICT use can tell us more generally about the technologies. These arise from the potential of the technological innovations in everyday communication and information access to address cognitive, educational, social, or psychological challenges that d/Deaf people might typically face.

Akamatsu, Mayer, and Farrelly (2006), for example, considered the potential impact of new mobile communication technologies on d/Deaf students' socioemotional developmental delays. They found that the provision of two-way pagers to both d/Deaf young people and their parents would positively influence the degree of independent activity that parents felt comfortable for their children to undertake and enhance the young people's confidence and independent living skills. Barak and Sadovsky (2008) set up a study to evaluate Internet use as a mediator of psychological well-being. They compared Internet use between d/Deaf students and hearing students and demonstrated that "on measures of loneliness and self-esteem, the 'Deaf/HOH' students who used the Internet intensively had scores similar to those of hearing students, whereas those who used the Internet less intensively had significantly lower scores" (p. 239). The impact of technologies on literacy for deaf children has also been explored. Dowaliby and Lang (1999) used an experimental procedure to compare different kinds of computer-delivered adjunct materials to support understanding. More recently, Okuyama and Iwai (2011) have analyzed the influence of texting on literacy in a comparative study of the content of d/Deaf and hearing students' messaging.

As the information and communication technologies themselves progress, the scope of the research questions investigating impact and effects of technological interventions and/or technology use are also changing. In particular, the incorporation into everyday devices of visual technologies that are quick enough to carry signed communication has opened up many new possible fields of enquiry. Snoddon (2010), for example, investigated the implications for d/Deaf children's multiliteracy of video recording and editing technologies. Rather than focusing on the commonly observed deficits in d/Deaf children's abilities to read written language, she considered the ways in which the new technologies enable ASL literacy. Central to ASL literacy is the social practice of learning to *read* ASL "texts," including the embedded cultural discourse(s) within them. This study investigated the impact on Deaf children of their involvement in the production and reading of

ASL texts, facilitated by easy access to technologies enabling the recording and editing of visual texts. It concluded that students' attitudes to their own use of ASL were positively affected, and ASL literacy practices such as the drafting and editing of stories also served to strengthen Deaf identities.

The new information and communication technologies also prompt questions about their specific use by d/Deaf people. Such studies are often undertaken to illuminate broader issues of technological design or practice through investigation of unique technological adoption practices of a community of users with specific characteristics and needs. Historically, learning from how d/Deaf people adopt, adapt, and use a technology has prompted a host of design solutions, many of which are now universal conditions within technologies. Predictive texting, for example, first arose in the context of speeding up typing for TTD (Telecommunications Device for the Deaf) users. The apparently new revolutions in how young people use written language in text communications raises a wry smile among Deaf people whose idiosyncratic contractions of written language in TTY predate this revolution by several decades. Conversely, e-com acronyms such as LOL (Laugh Out Loud) and OMG (Oh My God) are finding their way into signed languages as fingerspelled components, although in some cases used with an irony not always apparent in the original (Schneider, Kozak, Santiago, & Stephen, 2012).

Thus far, we have explored two kinds of questions that new communication and information technologies generate in the context of research involving d/Deaf people: broad-based sociological ones, and those which focus on how technologies are impacting directly on d/Deaf people. To some extent, this division is artificial because, as we argue in our discussion of the contribution of Actor Network Theory in Chapter 6, how we use technologies influences who we are and vice versa. However, we have made the distinction at this stage in order to draw attention to the fact that the intersection of information and communication technologies with being d/Deaf is not simply a matter of functional advantage/disadvantage, or practical benefit. It is fundamentally about participation in new possibilities with the potential to reshape how people know and are known. In the next section we examine how the new technologies are changing aspects of the research process.

NEW TECHNOLOGIES AND NEW RESEARCH PROCESSES

Advances in information and communication technologies do not just exert influence on research involving d/Deaf people by the questions they prompt but also by their influence on the research process. By research process, we mean all stages in the execution of a piece of research, including recruitment, data capture, data analysis, and dissemination/publishing.

Recruitment and Participation

As we discuss in Chapter 5, populations of d/Deaf people(s) are highly heterogeneous. In childhood and from an educational perspective, deafness is regarded as a low-incidence condition (Gray, 2006). In general population terms, its prevalence increases with age, becoming a part of the majority of people's lives after the age of 70 (Ha-Sheng, 2012). In cultural terms, Deaf people(s) are highly dispersed language-using groups whose nation(s) has no geographical existence but where pockets of high density exist (Kusters, 2010). These conditions, from whichever perspective, can make recruitment to research studies very challenging and have acted as a barrier to participation of large numbers of d/Deaf people in generating data, particularly with respect to Deaf sign language users.

Information and communication technologies create new possibilities for the recruitment and participation of d/Deaf people in research as they do for other marginalized, dispersed, or heterogeneous groups in other contexts (Bowen, Williams, & Horvath, 2004). The Web is packed with bounded and specialized spaces where people with shared interests, characteristics, or identities can and do choose to meet. Their functions encompass the social, the supportive, the informative, and the educational, with many Web spaces fulfilling more than one of these simultaneously. They also vary in degrees of formality. Compare, for example, young d/Deaf people who set up Facebook pages and invite their "friends" to join them, with moderated discussion boards for parents of d/Deaf children such as the National Deaf Children's Society's (NDCS) "Parent Place" in the United Kingdom (NDCS, 2012).

What is important from a recruitment for research point of view is that they are all spaces where (1) one might expect to locate a high density of people with whatever life experience or personal/group characteristics that are of relevance to a given research study; (2) they break through geographical barriers to recruitment in reaching a wide range of potential participants without having to travel; and (3) they provide a cost-effective means of informing a broad spectrum of people about research in which they might want to participate.

This recruitment potential can be capitalized upon through advertisements on Web sites or targeted e-mails through listserves, or through electronic snowball strategies where one participant then uses her or his own e-networks to pass on news of the research study and extends the invitation to participate. This form of extended message/information transfer is sometimes referred to as an item going "viral." Its impact lies in the *compound* effects of one message being relayed to multiple members of an individual's own electronic network, whose members in turn pass it on through their own social or professional networks of many additional members. This compound effect is what distinguishes it from "word of mouth" (or "sign of hand") approaches, which more commonly engage one person at a time although having a cumulative effect.

There are many examples worldwide of items, in everyday life, that have gone viral in Deaf communities through social networking, mobile telephony, and Web access, which demonstrate the potential power of this effect for research purposes. For a notable example, see "Limping Chicken" in the United Kingdom. The Web site was set up initially in response to a comment on a national TV documentary from a notetaker employed to support a Deaf student at University. She explained she was unable to stay for the whole of the lecture that the student was attending because she had to take a sick chicken to the vet. What initially provoked humorous outrage, spreading like an electronic wildfire among Deaf people, spawned a well-respected contemporary Deaf news and views Web site.

Of course, such electronic recruitment methods carry with them associated ethical concerns. One of the new challenges of Web technologies, in particular, is the blurring of boundaries between what is considered private and what is considered public (Bowker & Tuffin, 2004; Waskul & Douglass, 1996). Just because a specialized Web space exists that is open to all who might need it (such as a parent support or information site), does that mean that a researcher who can also access it can use this space for a professional purpose such as recruiting research participants? Its public nature, as defined by its accessibility, does not necessarily imply that it is not private, in the sense that only legitimate users, however defined, have a right of participation.

Even if we accept that a user of a Web site (who reads the pages) might not qualify as a member of the community of the site (those who participate/have a shared identity), such a distinction is not in all cases pertinent to the ethics of Web-based recruitment. Imagine a Deaf researcher doing a project on the contribution of involvement in sports to Deaf cultural identity. Is it ethical for the researcher to use her membership to an online Deaf sports forum to recruit interviewees? Or will the change in identity (from member to researcher) offend other users of that forum? Or will the researcher's insider identity as a Deaf sports forum member of many years standing mean that her attempt to recruit her peers through this medium is regarded as quite legitimate?

While the Web offers many new opportunities for speedy, targeted, cost-effective and broad-based recruitment, it also raises new kinds of problems. Web spaces, of whatever variety, extend and challenge the meaning of many notions that are of relevance to recruitment practices, such as "membership," "communities," "the public," "insiders," and "privacy." Consequently, researchers are challenged to justify ethically as well as functionally, why, not just how, the new recruitment channels that ICT offers are appropriate.

Of course, this kind of consideration is not unique to research involving d/Deaf people. However, it takes on another dimension because of the many ways in which the new information and communication technologies have become culturally embedded among Deaf people. For younger Deaf researchers, in particular, who grew up digital and whose knowledge and social communities are inextricably interwoven with text communication, social networking, online fora, and Web-based visual communication, it is not only a highly efficient but a *culturally appropriate practice* to use these methods to recruit and inform about research studies they might be running.

For example, a research study might have a sign language–accessible Web site where potential participants view the information and consent materials before they sign up to the study. The recruitment problem lies in getting potential participants to access that Web site in the first place. Sending an e-mail and/or text message to a wide constituency of other Deaf people directing them to take a look at the Web site and pass on the information quickly ensures many hits on the project Web site. Such community-based information nudging through text and e-mail is not unusual for a wide range of issues, be they social or professional, within Deaf communities. This recruitment step of electronically directing attention toward participant opportunities is consequently becoming more frequently used.

That said, one person's culturally appropriate practice can be another person's biased sampling strategy. The biases that can be created through Internet recruitment and how these might be avoided (for example, in randomized controlled trials) have become their own topics of research in fields as diverse as cancer (Im, Chee, Tsai, Bender, & Lim, 2007), epilepsy (Bergin et al., 2010), women's health (Klovning, Sandvik, & Hunskaar, 2009), multiple sclerosis (Miller et al., 2010), and smoking (Ramo, Hall, & Prochaska, 2010). Such issues of Internet recruitment bias and whether and how they are of significance remain hardly explored in studies involving d/Deaf people where once again the highly variable nature of the population(s) we refer to as deaf or Deaf is bound to exert influence (see Chapter 5).

Data Capture

The new information and communication technologies, including e-mail, the Internet, text messaging, and Web-based telephony (whether in spoken or signed languages), are also creating new means of capturing data in the first place. Their advantages are often described in terms of what they can avoid. For example, if someone is unable to travel (whether researcher or researched), ICT offers a means of long-distance participation (Rife, 2010). If someone is unable to use spoken language, ICT can nonetheless facilitate participation (Ison, 2009). Far less attention has been paid to what these new means of data collection can enable and exploit because their means of data capture can be tailored to the specific strengths or preferences of participants.

In this respect a common misperception among those new to research involving d/Deaf people is that one of the great advantages of some of the new communication technologies is their lack of dependence on sound. It is assumed that d/Deaf people can participate in the same way that hearing people can because you do not need to be able to hear to complete an e-mail interview, fill in a questionnaire on the Web, or complete an online diary or blog. For the many who lose their hearing in later life, this assumption about the inclusionary effects of non-sound-based technologies is often true. Filling in an online questionnaire is likely to pose far fewer difficulties than a telephone interview, for example, provided you are IT literate. But for the vast majority of d/Deaf people who have been deaf from birth or early childhood, the assumption that lack of dependence on hearing in data collection means greater inclusion is not axiomatic. The reasons why, however, are varied because the population of potential participants is also varied.

Childhood deafness commonly interferes with literacy (in the written word) with many deaf children not reading at age-level norms (Marschark & Spencer, 2009) with problems persisting into adulthood (Marschark, Lang, & Albertini, 2002). Therefore, for some deaf spoken language users, a face-to-face interview where it might be possible to use lipreading and audition could create fewer barriers to contributing data than a seemingly sound-neutral means of data collection that is nonetheless reliant on good literacy.

From a different perspective, sign language users who also use the written language of their home country are not necessarily balanced bilinguals (Knoors & Marschark, 2012). Expression and comprehension might be stronger in one language than another, as is often the case among hearing spoken language users of more than one language. Therefore, a written means of data collection is likely to create additional barriers to participation which might not be visible (Okuyama & Iwai, 2011). Completing a written survey, for example, can in effect become a test of literacy or second language competence—a fact that research studies do not necessarily acknowledge.

Bowker and Tuffin (2004), for example, in their study of the online medium for discursive research with and about disabled people, did not anticipate that their means of data collection which was designed to cohere with the topic of their research could actually result in exclusion. Compare their opening proposition:

> ...irrespective of physical coordination, mobility, and speech capacity, the textual nature of online interaction affords people with diverse operating techniques the capacity to participate. Hence, the

online medium may offer an ideal and equitable environment for conducting research about people with disabilities. (p. 230)

with their later adaptation:

The high degree of literacy required to participate in online interviews because of the textual nature of online communication meant the online setting was inaccessible to three deaf participants. Consequently, these interviews were conducted in a face-to-face setting via tape-recorder. Sign language interpreters were present to translate English into Sign and vice versa. (p. 233)

The consequences of this adaptation for the validity of the study's findings are not discussed. The face-to-face data are treated no differently for analysis purposes than the online data, and the implications of translation are ignored. In Chapter 6 we argue that movement across modalities/languages has significance for Deaf people in ways that are often missed by researchers. Interpretation, transcription, and translation all involve *re-presenting* participants rather than simply transferring identities from one context to another. This re-presentation for Deaf people may be seen as an eradication of identity because sign language, an important part of that identity, has no written form. We argue in Chapter 6 that this re-presentation of what it means to be Deaf has political and ethical implications.

Returning to the proposition that new information and communication technologies offer new opportunities to play to the strengths of Deaf people, the use of video combined with the Internet is a powerful example. The higher resolution of Web cams and the faster speeds of Internet connections make the transmission of sign language on the Web and the reading of online materials in sign language a viable proposition for many people using what might be regarded as everyday hardware and software, rather than specialist equipment. Consequently, it is entirely feasible and increasingly common to elicit and collect data in sign language over the Web. At its simplest, these methods entail the translation (or initial creation) of data collection instruments in sign language that are then hosted on Web pages. Surveys and questionnaires are good examples of this approach. Where the answers required are to closed questions with fixed choice categories, the participant who has viewed the question in sign language can simply click her or his answer from the choices provided or interact with the survey instrument using a touch screen interface (Graybill et al., 2010). Digital filming and digital transfer technologies enable the easy creation and uploading of the video clips in the first place. A few lines of programming can ensure that the data are automatically downloaded to a secure repository for later analysis.

Although this approach is becoming more commonly used, there is little formally written about it from a methodological perspective.

Rogers and colleagues applied online data collection methods to a study of the the psychometric properties of the British Sign Language (BSL) versions of the Patient Health Questionnaire, the Generalised Anxiety Disorder 7-item Scale, and the Work and Social Adjustment Scale (Rogers et al., 2012). Having completed a rigorous translation process into BSL of the standard assessments, the recruitment of a large enough sample of Deaf people to complete the pilot versions was required in order to test the reliability and validity of the BSL versions. By hosting the pilot versions online they were able to recruit a large enough sample of the general population of Deaf people with enough diversity, that is, including those with a clinical history of mental health difficulties, to establish whether the items measured robustly enough what they were intended to measure. Indirectly, they were also able to test out the acceptability and feasibility of this form of delivery in clinical practice. Furthermore, the software used to host and deliver the items on the Web included the possibility of automatic data transfer into the software to be used for statistical analysis in an anonymized form. Geography was no barrier to recruitment to the pilot; sign language use was no barrier to participation; size of sample and diversity could be achieved despite a dispersed population; the means of data collection could seamlessly interface with the means of analysis.

A more difficult application of data collection in sign language over the Web concerns those situations in which it is important to be able to capture what a participant might sign back as her or his answer. For example, online synchronous interviews that are carried out in sign language in much the same way as a spoken language telephone interview might be; or asynchronous applications, as in the case of open-ended questions within an online survey requiring extended responses, rather than fixed-choice answers. Visual blogs (sometimes referred to as vlogs) can be filmed and then uploaded to the Web. For research purposes it would be more efficient and straightforward if participants could simply log onto a Web site and sign in their vlog via their personal Web cam and that data be remotely captured. Bespoke adaptations of technologies such as FlashPlayer are making all of these possibilities a reality.

In a study of terminology within genetic counseling involving Deaf people, Belk (2014) created an online questionnaire in BSL with both closed and open questions in response to which participants signed their answers via Web cam. The answers were recorded and securely stored without the researcher being actually online at the time. The questions followed on from participants having viewed different scenarios in which a fictional genetic counseling situation was played out.

The advantages of this data collection method, however, did not just lie in its accessibility and its enabling of participants' language preference. As a hearing researcher but not a native signer, it enabled the lead researcher to remove herself from the data she was collecting lest her own levels of linguistic competence influenced the language that participants used in their responses. In a study concerned with terminology and how participants expressed genetic concepts, this distancing was vital. It is well recognized that skilled signers will nonetheless adjust their level and style of expression to match the needs of a less skilled (usually hearing) signer with whom they are communicating. Secondly, the possibility of participants asynchronously signing their answers, their thoughts, ideas, and responses, created itself a wealth of linguistic data that was pertinent to the topic of the research. These qualitative data bites were themselves analyzed as narrative data (see Chapter 6), as well as for the content of the information they contained.

Beyond specific adaptations and applications of online sign language technology for data collection, there is a broad interest in the general sociological literature about the potential of computer-mediated communication (CMC) for generating its own data, rather than being used as a means to generate data. CMC is a generic term used to refer to e-mail, discussion boards, chat rooms, and instant messaging applications (Ison, 2009). CMC technologies leave trails that are not necessarily provoked by research intent but naturally occur in the course of people communicating around specific issues and which can be analyzed by researchers. As Gill and Elder (2012) discuss, the Internet generates its own archive as well as being the means through which information can be archived. There is, without a deliberate process of recruitment, a plethora of data available for analysis, an increasing amount of which is in signed languages.

Waskul and Douglass (1996) argue that CMC is not just a technological application that is producing new information and new means of communication; it is a "technosocial phenomenon" (p. 129). Online applications create new social spaces in which participants can take on different identities whether through the anonymization of their own and/or the adoption and performance of another. In its extreme manifestation, the "second life" application enables participants to take on a whole new persona and/or lead a parallel life within a virtual world (Second Life, 2012). Within the second life world, you can, for example, buy real estate, perform the ritual of the Hajj, visit the Estonian Embassy, or get married. Online shared social spaces are contexts that can create their own cultural rules and practices. They are places where relationships do not necessarily conform to usual rules (join Facebook to find out how many "friends" you can have or Twitter to develop a legion of "followers"). These spaces influence language itself in creating new dialects, grammars, and vocabulary, for example, "PRW x-(C4N" ("Parents are watching, angry, ciao for now"). Consequently, the naturalistic data to be studied lie not just in what is said but in *how* it is engendered and how it is expressed within the medium where it is manifest:

> It is a context where the medium (computers, modems, and other technology) and the social environment (the setting or context) become intertwined elements of communication. The unique form of on-line interaction transforms social spheres into new social environments with new patterns of interaction, feeling, and belief. (Waskul & Douglass, 1996, p. 129)

The scale of this idea is important in thinking about technology's influence on research involving d/Deaf people. It is too easy to adopt a reductionist approach that focuses attention on the ways in which the information and communication potential of technology can create new opportunities or counterbalance apparent deficits. Instead, there are much bigger questions of interest, such as the ways in which they are generating new forms of knowledge out of the *routine* participation of d/Deaf people in the online communicative exchanges. Casper and Morrison (2010) remark, "what we know is inextricably bound up with how we know" (p. 121). That *how* is changing at a rapid pace for young d/Deaf people in particular. The artifacts of routine technosocial engagement, bulletin boards, e-mail, instant messaging, chat rooms, and social networking are evidence that should cause us to question the limits of our knowledge about young d/Deaf people's social, linguistic, and cultural development. Such data do not have to be specially captured; they are simply present but require our attention, understanding, and analysis.

Analysis

The use of information and communication technologies for data collection entails also some added advantages for the analysis of data, whether quantitative or qualitative. In terms of effort, many of the new means of data capture enable a usual step in data processing to be left out. For example, if the sample is textual and gathered through an online medium (e.g., e-mail interviews, blogs, chat room messages), then there is no need to transcribe the data. It is already in an orthographic form. If the data capture includes knowing how frequently something occurs, such as how many texts were sent, how many times a Web site was visited, how many people contributed to a discussion, and so forth, these data can be counted automatically. For example, Akamatsu et al. (2006) in their study of the impact of two-way pager use on deaf young people's independence were able to use a commercial company to supply a readout of the frequency of text/pager use without accessing messages themselves. Bowe (2002) in a study of Deaf and hard-of-hearing Americans' use of instant messaging and e-mail used a software application that automatically tabulated answers to his online questionnaire and regularly sent him updates of results.

For data captured in signed languages, the new technologies have significantly advanced the processes of data analysis. Particularly in relation to qualitative data, whether captured online or separately filmed, the easy digital interface that now exists between video capture and computer software has brought crucial advantages. Video data can be uploaded with ease to a computer, where it might be then transferred to qualitative data analysis programs such as QSR NVivo, the latest versions of which are equipped to handle video data. Within such programs it is now possible to do to video data what has long been possible with textual data (Stone & West, 2012). Segments can be tagged and reorganized for thematic analysis in just the same way as written transcripts can. The significance of this advance, however, lies not just in the effort it might save. It also breaks down the previous necessity to have to translate data in order to make it amenable to analysis using sort and retrieve software applications (Temple & Young, 2004).

In the past there were difficult choices to be made for the qualitative analysis of data in a signed language. Its translation, in order to produce a transcription, carried with it questions of how to represent a participant in language she or he did not use (see Chapter 7). It also broke the vital link between the form in which knowledge is produced and the means by which it is known. Data generated in a signed language that is then translated into the written form of the dominant spoken language literally eradicates the visibility, and thereby the identity, of those who have produced the data. This has been a particularly sensitive political act in a context where Deaf people's legitimacy as users of a largely unrecognized language remains a significant sociopolitical struggle (Young & Ackerman, 2001). On the other hand, sustained qualitative analysis of substantial amounts of sign language data without the use of sort and retrieve software is difficult. One of the great advantages of programs such as NVivo and Atlas Ti is that they introduce a degree of checking into one stage of the analysis process. By thematically organizing data and/or tagging data, it is possible for the researcher to be challenged about such issues as whether the major theme seen in the data is really that big, or shared that broadly, among participants. Looking at (visually reading) sign language interviews and drawing up an analysis from that process alone leaves out such checks and challenges.

Dissemination/Publishing

Online and digital technologies are, in the wider world, engendering a revolution in publishing, as evidenced by the growing market for e-books and e-readers. Beyond the medium itself, there is also significant interest in the ways in which the interface is changing the relationship between the reader and what is read (Keegan, 2010). For example, when reading an e-book on applications like iPad and Kindle, the reader can hover over words and check their meaning automatically via online dictionaries. Hybrid forms of publishing are emerging which embed video links into the written text, known as "vooks" (Rich, 2009). More radically, the reader can choose to write her or his own text in response to what she or he read and have it pinned behind the authors' text. One reader, retracing the steps of a character in Robert Louis Stevenson's novel *Kidnapped*, appended the blog of his journey to the book's original text and e-published it (Wright, 2009). In these and many other previously unimagined ways, books are becoming *personalized* to the reader through processes of co-creativity and futuristic co-publishing.

In research involving Deaf people, this re-examination of the text and its author–reader relationship has had a different focus. It is now possible for "the text" to be a signed text. Publishing, including academic peer-reviewed publishing, can occur in and through signed language. The Fourth International Deaf Academics and Researchers Conference held in Dublin, Ireland, in 2008, for example, published their proceedings on a DVD in International Sign Language. In such publications, the reader is the viewer and the author is, quite literally, seen. This seeing is important because potentially the reader discerns a whole host of additional information from the visibility of the author that may not be "in" the text. For example, characteristics of an author's signing may reveal the school she went to as a child, the region where she lives, or whether she is signing in her first, second, or third language. Some aspects of identity are de facto visible, such as age and sex. Others, the author might choose to reveal through language use. For instance, it is possible to recognize someone's sexuality by choice of lexical items and style of signing if using gay-sign register or a gay-sign variant (Silverman Kleinfeld & Warner, 1996).

The implications of the visible text for academic publishing are only just beginning to be explored with the launch of the world's first peer-reviewed academic journal in a signed language, the *Deaf Studies Digital Journal* (DSDJ, 2009). The significance of this development does not lie solely, or even primarily, in issues of accessibility—academic papers available in ASL like they might be available in Dutch or Russian. Rather this is a form of publishing in which the medium facilitates and exploits styles of thinking and expression that are part and parcel of the properties of the language being used, not just which language. Stokoe (1979) pointed out many years ago that signed languages work in *four* dimensions.

Speech has only one dimension—its extension in time; writing has two dimensions; models have three; but only signed languages have at their disposal four dimensions—the three spatial dimensions accessible to a signer's body, as well as the dimension of time. And

> Sign fully exploits the syntactic possibilities in its four-dimensional channel of expression. (Sacks, 1989, p. 89)

Four dimensions create possibilities for the manipulation of ideas, structuring of thoughts, leaps of imagination, and their expression which are unavailable in spoken and written languages. Bahan's (2009) article on "Sensory Orientation" published in ASL is an excellent example of the exploitation of the properties of a signed language for the expression of complex, multilayered, critical, and conceptual thinking. By contrast, even those (nonsigning) authors who might think in three or more dimensions are confined usually to two in communicating those thoughts.

Once again the medium is not just the channel of the message but a co-constructor of its content, too. Peer-reviewed journals in signed languages open up new styles of academic discourse because the properties of the medium influence and structure styles of thought as well as expression. To regard them simply as journals where an academic paper is presented in a signed language is to diminish their long-term significance. The language we use influences how we think, and the medium in which we express ourselves influences the possibilities of what it is we can show and tell.

CONCLUDING THOUGHTS

This chapter has been concerned with the influence of information and communication technologies on research with, by, and about d/Deaf people. It has considered the new kinds of research question that these technologies provoke, the new forms of data capture and analysis that are available, and the influence of new means of publication that are now possible. Throughout, we have been concerned to move beyond a notion of new technologies facilitating new adaptations *for* d/Deaf people—whether as researchers, participants, or readers. Instead, we have pointed to the challenges that the uses of the new information and communication technologies bring to our notions of what counts as data and the new forms of research participation and academic discourse that are now possible.

From this perspective, the influence of technology is not a compensatory one that supports inclusion. It is an iconoclastic one, which releases potential, changes the rules of participation, breaks down old certainties, and challenges us to know and be known differently. Therefore, exploring the influence of technology of necessity involves an examination of how its use positions d/Deaf people within the research process. Access to the means to take part in research is not necessarily an indicator of the inclusive effects of technology for Deaf people. If the established hierarchy of knowledge and its form of expression (written language) prevails, then Deaf identities and epistemologies will continue literally to be written out of intellectual history. Throughout this book we argue that the many ways in which it is possible to experience being d/Deaf are a warning to researchers that one person's preferred means of participating in research may present barriers for another person. The new possibilities brought by advances in ICT do not change this proposition.

REFERENCES

Akamatsu, C. T., Mayer, C., & Farrelly, S. (2006). An investigation of two-way text messaging use with deaf students at the secondary level. *Journal of Deaf Studies and Deaf Education, 11*(1), 120–131. doi: 10.1093/deafed/enj013

Bahan, B. (2009). Sensory orientation. *Deaf Studies Digital Journal, 1*(1).

Barak, A., & Sadovsky, Y. (2008). Internet use and personal empowerment of hearing-impaired adolescents. *Computers in Human Behavior, 24*, 1802–1815. doi: 10.1016/j.chb.2008.02.007

Belk, R. (2014). *Genetic counselling and terminology in BSL.* PhD thesis, Manchester, UK.

Bergin, P. S., Ip, T., Sheehan, R., Frith, R. W., Sadleir, L. G., McGrath, N., Ranta, A., & Walker, E. B. (2010). Using the Internet to recruit patients for epilepsy trials: Results of a New Zealand pilot study. *Epilepsia, 51*(5), 868–873. doi: 10.1111/j.1528-1167.2009.02393.x

Bowe, F. (2002). Deaf and hard of hearing Americans' instant messaging and e-mail use: A national survey. *American Annals of the Deaf, 147*(4), 6–10. doi: 10.1353/aad.2012.025

Bowen, A., Williams, M., & Horvath, K. (2004). Using the internet to recruit rural MSM for HIV risk assessment: Sampling issues. *AIDS and Behavior, 8*(3), 311–319. doi: 10.1023/B:AIBE.0000044078.43476.1f

Bowker, N., & Tuffin, K. (2003). Dicing with deception: People with disabilities' strategies for managing safety and identity online. *Journal of Computer Mediated Communication, 8*(2). doi: 10.1111/j.1083-6101.2003.tb00209.x

Bowker, N., & Tuffin, K. (2004). Using the online medium for discursive research about people with disabilities. *Social Science Computer Review, 22*, 228–241. doi: 10.1177/0894439303262561

Burgess, J., Green, J., Jenkins, H., & Hartley, J. (2009). *YouTube: Online video and participatory culture.* Cambridge, UK: Polity Press.

Carr, N. (2010). *The shallows: How the internet is changing the way we read, think and remember.* London: Atlantic Books.

Casper, M. J., & Morrison, D. R. (2010). Medical sociology and technology: Critical engagements. *Journal of Health and Social Behaviour, 51*(1 (Suppl)), S120-S132. doi: 10.1177/0022146510383493

Crasborn, O. (2010). What does "informed consent" mean in the internet age? Publishing sign language corpora as open content. *Sign Language Studies, 10*(2), 276–290. doi: 10.1353/sls.0.0044

De Clerck, G. A. (2010). Deaf epistemologies as a critique and alternative to the practice of science: An anthropological perspective. *American Annals of the Deaf, 154*(5), 435–446.

Dowaliby, F., & Lang, H. (1999). Adjunct aids in instructional prose: A multimedia study with deaf college students. *Journal of Deaf Studies and Deaf Education, 4*(4), 270–282. doi: 10.1093/deafed/4.4.270

DSDJ. (2009). Deaf Studies Digital Journal homepage. Retrieved November 23, 2012, from http://dsdj.gallaudet.edu/

DSRU. Deaf Studies Research Unit (1993). *Dictionary of British Sign Language.* London: Faber and Faber.

Gill, F., & Elder, C. (2012). Data and archives: The Internet as site and subject. *International Journal of Social Research Methodology, 15*(4), 271–279. doi: 10.108 0/13645579.2012.687595

Gray, P. (2006). National audit of support, services and provision for children with low-incidence needs. *DfES Research Report* (Vol. 729). London: DfES.

Graybill, P. J. A., Dean, R. K., Demers, S., Finigan, E. G., & Pollard, R. Q. (2010). A community participatory approach to adapting survey items for Deaf individuals and American Sign Language. *Field Methods, 22*(4), 429–428. doi:10.1177/1525822X10379201

Grimes, M., Thoutenhoofd, E. D., & Byrne, D. (2007). Language approaches used with deaf pupils in Scottish schools: 2001–2004. *Journal of Deaf Studies and Deaf Education, 12*(4), 530–551.

Ha-Sheng, L. K. (2012). Age-related hearing loss: Quality of care for quality of life. *The Gerontologist, 52*(2), 265–271. doi: 10.1093/geront/gnr159

Im, E. O., Chee, W., Tsai, H. M., Bender, M., & Lim, H. J. (2007). Internet communities for recruitment of cancer patients into an internet survey: A discussion paper. *International Journal of Nursing Studies, 44*(7), 1261–1269. doi: 10.1016/j.ijnurstu.2006.07.003

Ison, N. L. (2009). Having their say: Email interviews for research data collection with people who have verbal communication impairment. *International Journal of Social Research Methodology, 12*(2), 161–172. doi: 10.1080/13645570902752365

Keegan, V. (2010). The digital reading revolution. Retrieved October 14, 2010, from http://www.guardian.co.uk/commentisfree/2010/oct/14/digital-reading-ebook-kindle-ipad

Klovning, A., Sandvik, H., & Hunskaar, S. (2009). Web-based survey attracted age-biased sample with more severe illness than paper-based survey. *Journal of Clinical Epidemiology, 62*(10), 1068–1074. doi: 10.1016/j.jclinepi.2008.10.015

Knoors, H., & Marschark, M. (2012). Language planning for the 21st century: Revisiting bilingual language policy for deaf children. *Journal of Deaf Studies and Deaf Education, 17*(3), 291–305. doi: 10.1093/deafed/ens018

Kusters, A. (2010). Deaf utopias? Reviewing the sociocultural literature on the world's "Martha's Vineyard situations." *Journal of Deaf Studies and Deaf Education, 15*(1), 3–16. doi: 10.1093/deafed/enp026

Lang, H. (2000). *A phone of our own: The deaf insurrection against Ma Bell.* Washington, DC: Gallaudet University Press.

Marschark, M., Lang, H., & Albertini, J. (2002). *Educating deaf students: From research to practice.* New York, NY: Oxford University Press.

Marschark, M., & Spencer, P. E. (2009). Evidence of best practice models and outcomes in the education of deaf and hard-of-hearing children: An international review (pp. 1–294). National Council for Special Education (Ireland).

McCleary, L. (2003). Technologies of language and the embodied history of the deaf. *Sign Language Studies, 3*(2), 104–124. doi: 10.1353/sls.2003.0002

McLuhan, M. (1964). *Understanding media: The extensions of man.* London: Routledge & Kegan Paul.

Miller, D. M., Fox, R., Atreja, A., Moore, S., Lee, J. C., Fu, A. Z., Jain, A., Saupe, W., Chakraborty, S., Stadtler, M., & Rudick, R. A. (2010). Using an automated recruitment process to generate an unbiased study sample of multiple sclerosis patients. *Telemedicine Journal and E-Health*, *16*(1), 63–68. doi: 10.1089/tmj.2009.0078

NDCS. National Deaf Children's Society (2012). Parent Place. Retrieved November 23, 2012, from http://www.ndcs.org.uk/applications/discussion/

Okuyama, Y., & Iwai, M. (2011). Use of text messaging by deaf adolescents in Japan. *Sign Language Studies*, *11*(3), 375–407. doi: 10.1353/sls.2011.0001

Power, D., Power, M. R., & Rehling, B. (2007). German deaf people using text communication: Short message service, TTY, relay services, fax, and e-mail. *American Annals of the Deaf*, *152*(3), 291–301. doi: 10.1353/aad.2007.0030

Power, M., & Power, D. (2004). Everyone here speaks TXT: Deaf people using SMS in Australia and the rest of the World. *Journal of Deaf Studies and Deaf Education*, *9*(3), 333–343. doi: 10.1093/deafed/enh042

Ramo, D. E., Hall, S. M., & Prochaska, J. J. (2010). Reaching young adult smokers through the Internet: Comparison of three recruitment mechanisms. *Nicotine & Tobacco Research*, *12*(7), 768–775. doi: 10.1093/ntr/ntq086

Rich, M. (2009). The Vook: A picture book, but the pictures move. *New York Times*, November 30. Retrieved November 10, 2010, from http://artsbeat.blogs.nytimes.com/2009/09/30/the-vook-a-picture-book-but-the-pictures-move/

Rife, M. C. (2010). Ethos, pathos, logos, kairos: Using a rhetorical heuristic to mediate digital-survey recruitment strategies. *IEEE Transactions on Professional Communication*, *53*(3), 260–277. doi: 10.1109/tpc.2010.2052856

Rogers, K., Young, A. M., Lovell, K., Campbell, M., Scott, P., & Kendall, S. (2012). The British Sign Language versions of the Patient Health Questionnaire, the Generalized Anxiety Disorder 7-Item Scale, and the Work and Social Adjustment Scale. *Journal of Deaf Studies and Deaf Education*, *18*(1), 110–122. doi: 10.1093/deafed/ens041

Sacks, O. W. (1989). *Seeing voices: A journey into the Deaf world*. Berkeley: University of California Press.

Schneider, E., Kozak, L., Santiago, R., & Stephen, A. (2012). The effects of electronic communication on American Sign Language. *Sign Language Studies*, *12*(3), 347–370. doi: 10.1353/sls.2012.0004

Second Life. (2012). Homepage. Retrieved November 10, 2010, from http://secondlife.com/

Seymore, W., & Lupton, D. (2004). Holding the line online: Exploring wired relationships for people with disabilities. *Disability and Society*, *19*(4), 291–305. doi: 10.1080/09687590410001689421

Silverman Kleinfeld, M., & Warner, N. (1996). Variation in the Deaf community: Gay, lesbian and bisexual signs. In C. Lucas (Ed.), *Multicultural aspects of sociolinguistics in Deaf communities* Washington, DC: Gallaudet University Press.

Snoddon, K. (2010). Technology as a learning tool for ASL literacy. *Sign Language Studies*, *10*(2). doi: 10.1353/sls.0.0039

Stokoe, W. (1979). *Syntactic dimensionality: Language in four dimensions*. Paper presented at the New York Academy of Sciences, New York.

Stone, C., & West, D. (2012). Translation, representation and the Deaf "voice." *Qualitative Research*. doi: 10.1177/1468794111433087

Temple, B., & Young, A. (2004). Qualitative research and translation dilemmas. *Qualitative Research, 4*(2), 161–178. doi: 10.1177/1468794104044430

Valentine, G., & Skelton, T. (2008). Changing spaces: The role of the internet in shaping Deaf geographies. *Social and Cultural Geography, 9*(5), 469–485. doi: 10.1080/14649360802175691

Waskul, D., & Douglass, M. (1996). Considering the electronic participant: Some polemical observations on the ethics of on-line research. *The Information Society, 12*(2), 129–139.

Wright, T. (2009). Kidmapper. Retrieved November 10, 2010, from http://www.timwright.typepad.com/kidmapper/

Young, A. M., & Ackerman, J. (2001). Reflections on validity and epistemology in a study of working relations between deaf and hearing professionals. *Qualitative Health Research, 11*(2), 179–189. doi: 10.1177/104973230101100204

9

(In)conclusion

Readers of this book who are looking for an argument that builds incrementally to a conclusion will be disappointed. Those who enjoy discussion of possibilities and uncertainties will feel more at home with the idea of writing about a set of issues and axes that are central in social research which involves d/Deaf people. We have chosen to focus on a few of these, including definition and identity, epistemology and ethics, but we show how these slip into other aspects of being d/Deaf that impact on research processes, for example, ontology and politics.

Research with d/Deaf people has largely grown and developed within psychology, linguistics, audiology, education, and Deaf studies. We discuss some of this research but play with the ideas and concepts in ways which differ from how they have been treated within their own disciplines. We hope that readers new to social research will find the perspectives and practices we discuss offer valuable insights into ways of looking at the social realities of d/Deaf people's lives. Social research at its best opens up social worlds and muddies the boundaries between what is seen as social and what is deemed to be "natural." This is evident, for example, in changing perspectives on what is natural for women, disabled, and d/Deaf people. Social research helps to undermine certainties and grand narratives which limit people's lives.

Some social research with d/Deaf people is already under way, for example, by researchers quoted in this book. However, it is time to look at the broad sweep of what is available in terms of, for example, epistemological and ontological positions and to discuss the consequences as well as the advantages of taking specific stances toward the research process. Social constructionism and postmodernism have been used but rarely are the consequences of adopting them taken on board. Although we have not labeled ourselves as either of these, we describe our position in detail and argue that if researchers do not address their epistemological stance, one will be imputed and their research will be judged accordingly.

Our epistemological position is that there is no objective truth in the sense of a truth that is independent of who is doing the research. This is more than a question of perspective. It is an issue of process as well as end point. This book is ultimately about choices and consequences. We follow what seem to be individual choices in the research process to show how they build and impact on each other. Who triggers the data, how it is put together, and the intended reader/audience are all significant. This is as much the case with research methodologies and methods which are traditionally viewed as positivist, such as surveys, as it is with those associated with social constructionist perspectives such as interviews. Indeed, we argue in the book that suggesting that any methodology or method is per se the only way to do research itself smacks of the positivism that is used to dismiss others.

We do not attempt to fix a definition of what it means to be d/Deaf. Each of the different perspectives on being d/Deaf may make valuable contributions in specific circumstances. There is, in line with our epistemological stance, no correct "model" or approach which outshines all others in all circumstances. We are more interested in the relationship between definitions and their consequences so that although identity matters, issues of representation also matter.

Researchers represent participants in their research when they interpret, transcribe, or translate what has been spoken/signed or work with others to do so. What may be perceived as merely tools or techniques also create representations of d/Deaf people and imply consequences for the ways research is produced. Issues of representation raise the question of the extent to which researchers should differentiate and divide populations or set nuances aside. We argue that although it is important to differentiate the different ways in which it is possible to be d/Deaf and to understand identities as situational, fluid, and contextual, it may also sometimes be important to set the nuances aside to argue for the opening up of the academy. This is a position that will be recognized by other marginalized groups, including women who marched together to improve the lives of women generally. Black, working-class, and lesbian women challenged academics' assumptions that they could represent all women.

In a similar way, some Deaf researchers quoted in this book query how being Deaf has been represented and argue for the need to drop the use of "d/Deaf." However, it would be problematic to distinguish anything distinctive about Deaf epistemologies if deaf people who did not consider themselves culturally Deaf were included. As with other concerns which we raise in the book, this issue begs the question: Who decides when it is time to move on? Has the argument for Deaf cultures and ways of knowing been won so that Deaf people can be subsumed into a general deaf population? There are not many social researchers who do not work directly and regularly with d/Deaf people who would recognize the issues raised in this book. Nor indeed would they see the need to read this or any other literature relating to working with d/Deaf researchers. This suggests that it is still business as usual.

Our basis for deciding which research methodologies and methods to use is not just based on the research question, as this may be approached in more than one way. The significance of the research question is often cited in general research texts with examples of how

"how many" questions being more suited to questionnaires and "how" questions being the domain of in-depth interviews. However, to this we need to add a consideration of the epistemological stance of the researchers. If we accept that researchers cannot remove their own influence from their research, then we need to find some other criteria for deciding how to carry out research. We suggest some alternatives, for example, the ethics and politics of research.

The desire to address the exclusion of d/Deaf people from the academy, as well as the exclusion of other groups such as women, people from minority ethnic communities, and disabled people, may feature heavily in decisions about who should do research and how it should be done. These choices are not based on any methodology or method itself being more ethical than any other or any researcher being automatically included or excluded. The positioning of d/Deaf researchers within academic research is an ethical stance where the definition of ethical considerations is not restricted to issues that would be relevant in an institutional review board. Nor is it a matter of situational ethical issues that arise in the field. It is also one which is imbued with politics—an ethical position that recognizes that all researchers are not viewed as equal in the academy and that values attempts to open up traditionally restricted and restrictive academic institutions to other ways of knowing and behaving.

Writing this book has been an intellectual and personal journey for us both. Questioning what one knows is both rewarding and unsettling. Encountering and engaging with the ideas in research with d/Deaf people has changed the ways we both view knowledge production and carry out our research, in different ways. As we discuss in the introduction, we started from different bodies of literature and areas of research. Alys's starting point is the academic literature developed by researchers working with d/Deaf people, although she has always had a broader interest in general social research writing. Bogusia's starting point is her reading of social research methodology across a number of areas. Through this she became interested in occasionally dipping into research with d/Deaf people, and it has led her to rethink some of the ways she writes about concepts such as language and narrative with people who are not d/Deaf. This difference in starting points is significant for what is contained in this book and for how it will be received by readers. Throughout its writing we have struggled to think of a title for the book that would entice social researchers from a range of disciplines to pick it up off the shelf. Research with d/Deaf people is usually seen as a specialist concern and writing in this area is for an audience which is already immersed in the field. The challenges to established ways of thinking and knowing are rarely generally recognized. In this book we point to some of these challenges for researchers who may have little knowledge of the issues, for example, around understanding language, identity, ethics, and politics in the context of d/Deaf people's lives. We also aim to stimulate dialogue with scholars well versed in the existing literature on research with d/Deaf people.

Many of the chapters at some point address the consequences of arguing that there is no objective viewpoint from which to judge truth claims in research. This is usually presented in terms of the insider/outsider debate, which runs through both social research generally and specifically in research with d/Deaf people. We discuss the intellectual arguments around the shifting nature of such supposed binaries and argue that investigating a researcher's influence cannot be limited to the researcher's hearing/deaf status or language use. These may be significant or not. We argue that researchers' intellectual autobiographies influence their choice of topic, how they carry out research, and how they write up the findings. We spell out our views on a number of issues such as insider/outsider debates as well as on the status of research.

There may be people who find it difficult to swallow the idea that two hearing women have written a book about research with d/Deaf people. Is this because we are hearing or women? Or is it both? Both of us witness examples of discrimination at work and in everyday life. Our own experiences of racism, sexism, and class divides form the lens through which we have written this book. Feminism has proved particularly seductive here, and its influence is apparent not only in the feminist literature we use but in our interpretations of all the literature we present. Our experiences have influenced the literature we recognize as appropriate and the perspective we take on it. This is the case for all researchers.

Arguments that hearing researchers will never understand d/Deaf people's lives focus on one aspect of their lives and leave hearing researchers between a rock and a hard place—named as the oppressor if they do not attempt to take notice of d/Deaf research and charged with treading on territory that is not theirs if they do. Hearing researchers may well understand and experience other aspects of living in an unequal social world that is reflected in academic life. The fact that we recognize that one of us is an insider to some extent (in terms of Deaf circles) and the other an outsider in these terms is important. We start from different positions and bring different academic baggage with us. Researchers are nevertheless defined by more than their hearing/deaf status, and throughout the book we argue that using one axis to decide whether someone is an insider or not misrepresents the complexity of human experience and constructs people as "mouthpieces" for essentialized identities. In a similar way, we would not expect d/Deaf researchers to stay within the confines of research with d/Deaf people.

We sincerely look forward to the dialogue that this book will generate, the ways in which it will become an artifact of its time and that others will move the debates forward. Social research is poorer for not attending to the insights, complexity, and challenges of studies which involve d/Deaf people, whether as producers, participants, leaders, or critics.

Author Index

Subject Index